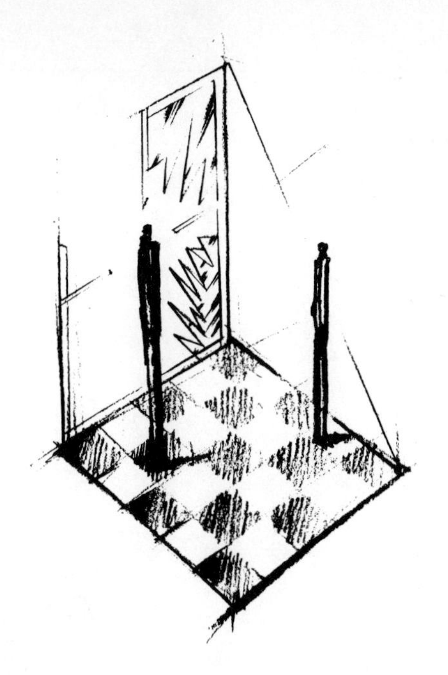

THE BROKEN WINDOW

Purdue University Press
West Lafayette, Indiana

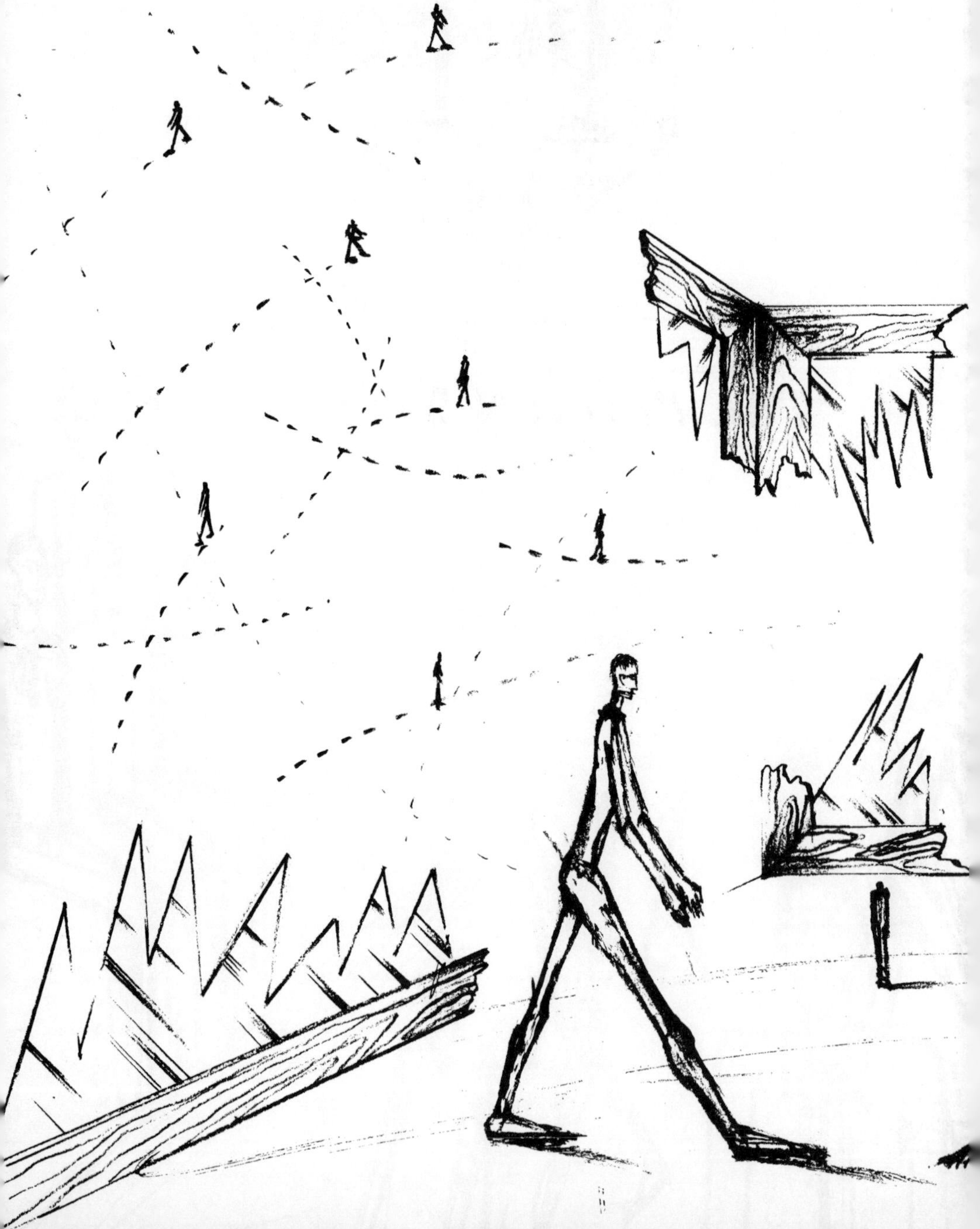

Jane Alison Hale

Window

Beckett's Dramatic Perspective

Book and jacket designed by Marlene Kennedy and illustrated by Alexandru Preiss

Printed in the United States of America

Library of Congress Cataloging-in-Publication Data

Hale, Jane Alison, 1948–
The broken window.

Bibliography: p.
Includes index.
1. Beckett, Samuel, 1906– —Dramatic works.
2. Beckett, Samuel, 1906– —Technique. 3. Drama—Technique. 4. Perspective in literature. I. Title.
II. Title: Beckett's dramatic perspective.
PR6003.E282Z6673 1986 842'.914 86–9447
ISBN 0–911198–82–2

CONTENTS

INTRODUCTION

The problem of seeing in an indeterminate world has long preoccupied Samuel Beckett. In his works, human beings no longer occupy a stable and privileged point in space and time from which they may visually organize, give meaning to, and institute relationships with other beings and objects. Instead, they find themselves drifting in and out of vague, undefined fields of vision in which the objects of their gaze appear, disintegrate, combine, separate, approach, and fade away in unpredictable fashion. The subjects themselves are victims of the same instability, and they call their own existence and its form into question at least as often as they interrogate the world around them. Indeed, the very boundary between the self and the world is an object of much confusion and speculation. In a 1934 essay entitled "Recent Irish Poetry," Beckett distinguished between the "antiquarians" and those who "evince awareness of the new thing that has happened, or the old thing that has happened again, namely the breakdown of the object," which he equates with "the breakdown of the subject," asserting that "it comes to the same thing—rupture of the lines of communication." He claims that "the artist who is aware of this may state the space that intervenes between him and the world of objects. . . . He may even record his findings, if he is a man of great personal courage."[1]

By his own admission, Beckett is not a philosopher;[2] his ideas may be (and have been) traced to numerous sources from Democritus of Abdera through Saint Augustine, Descartes, Geulincx, Pascal, Berkeley, Hegel, Schopenhauer, Husserl, Wittgenstein, Heidegger, and Sartre.[3] He is rather an artist—a writer sensitive to the specificity of his time and capable of translating it into literary and dramatic forms that affect his audience by their ring of truth and by their ability to translate for a collectivity what each of us has felt or suspected vaguely, intuitively, disturbingly. Beckett has defined the mission of the modern artist in the following terms: "To find a form that accommodates the mess, that is the task of the artist now."[4]

This study aims to explore how Beckett has experimented with new forms in drama in order to "accommodate the mess," and its organizing notion will be that of *perspective*. By perspective, I mean the representation of objects, including other people and the self, in respect to their spatial relationships with one another and with the eye of the observer. While this is a theme treated continually by Beckett both in his narrative fiction and in his drama, the drama adds an additional dimension to the problem: perspective is treated in words as well as in powerful, material images that are presented to the spectators' eyes. As Billie Whitelaw, Beckett's favorite actress, has so aptly said, "He writes paintings."[5] Ruby Cohn has characterized his latest television plays as "still lives in movement."[6] Beckett has created in his drama a type of perspective similar to that which has revolutionized the plastic arts during our century. In both domains, the same underlying esthetic and philosophical concerns are at work: how to formalize, in a specific artistic medium, the major shift that has taken place in the Western world regarding people's conception of the organization of that world and of their place in it. Before examining contemporary notions of perspective and their manifestations in Beckett's theater, a definition of the theory of linear perspective and a brief discussion of its implications for the era in which it flourished are in order.

The term *perspective* most often brings to mind a technique of painting born in Florence in the quattrocento which dominated Western art until the late nineteenth and early twentieth centuries. Painting in linear or geometric perspective consisted of treating the canvas no longer as a flat surface on which the painter portrayed isolated figures, but rather as a transparent plane, a "window" leading to a space beyond the painting, and of ordering objects and figures in geometrical relations meant to duplicate the arrangement of these forms as they appeared to the eye of the painter, which was situated outside the field under observation. Painters of these pictures presupposed that observers could, and would, view their work from a fixed, immobile vantage point corresponding to the one from which they conceived and executed the painting.

If linear perspective exerted such a strong and long-lasting influence on the visual arts, this was not due to the fact that artists had finally found the scientifically "true" or most faithful way of representing the world as it appears to the human eye, as was sometimes claimed by artists and art historians of past centuries. Rather, they had developed an esthetic technique that corresponded most satisfactorily to the imaginary structures of the generations for whom they painted.[7] For linear perspective was not merely an artistic phenomenon—it was the expression in the visual arts of a model of thought that pertained, to varying degrees and in different manifestations, in many domains of Western reality during the period of its influence.

Underlying the theory of linear perspective was the assumption of a divinely created order among all the elements of the world. While this order might not always be apparent to the imperfect perception of human beings, it was nonetheless an unquestionable reality. The task of people was not to create, but merely to discern, the rapports among the elements of the universe. Foucault has identified taxonomy, or the ordering of complex natures, as the key to the classical system of knowledge.[8] By creating tables that named and classified living beings according to their visible identities and differences, scientists would eventually be able to construct a faithful representation of the continuum of the universe and to understand the natural relationships among all things.

Closely related to the efforts of classical scientists in the field of natural history was the work done simultaneously in the domain of grammar. Syntax, which was the primary object of study for classical grammarians, can be characterized as a way of analyzing and ordering thought or of introducing linear perspective into discourse.

Painting in perspective was a method of analyzing a particular segment of the universal order, of discovering and expressing the spatial relationships among the elements selected for representation. Beckett has defined the impression of order and clarity experienced by most observers when they confront a work of classical art: "This is clear. This does not allow the mystery to invade us. With classical art, all is settled."[9] Classical space was abstract, autonomous, homogeneous, isotropic, systematic, and continuous. It was rational and stable and could be subjected to the mathematical operations of addition, subtraction, multiplication, and division. It existed independently of either the position in time and space or the qualities of the observer.[10]

When classical space informed a painting, individual objects or groups of figures were no longer represented in isolation on the canvas, as they had been in previous paintings; they were instead portrayed with the portion of space that surrounded them, and the entire pictorial space became homogeneous and unified, relating the individual elements to one another in rational, mathematically analyzable terms. This space existed before the objects themselves, and their form was determined by their relationship to the space in which they were represented.[11]

Artists were constrained by the logic of linear perspective to represent objects as they appeared to the human eye at a fixed, specific point in space that was always located outside the canvas. There was one, and only one, place from which a spectator might apprehend such a painting "correctly," by duplicating the point of view of the artist who had conceived and organized the space of the canvas, thereby allowing him to perceive reality in exactly the same fashion as had the painter.

Just as linear perspective in painting may be compared to the point of view of the natural scientists and grammarians of the same era, similar parallels prevail in other domains. In the theater, for instance, the spectators were meant to reproduce the vision of the dramatist: excluded from the spectacle, located in a privileged space exterior to the world of the representation from which they could cast an omniscient eye upon the totality of the drama, they inhabited the universe of the creator and shared his objective, all-encompassing, fixed point of view upon the represented reality.[12] The Italian perspective stage setting, whose guiding principle was the concept of unity of place, dominated Western theater from the seventeenth to the early twentieth centuries. The spatial unity of the perspective setting was achieved only by excluding the concept of time from the stage: "Only between the acts and scenes was time permitted to pass freely."[13] In the forthcoming discussion of Beckett's break with linear dramatic perspective, one of the innovations considered will be his attempt to portray the passage of time upon the stage.

The familiar image of the invisible fourth wall of the stage that is penetrated by the spectators' eyes grew out of the post-Renaissance theory of theatrical space.[14] Proust's description of his Hero's first visit to the theater provides an excellent summary of the assumptions that informed theatrical perspective from the time of the French classicists until at least the first decades of the present century:

> Il n'y avait qu'une scène pour tout le monde, je pensais qu'on devait être empêché de bien voir par les autres spectateurs comme on l'est au milieu d'une foule; or je me rendis compte qu'au contraire, grâce à une disposition qui est comme le symbole de toute perception, chacun se sent le centre du théâtre . . . . Et . . . sur la scène une table à écrire et une cheminée . . . signifièrent que les personnages qui allaient entrer seraient, non pas des acteurs venus pour réciter . . . , mais des hommes en train de vivre chez eux un jour de leur vie dans laquelle je pénétrais par effraction sans qu'il pussent me voir.[15]

The concepts of linear perspective may also be used to analyze the notion of the *Dieu mécaniste* who observed the world of his creation with an omniscient eye from above and beyond, never entering directly into the scene organized by his eye. Similarly, in politics, the King was situated outside the civil society. Because of its exterior, omniscient position, the eye of the King ordered society in its totality.[16]

Since the time of the Impressionists, linear perspective has lost its supremacy as the organizing principle of space in painting. If its long reign of influence was possible because of its close connection to the imaginary structures of a given society during a certain era, then its decline implies changes in those structures.

The objectively reproducible position of the observer exterior to the field of observation was one of the principal assumptions of linear perspective. Once the objectivity, stability, and very possibility of this position were called into question, it was inevitable that an esthetic rupture should occur.

Erich Auerbach characterizes this shift in literature as a dissolution of reality "into multiple and multivalent reflections of consciousness" and a portrayal of "not one order and one interpretation, but many, which may either be those of different persons or of the same person at different times."[17] He cites as examples of this changing perspective the works of Joyce, Woolf, and Proust. Proust constantly evokes the difficulty of knowing either oneself or another person because of the endless succession of "moi's" that inhabit each of us: "Ces êtres-là, tandis qu'ils changent par rapport à nous, changent aussi en eux-mêmes."[18] The Proustian universe is seen differently by each observer and changes its aspect daily, as we change within ourselves: "L'univers est vrai pour nous tous et dissemblable pour chacun. . . . ce n'est pas un univers, c'est des millions, presque autant qu'il existe des prunelles et d'intelligences humaines, qui s'éveillent tous les matins."[19] In his essay on Proust, Beckett speaks of the "*pictorial* multiplicity of Albertine," which is not merely "an effect of the observer's angle of approach," but also of the inward multiplicity of the object, "a turmoil . . . over which the subject has no control."[20] Elsewhere in the same essay, he emphasizes the turmoil of the subject as a barrier to perception: "The observer infects the observed with his own mobility" (p. 6). Unlike Beckett, however, Proust finds a means to resolve the dilemma of changing perspectives through art. While art is to Beckett the ultimate expression of human impotence, it represents to Proust a triumph over the fragmented universe created by the passing of time and by the variation of perceptions from one individual to another:

> L'oeuvre d'art était le seul moyen de retrouver le Temps perdu.[21]

> Par l'art seulement nous pouvons sortir de nous, savoir ce que voit un autre de cet univers qui n'est pas le même que le nôtre.[22]

If Proust exerted a tremendous influence on perspective in the twentieth-century novel, Pirandello's contribution to a new theatrical esthetic was no less revolutionary. He did away with the traditional fourth wall of the theater by taking a non-omniscient, partial, shifting point of view on his work and by obliging his spectators to follow suit.[23] Previously well defined boundaries between actors and the characters they portray, as well as between the audience and the scene it observes, break down in his work, which thus becomes a reflection upon the nature of theater, upon the conditions of perception, and upon the subtle, undefinable distinction between illusion and reality.

Wylie Sypher calls Pirandello's work "cubist drama" and sees in it an esthetic revolution comparable to the Cubists' influence upon the plastic arts:

> Just as the cubist broke up the object into various planes, or as photomontage gave its own sort of polyphonic vision by means of combined shots, so Pirandello offers a compound image in drama. He surrenders the literary subject while the cubist is surrending [*sic*] the anecdote, and treats this theatre as a plane intersecting art and life. . . .
>
> Pirandello "destroys" drama much as the cubists destroyed conventional things. He will not accept as authentic "real" people or the cliché of the theatre any more than the cubist accepts as authentic the "real" object, the cliché of deep perspective, the contour of volumes seen in the light of the studio—or under sunlight either. The object, say Gleizes and Metzinger, has no absolute form; it is only a passage in possible relationships, with many relevances that are never fixed. Except by a blunder we cannot drop the curtain on Pirandello's drama because there is no clear boundary between life and art. Nor can the cubist painter isolate or define his object. He can, however, represent its emergence into reality.[24]

The tension between the endurance and fixity of artistic forms and the fluidity and mobility of life underlies all of Pirandello's drama. As his Doctor Hinkfuss informs us in *Tonight We Improvise*, "The theatre is . . . art, yes, but it is also life. It is creation, yes, but not an enduring one: it is momentary. It is a miracle of form in motion! And the miracle, Ladies and Gentlemen, can be but momentary. In a moment, I create a scene in front of your eyes, and within that scene another one, and within that other, yet another."[25] Beckett's drama is also informed by a struggle between the static nature of artistic form and the fluidity of the life which that form is meant to convey to his audiences, and he makes extensive use of Pirandello's "play-within-a-play-within-a-play" technique as one means of introducing the motion of life into the fixity of art.

In both the form and the content of his drama, Pirandello deals with the same problems of perspective as do Proust and Beckett: the impossibility of observing one's own life and the consequent alienation from oneself; the fact that others perceive us in multiple ways, because we lead not one life, but as many lives as there exist eyes to watch them; and our resulting multiple personalities, which can be cured only if we resign ourselves to a permanent loss of identity.[26]

The human consciousness is thus no longer the neutral, stable "je" of Descartes's *cogito*, confronting an orderly and ultimately knowable world from the exterior, but a social and individual creation that becomes an integral part of the field of observation and whose position in space and time has a decisive influence upon the configuration of reality that it perceives. In Kierkegaard's words, "He whose eye chances to look down into the yawning abyss becomes dizzy. But the reason for it is just as much his eye as it is the precipice."[27]

Before beginning an analysis of Beckett's treatment of perspective in his dramatic works, it may be useful to discuss briefly certain changes that have taken place in the notion of perspective in several different fields of contemporary knowledge and research. The selection is necessarily arbitrary and limited, for it would obviously be impossible, given the scope of this study, to conduct such a survey for every domain of Western reality. An overview of the major shifts in perception of space, order, and the nature and position of the observer in a few important areas should, however, suffice to place this study in its contemporary context and to give weight to the argument that Beckett's work derives much of its power and appeal from its success in formalizing in its own domain certain concepts that cut across interdisciplinary boundaries in modern thought.

Time was injected into the field of science by the Second Law of Thermodynamics, which has taught humanity that the universe is mortal. This law challenged the long-accepted notion of the reversibility of physical processes by describing a universe where all the energy put into a system cannot be recuperated. All the elements and particles once thought permanent have now been discovered to be unstable and to exist in a continual process of transition. The laws, order, and rationality of the universe are no longer givens, and scientists have turned their attention to the study of transitions from chaos to order. With the loss of belief in the reversible world of equilibrium thermodynamics has come the realization that there is a limit to our control over nature.[28]

Since the formulation by Planck of quantum theory in 1900 and by Einstein of the theory of relativity in 1905, the observer has become an essential variable in scientific experimentation.

Formerly accepted a priori categories of time and space have been superseded by new definitions that take into consideration the spatiotemporal coordinates and the individual qualities of the observer, who thus enters the field of the observed. Heisenberg made imprecision and uncertainty one of the cornerstones of modern physics when he formulated his well-known principle of indeterminacy. Galilean science, which had been the dominant model since 1600, constituted the object of observation independently of the subject and posited the existence of a spatiotemporal domain whose reality and conditions were identical to all observers. Scientists thus worked under the assumption that a unique system of natural laws regulated the universe and that these laws acted independently of human beings and could be discovered by them.[29] Once the stable, external position of the observer was called into question, it became impossible to speak of isolated or separate phenomena, and the very notions of observer, observed, and observation became imprecise and undefinable. It may no longer even be possible to speak of a single universe, since the reality described by contemporary science has become a reality composed of many different worlds.[30]

The revolutionary impact of Planck's and Einstein's discoveries upon the world of science can be likened to that of Freud's discovery of the unconscious upon the Western world's conception of human beings' minds, their behavior, and their perceptions of the universe. Freud acknowledged the potential importance of his theory in a 1916 lecture: "I can assure you that the hypothesis of there being unconscious mental processes paves the way to a decisive new orientation in the world and in science."[31] The logic of the human consciousness loses its formerly privileged position as observer and decipherer of reality and gives way to a complex interplay between the conscious and the unconscious. The workings of the latter are hidden and not directly attainable to the human observer: "Human megalomania will have suffered its . . . most wounding blow from the psychological research of the present time which seeks to prove to the ego that it is not even master in its own house, but must content itself with scanty information of what is going on unconsciously in its mind."[32]

While Freud's psychological theory grew out of his treatment of patients suffering from obsessional neurosis and hysteria, the psychological disorder most typical of our own era is that of schizophrenia. In his pioneering work in this field, *The Divided Self*, R. D. Laing notes the specificity of schizophrenia to the twentieth-century Western world and calls upon psychologists to recognize the interrelatedness of psychological phenomena and the essential features of the society in which they arise.[33] Laing characterizes schizophrenia as an expression of "ontological insecurity" and notes its manifestation in the works of such modern authors as Kafka and Beckett and in the paintings of Francis Bacon. He describes the ontologically insecure person as an individual who experiences himself as more unreal than real, more dead than alive. Such a person has difficulty feeling autonomous and differentiating himself from the rest of the world. He lacks a sense of his own temporal continuity, consistency, and cohesiveness and may experience his self as partially divorced from his body. Lacking certainty regarding his own identity, he finds it impossible to share his experience with other people.[34] Compare this description to the words uttered by Kafka's young supplicant in *The Penal Colony*:

> There has never been a time in which I have been convinced from within myself that I am alive. You see, I have only such a fugitive awareness of things around me that I always feel they were once real and are now fleeting away. I have a constant longing, my dear sir, to catch a glimpse of things as they may have been before they show themselves to me. I feel that then they were calm and beautiful. It must be so, for I often hear people talking about them as though they were.[35]

Beckett's characters frequently express similar yearnings for a long-lost vision of the world as it must have been at some calmer and more beautiful epoch when it was still possible to perceive things as real, stable, and orderly.

Since Laing defines his approach as "existential psychology" and since Beckett is often referred to as the existentialist writer par excellence, it may be useful to turn now to the existentialist characterization of the human consciousness as put forth by Sartre in *L'Etre et le néant*. Sartre differentiates between two modes of being that he labels "pour-soi" and "en-soi." At the risk of a gross oversimplification, one might define the "pour-soi" as the mode of being of the human consciousness and the "en-soi" as the mode of being of things or objects.

Sartre discusses all the possible relationships of a human

being to the world in terms of the "pour-soi," or consciousness, which is the originator of these relationships. In relationships with things, for example, the consciousness is always the subject and calls things into existence by differentiating and establishing rapports among them. Relationships with other people are more complicated since, unlike things, people possess consciousnesses that exist independently of the perception of any given observer and thus do not wait for an observer's perception to endow them with existence. In addition, other people are capable of turning an observing consciousness into the object of their own perception. The consciousness may thus experience itself as both subject and object, though never simultaneously. Sartre characterizes relations between individual consciousnesses as a continual battle for dominance in the Hegelian master/slave mode: Who will be subject? Who object?

Another relationship examined by Sartre is that of the consciousness to itself. The consciousness strives constantly toward an unattainable state of "en-soi-pour-soi," i. e., a state of permanent, atemporal being that would be conscious of its own existence. Since it is not possible for the self to achieve the distance and separation from itself necessary for such observation, we can never become objects for ourselves.

Sartre obviously deals at length with the problem of perspective. For him, there is no such thing as a pure, total perspective. Just as, for Planck, all scientific procedures imply the adoption of a limited and limiting perspective, for Sartre "la perception ne se conçoit jamais en dehors d'une attitude vis-à-vis du monde."[36] Sartre states that geometric space—the pure reciprocity of spatial relationships (i. e., the concept of space that informed linear perspective)—is contrary to human reality.

In 1946, Eric Bentley characterized Sartre's Existentialist Theater as the "theater of the inner eye," by way of contrast with Brecht's Epic Theater, which he called "the theater of the outer eye."[37] In comparison with Beckett's drama, which could certainly be defined as a theater of the inner eye, Sartre's appears quite traditional, in style if not in content. Beckett has translated Sartre's ideas into new dramatic forms that convey with more immediacy and more esthetic potency many of the same philosophical concerns developed by the grand master of existentialism.

Nowhere is the rupture of linear perspective more evident than in the domain of the contemporary visual arts. Early in his career, Beckett published several critical texts on modern art, especially on the painting of his friends Bram and Geer van Velde, in which he discusses the breakdown of linear perspective and the new vision that has come to replace it. In "La Peinture des van Velde ou le monde et le pantalon," he characterizes Bram's painting as the representation of isolated things in suspense and remarks of it: "Impossible de mettre de l'ordre dans l'élémentaire."[38] Geer's work portrays shifting planes, vibrating contours, an equilibrium that breaks down and reforms under the eye of the beholder. Of this continuous movement—undoing, redoing, coming, and going—Beckett says: "On dirait l'insurrection des moléçules [*sic*], l'intérieur d'une pierre un millième de seconde avant qu'elle ne se désagrège."[39] Both brothers confront the dilemma of how to represent change: Bram, change in space; Geer, change in time. They choose different solutions: where Bram artificially arrests the process of change in order to attempt to seize an object in isolation and immobility, Geer paints things in succession, agitated by a time that prevents us from seeing them, and makes of this blinding succession the very object of his representation. Geer's treatment of time thus seems quite similar to Proust's portrayal of the past, which Beckett describes as "agitated and multicoloured by the phenomena of its hours" (*Proust*, p. 5). Beckett concludes that both painters' goals are unrealizable and claims that the power of these artists' work lies in their calm acceptance of the impossibility of representation.[40]

In another text on the van Veldes, Beckett suggests that the originality of their painting derives from their attitude of mourning vis-à-vis the object of representation, or the "deuil de l'objet."[41] Having accepted the loss of the object, they choose as their goal the representation of the conditions of its escape and accept the task of painting that which renders painting impossible. Theirs is thus a "peinture d'acceptation, entrevoyant dans l'absence de rapport et dans l'absence d'objet le nouveau rapport et le nouvel objet,"[42] just as, for Mallarmé, the goal of art was to create "la notion d'un objet, échappant, qui fait défaut."[43] Beckett later generalized this acceptance of the impossibility of art to represent when he defined the modern artist's condition in a now-famous passage from his "Three Dialogues": "The expression that there is nothing to express, nothing with which to express, nothing from which to express, no power to express, no desire to express, together with the obligation to express."[44]

In summary, then, Beckett sees the task of modern art to be the attempt at visual representation of movement—shifting contours, disintegration and reintegration of objects in space and time before the eyes of the painter and the spectator. This art is characterized by the absence of objects and the absence of relationships among objects, as well as by the impossibility of order. All of these factors point to the impossibility of representation, which thus becomes the only conceivable subject matter for the modern artist and which creates an art unabashedly self-conscious in its relentless questioning of the possibility of its very existence. This self-consciousness, which is also a fundamental characteristic of modern literature, calls to mind Sartre's description of the human consciousness' compelling yet unfulfillable need to observe itself. Beckett fully realizes the widespread implications of the type of painting he analyzes when he says of the brothers van Velde: "C'est qu'au fond la peinture ne les intéresse pas. Ce qui les intéresse, c'est la condition humaine."[45]

Instead of relying solely upon Beckett's views of modern art in order to point out, in an admittedly tautological manner, the relations of his work to those of modern artists, it will be useful to examine a brief sampling of other statements on the subject to see what light they can throw upon this discussion of the breakdown of linear perspective in modern art.

In their overview of the history of perspective in geometry and art, Albert Flocon and René Taton assert that since the theory of linear perspective has given rise to no new discoveries in the field of mathematics or of painting for over a century, it has been abandoned by practitioners in both domains. For this theory supposes a Euclidean structure of physical space that contradicts contemporary concepts of the structure of the physical universe. What is more, technological innovations such as cameras, radar, telescopic lenses, microscopes, and aerial pictures, which afford constantly changing points of view, including close-ups and long-distance shots, have rendered obsolete the construct of space as tranquil, stable, and measurable with the ruler and compass.[46] In *Proust*, Beckett comments upon the capacity of photography to decompose objects: "The most modern applications of photography can frame a single church successively in the arcades of all the others and the entire horizon in the arch of a bridge or between two adjacent leaves, thus decomposing the illusion of a solid object into its manifold component aspects"(p. 34). Susan Sontag views the invention of the camera as a major contribution to a new theory of perspective in painting:

> The large influence that photography exercised upon the Impressionists is a commonplace of art history. . . . The camera's translation of reality into highly polarized areas of light and dark, the free or arbitrary cropping of the image in photographs, the indifference of photographers to making space, particularly background space, intelligible—these were the main inspiration for the Impressionist painters' . . . experiments in flattened perspective and unfamiliar angles and decentralized forms that are sliced off by the picture's edge. ("They depict life in scraps and fragments," as Stieglitz observed in 1909.)[47]

Indeed, the Impressionists are often described as the founders of modern painting, the first group of artists to effect a definitive break with linear perspective and the notion of immutable, permanent space that it implied. They attempted in their works to capture the fleeting instant, to represent objects and landscapes as they appeared to a particular human eye at a specific moment under particular atmospheric conditions—all variables which could never be reproduced and which rendered the treatment of time and space in each canvas unique and specific to the momentary vision, or impression, of the individual artist. The Impressionists also insisted upon the materiality of the canvas as a flat surface covered with pigment which the spectator looked at, and not through.[48]

Cézanne, who was associated for a time with the Impressionists, broke from them in order to explore different avenues of experimentation regarding form, color, and spatial organization in painting. He was the first artist to abandon the convention of the unique point of view in painting, for even the Impressionists had retained this element of linear perspective. Cézanne experimented with the presentation of objects from two different angles of vision in several of his still lifes and landscapes. This innovation is of course now familiar thanks to the later work of the Cubists, upon whom Cézanne exerted a great influence. With Cézanne, the material surface of the canvas definitively regained the ascendancy over depth which it had lost since the quattrocento and which had begun to assert itself in the Impressionists' works; a painting was no longer a transparent window leading the eye to a rational space beyond it that was subject to the same rules and obeyed the same principles in all paintings, but a space of its own which invented, for each composition, an organization unique to the work at hand.

The Cubists, led by Picasso and Braque, took Cézanne's work a step further, decomposing objects into their geometric elements and representing them from multiple points of view. Writing of them in 1913, Apollinaire defined their new concept of space as the "fourth dimension."[49] The Cubists' experiments with pictorial space led them quite naturally to explore the technique of collage—the juxtaposition of fragments of actual objects on the surface of the canvas. This method made final the break with the idea of the canvas as a window pointing to depths beyond it, for it created a space that lay concretely in front of the picture plane.[50]

Alberto Giacometti, whose sculptures are often compared to Beckett's literary and dramatic images, describes the problem of painting a glass upon a table in terms that recall Beckett's description of the van Veldes' attempts to represent change:

> Chaque fois que je regarde le verre, il a l'air de se *refaire*, c'est-à-dire que sa réalité devient douteuse, parce que sa projection dans mon cerveau est douteuse, ou partielle. On le voit comme s'il *disparaissait* . . . resurgissait . . . disparaissait . . . resurgissait . . . . Toute la démarche des artistes modernes est dans cette volonté de saisir, de posséder quelque chose qui fuit constamment.[51]

Giacometti's statement manifests the same attitude towards art as an impossible, yet urgently necessary, task that dominates Beckett's critical and fictional writings.

Beckett's revolutionary dramatic perspective is informed by his concepts of the impossibility of establishing a "correct" point of view upon a given object, the doubtful reality of every object exterior to the self, the fragmentary nature of all perception, the continual change undergone by the objects of our vision, as well as the artist's (unrealizable) will to seize and give permanent form to a constantly fleeing vision.

Chapter 1

"IN BOUNDLESS SPACE, IN ENDLESS TIME":

Time, Space, and Movement in Beckett's Work

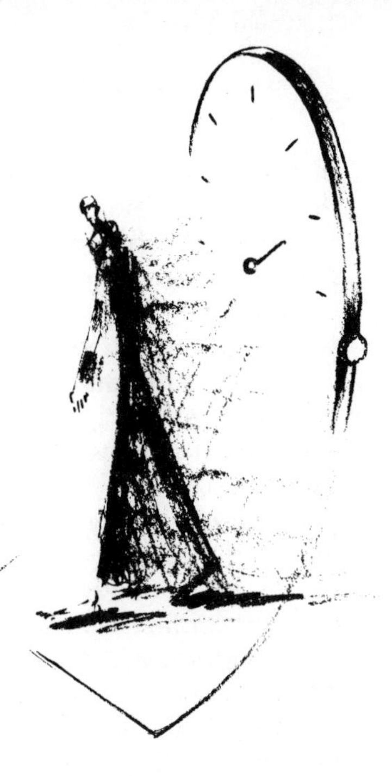

Space, time, and movement: the three basic obstacles to vision in the Beckettian universe. Place, time, and action: the three unities of classical French theater, which suggest the same way of seeing the world as does painting in linear perspective. Classical art, whether dramatic or plastic, separated the time and space of the observer from those of the phenomenon observed, thus rendering vision possible. Beckett puts it this way: "The classical artist assumes omniscience and omnipotence. He raises himself artificially out of Time in order to give relief to his chronology and causality to his development" (*Proust*, p. 62). Perspective was possible in the post-Renaissance theater because the dramatist and, therefore, the viewer were removed from the time, place, and action of the drama, and they possessed a stable and omniscient point of view that was clearly differentiated from that of any of the characters. Such stability was possible only in an era when people believed in the existence of another world—another kind of time and place—whose perspective they could imitate while viewing or creating works of art.

In Beckett's drama, on the other hand, the only point of view available to the dramatist and the spectators is as partial as that of the characters; we move along with them in the fragmented time and space that compose their universe, and while we may see them from a different perspective than that from which they see themselves, our vision is no more reliable nor stable than theirs. For we are observing people drifting purposelessly through the same undefinable, formless time and space that we ourselves inhabit; in our age, there exist no others. Vision in perspective requires distance between subject and object, in the theater as elsewhere. When limits are vague and constantly eroding, "here" and "there" and "now" and "then" become confused; continual movement, or "déplacement," which is the primary characteristic of Beckett's (and our) conception of space and time, impedes perception, whose prerequisite is stability. Now that our only conceivable universe is the one in which we live, there is no way to step outside it, even in our imagination, in order to escape the continually changing point of view inherent to observers who stand in the middle of their field of observation and who find themselves necessarily subject to all of its influences. Beckett states the problem in these words: "What elsewhere can there be to this infinite here?" (*Texts for Nothing*, 6, p. 102). The only believable alternative to the world in which we live is one in which we do not exist: if we call our universe into being by looking at it, when we no longer look, there remains precisely nothing. As long as God's eye organized the universe from above and beyond, an individual's perception was less problematic, for reality did not depend upon the human consciousness for its very existence. When Bishop Berkeley said "esse est percipi," he meant that our being comes from being perceived in the eye of God. When Beckett uses the same words at the beginning of *Film*, he is referring to the unstable, blurred, yet unavoidable self-perception that is now the only possible source of being: "All extraneous perception suppressed, animal, human, divine, self-perception maintains in being" (p. 11). Now that no above nor beyond is conceivable, there is no position from which to see. Indeed, there may no longer be anything left to see, either: "I see nothing, it's because there is nothing, or it's because I have no eyes, or both" (*The Unnamable*, p. 410).

Beckett has stated that he turned to the theater as a respite from the ordeal of writing novels, where "on s'avance dans le noir," and that he finds it comforting to work in a medium which requires an artist to submit to certain rules and constraints, no matter how much he may seem to challenge them.[1] One of the inescapable realities of the theater that Beckett has had to confront is its visuality. As Hugh Kenner points out, "The drama is a ritual enacted in an enclosed space into which fifty or more people are staring."[2] Vision, or rather the impossibility thereof, is a recurrent theme in Beckett's work. What, then, do these fifty or more people see when they cast their eyes upon the Beckettian stage? Actors, or parts of them. Sets, occasionally. Action, less and less often. Why do they continue to look? What compels them to fix their gaze upon a scene practically devoid of all the elements traditionally associated in many people's minds with theater? The word *theater* comes from the Greek *thea*, for the act of seeing. If, as Beckett often suggests, there is nothing left to see, or at least no way of seeing whatever might be left, is theater then impossible? Not any more so than a novel like *The Unnamable*, which is written about the impossibility of writing, indeed, even of speaking. Just as the voice in *The Unnamable* assails us with a description of the conditions that prevent it from speaking what it feels compelled to speak, so the characters of Beckett's theater communicate the impossibility of seeing what they long to see and explore in language, gesture, and images the barriers that impede their vision. We accompany them on their journeys through space and time in search of the right place and the right moment—the location of the unseeable, unnamable object that constantly eludes their ceaseless efforts of perception.

Beckett has indeed broken radically with the classical unities in order to create images of a new kind of time and space in his drama. His plays, however, have often been described as classical in their own right. This is so, not because Beckett follows the precepts of classical theatrical esthetics, but because he has found new techniques, more relevant to the imagination of his twentieth-century spectators, that enable him to portray a fragmented, fluctuating, and unseeable universe in a unified and esthetically satisfying dramatic form. Before exploring the mechanisms of Beckett's drama and their relation to the problem of perspective, it is necessary to define the categories of time, space, and movement that act as veils upon the eyes of Beckett's characters and audiences. For, in the Beckettian oeuvre, "space and time conceal—from a being whose deepest need is to see."[3]

Beckett's essay on Proust provides valuable insight into the workings of time and perspective in the writings of Beckett as well as Proust. Beginning with an allusion to Proust's "perspectivism," Beckett proceeds to examine "that double-headed monster of damnation and salvation—Time" (p. 1). He discusses how time acts upon desire to impede one's perception of other people and of oneself—a concern central to the works of both

Proust and Beckett. He asserts that the self, and its desires, change constantly over time and can therefore never coincide with the objects they pursue:

> We are not merely more weary because of yesterday, we are other, no longer what we were before the calamity of yesterday. . . . The aspirations of yesterday were valid for yesterday's ego, not for to-day's. We are disappointed at the nullity of what we are pleased to call attainment. But what is attainment? The identification of the subject with the object of his desire. The subject has died—and perhaps many times—on the way. For subject B to be disappointed by the banality of an object chosen by subject A is as illogical as to expect one's hunger to be dissipated by the spectacle of Uncle eating his dinner. (P. 3)

If the self changes daily, so, therefore, does the world: "the world being a projection of the individual's consciousness. . . . The creation of the world did not take place once and for all time, but takes place every day" (p. 8).

Beckett describes the Proustian answer to the problem of time as "the identification of immediate with past experience" (p. 55), or the workings of "involuntary memory" (p. 19), which enable "the communicant . . . [to be] for the moment an extra-temporal being" (p. 56). Such an experience conquers time and, with it, death: "The Proustian solution consists . . . in the negation of Time and Death, the negation of Death because the negation of Time. Death is dead because Time is dead" (p. 56). But Proust's involuntary memory is, by definition, an accidental occurrence that cannot be summoned by the will. How, then, can an individual conquer time other than sporadically and unexpectedly at the rare moments that trigger the involuntary memory? Proust's answer is clear to Beckett: "He understands the necessity of art. For in the brightness of art alone can be deciphered the baffled ecstasy that he had known before the inscrutable superficies of a cloud, a triangle, a spire, a flower, a pebble" (p. 57).

Beckett regards art differently: it is not a salvation, as for Proust, but an impossible task doomed to failure from the outset. While he asks the same questions about time as Proust and supplies many of the same answers, the ultimate solution continues to elude him. For Proust, "the workings of involuntary memory . . . restore the individual integrity of things in the paradisiac joy of the past resuscitated and made timeless."[4] For Beckett, escape from time is impossible and things therefore remain fragmented, changing, imperceptible, and unrepresentable.

The most Beckettian art seems willing or able to achieve is not a Proustian victory over time and space, but images of the time and space from which not even art can deliver us. Beckett described such an image of time in his "Director's Notebook" for the 1971 Berlin production of *Happy Days*: "Relate frequency of broken speech and action to discontinuity of time. Winnie's time experience incomprehensible transport from one inextricable present to the next, those past unremembered, those to come inconceivable."[5] Similar descriptions of the spasmodic, discontinuous movement of a time whose end is inconceivable appear throughout Beckett's texts. Consider these two examples from an early and a recent work:

> It's every second that is the worst, it's a chronicle, the seconds pass, one after another, jerkily, no flow, they don't pass, they arrive, bang, bang, they bang into you, bounce off, fall and never move again, when you have nothing left to say you talk of time, seconds of time, there are some people add them together to make a life, I can't. (*The Unnamable*, p. 395)

> Close-up of a dial. . . . One hand only. . . . It advances by fits and starts. No tick. Leaps from dot to dot with so lightning a leap that but for its new position it had not stirred. . . . despair certain nights of its ever attaining the last. (*Ill Seen Ill Said*, pp. 45–46)

For Beckett, time's movement, from which there is no escape, thwarts the self's desire to perceive its own identity as a changeless essence, to add up the unconnected seconds of its days to make a life it can call its own, to salvage the fragments of its existence and integrate them into a comprehensible whole. Such a feat is possible only in a domain where time as we know it does not exist, and such a domain is as nonexistent as is the essential self that we all long to perceive. Bergson spoke of this essential self as "ce moi réel et libre, qui est en effet étranger à l'espace. . . . [et] que nous apercevons . . . toutes les fois que, par un vigoureux effort de réflexion, nous détachons les yeux de l'ombre qui nous suit pour rentrer en nous-mêmes."[6]

Beckett's characters often close their eyes in an attempt to see the real "me" who resides within, but without success.

The unquenchable desire to rejoin the essence of the self calls to mind the philosophy of Schopenhauer, which exerted an undeniable influence upon Beckett's work. The origin of the perceiver/perceived split in the self lies in the feeling of separation from the essence of being, or in what Schopenhauer calls the "principle of individuation" that keeps us from experiencing the underlying unity of the universe. Schopenhauer drew heavily from Indian philosophy in his concept of the Will as the inmost nature of all things, the "thing-in-itself." The Will is independent of time and space, irrational, unifies subject and object, and expresses itself as an endless striving to be. Individuality, whose principles are space and time, which are subjective creations of the intellect, is illusory. Salvation for Schopenhauer resides in acceptance of the ancient Vedic formula "This thou art." One of the paths to enlightenment consists of esthetic experience; contemplation of a work of art permits observers to feel a unity with the object they behold, thereby escaping individuality. Music is the highest art form, since it embodies the Will: "The other arts . . . speak only of shadows, but it speaks of the thing itself."[7] Beckett analyzes the significance of music in the work of Proust in terms of Schopenhauer's philosophy (*Proust*, pp. 70–72), and his own use of music in drama bespeaks a close affinity with the views of the German philosopher. Schopenhauer's concept of the unifying power of art seems, however, to coincide more exactly with that of Proust than with that of the more pessimistic Beckett, who, while he clearly considers art a striving of the Will, holds forth no hope that the veil of Maya, the principle of individuation that gives birth to isolated phenomena, can ever be lifted from the eyes of humanity.

Like Schopenhauer's Will, the "true" Beckettian self exists outside of both space and time. Like Descartes's "je," it is "une substance dont toute l'essence n'est que de penser, et qui pour être n'a besoin d'aucun lieu."[8] But just as Beckettian man, and woman, can never escape from the fluctuations of time which prevent them from being and perceiving a stable self, so are they condemned to change positions constantly in an earthly space from which there is no issue and in which there is no fixed point for them to occupy that would afford a complete and clear view of the constantly shifting field around them, or which would permit them to remain still long enough so that they might be the same subject from one instant to the next. The self is unattainable because each time we change places to look for it, we have become other in terms of both space and time, and both the object and subject of our search have vanished.

Voyages have long been used in literature as metaphors for human life, and Beckett often borrows this image to portray his characters' movement through the space and time of their earthly existence. Sometimes, and most frequently in the early works, the journey takes place at least nominally in geographical space: Watt goes to Knott's house; Mercier and Camier traverse the countryside by train, bicycle, and foot; Molloy sets off in search of his mother; Moran pursues Molloy; Pozzo and Lucky are going to the fair; Maddy Rooney fetches her husband at the train station. All of these trips, however, may be read on another level as descents into the inner realm of consciousness, a voyage made explicit in such other Beckettian works as *The Unnamable, Krapp's Last Tape, Embers, Eh Joe, Not I, That Time*, and *A Piece of Monologue*, to name but a few.

Molloy, who participates in both types of journey, explains why he gave up his wanderings in the outside world to stay in the isolation of his mother's room:

> Though I fail to see, never having left my region, what right I have to speak of its characteristics. No, I never escaped, and even the limits of my region were unknown to me. But I felt they were far away. But this feeling was based on nothing serious, it was a simple feeling. For if my region had ended no further than my feet could carry me, surely I would have left it changing slowly. For regions do not suddenly end, as far as I know, but gradually merge into one another. . . . however far I went, and in no matter what direction, it was always the same sky, always the same earth, precisely, day after day and night after night. On the other hand, if it is true that regions gradually merge into one another, and this remains to be proved, then I may well have left mine many times, thinking I was still within it. But I preferred to abide by my simple feeling and its voice that said, Molloy, your region is vast, you have never left it and you never shall. And wheresoever you wander, within its distant limits, things will always be the same, precisely. It would thus appear, if this is so, that my movements owed nothing to the places they caused to vanish, but were due to something else, to the buckled wheel that carried me, in unforeseeable jerks,

> from fatigue to rest, and inversely, for example. But now I do not wander any more, anywhere any more, and indeed I scarcely stir at all, and yet nothing is changed. And the confines of my room, of my bed, of my body, are as remote from me as were those of my region. . . . And the cycle continues, joltingly, of flight and bivouac, in an Egypt without bounds. . . . And when I see my hands, on the sheet, . . . they are not mine, less than ever mine. (*Molloy*, pp. 65–66)

This lengthy and most important passage summarizes the characteristics of Beckettian space as well as the perceptual problems related to it. The opening words, "I fail to see," refer on one level to Molloy's doubt about his right to speak of his region's characteristics. However, one may also read them as a commentary upon Molloy's lack of visual perspective, which has been hindered by his inability to stand outside the space he calls his "region," in spite of all his wandering. The reason he offers for never leaving his region is simple: its boundaries seemed too far away. But he admits that his notion of their distance from him might have been due merely to the fact that they were shifting and therefore imperceptible. Indeed, he may even have crossed them without knowing it. At any rate, wherever he has roamed, space has always appeared the same to him, and he thus attributes his compulsive movement to an unknown force—"the buckled wheel"—which continues to jolt him by fits and starts even now, when he has ceased his travels in the world outside his mother's room. He still fails to see and is no closer to leaving his region than before: however circumscribed its limits, they remain untraversable. Wherever he goes, either in the countryside or in his inner "region," he will encounter nothing but "the same, precisely": a space where all is in motion, whose confines cannot be escaped, and where the self perceives its various parts as foreign objects, fragments created by the mobility of the space and time in which it is imprisoned. While the self is never the same from one moment to the next and space and time never remain stable enough to permit vision, one still, paradoxically, encounters "the same, precisely" wherever one wanders in Beckett's universe: the same flux, uncertainty, and invisibility.

The Beckettian inward journeys thus prove to be no more fruitful than movement towards a goal in the external world. In both cases, the goal, as well as the traveler, changes constantly, and the voyages wind up resembling the "vicious circule" of the Joycean purgatory once described by Beckett: "Movement is non-directional—or multi-directional, and a step forward is, by definition, a step back. . . . And no more than this; neither prize nor penalty; simply a series of stimulants to enable the kitten to catch its tail."[9] As we all know, the kitten never catches its tail, just as the Beckettian voyager never catches up with himself, either in space or in time. Perhaps nowhere in the Beckettian oeuvre is there a clearer image of the circular, non-directional, meaningless movement of our existence than in *The Lost Ones*, Beckett's description of life in a closed cylinder where there are no names, no voices, no stories, no reasons—nothing but moving and resting. Ionesco interprets this text as a picture of a humanity yearning to escape from the world to which it has been abandoned toward a higher realm which it knows to be no longer accessible: "Il s'agit dans ce texte . . . de la longue, interminable agonie de l'humanité entière jetée, abandonnée, dans ce trou qu'est le monde ou dans les limbes, cherchant péniblement à remonter vers les cercles supérieurs au-delà de ce monde justement, vers un ciel ardemment désiré et inaccessible."[10]

While the inescapable time and space of this hole we call the world bar us from satisfying our ardent desire for another, it is, paradoxically, the predicament of desire that calls earthly time and space into being. For to desire means, at one and the same time, "to long or hope for" and "to feel the loss of."[11] Although Winnie in *Happy Days*, for example, is transported "from one inextricable present to the next," her thoughts are constantly directed to an imperfectly remembered past or to an unknowable future, thus negating her perception of her existence in each of her inextricable presents. Just as the perpetual, unsynchronized motion of time and desire keep us from being ourselves in the present, so the fluctuations of space preclude our experiencing what Heidegger termed the "dasein," or "being there." Beckett's characters are never fully "there" nor "here," because their desires take them from one undefinable, uninhabitable place and time to another, whose boundaries are equally uncertain, and which comes no closer to satisfying their need than did the place and time they have just left: "So I went . . . , straining towards an issue . . . my mind panting after this and that and always flung back to where there was nothing" ("The Calmative," p. 44).

Near the end of *Endgame*, Hamm announces to Clov: "I was never there" (p. 74). The voice of *Texts for Nothing* has the same problem regarding its present location—it is unable to believe itself "there": "I don't know where I am. . . . The first thing would be to believe I'm there, if I could do that I'd lap up the rest, there'd be none more credulous than me, if I were there" (Text 5, pp. 95, 98). As evidenced by her name, Miss Fitt, of *All That Fall*, experiences a similar dilemma: "I suppose the truth is I am not there, Mrs. Rooney, just not really there at all" (p. 55). Later in the same play, Maddy tells Dan of an amazing discovery made by a psychiatrist about one of his patients: "The trouble with her was she had never really been born!" (p. 84). Similar references to people who have never been born occur frequently in Beckett's work.[12] We read, for example, in *Texts for Nothing*, that "one is frightened to be born, no, one wishes one were, so as to begin to die" (Text 5, p. 95). Just as the creation of the world takes place every day, so the birth of the self is not one definitive event delimited by identifiable temporal/spatial boundaries, but a continual process which is over the moment it has begun and therefore without beginning or end. Because of the multiplicity of "I's" that inhabit successively a different time and space inaccessible to any past or future self, all births are abortions, and the true self, which would live in the "here" and "now," is never born: "Today is the first day, it begins, . . . all adown it I'll be born and born, births for nothing, and come to night without having been" (*The Unnamable*, p. 400). As Beckett notes in the passage from *Texts for Nothing* cited above, the same perpetual motion of space and time that renders birth impossible also calls into question the likelihood of the ending we know as death.

Desire transports us out of our present situation toward a time and space which are not yet or which are no more. Without desire, we could live fully in our present; we could experience and perceive ourselves as complete beings anchored firmly in a changeless spatiotemporal dimension. Yet it is desire, or, as Beckett calls it, need, "that is the absolute predicament of particular human identity."[13] Compare these words to Sartre's characterization of desire: "L'homme est fondamentalement *désir d'être*. . . . La réalité humaine est désir d'être-en-soi."[14]

Sartre's atemporal être-en-soi is as impossible a goal for the human consciousness as is the freedom from desire for which

Beckett's characters yearn. And for Sartre, as for Beckett and Proust, it is time that stands in the way:

> C'est le temps qui me sépare . . . de la réalisation de mes désirs. . . . Sans la succession des "après," je serais *tout de suite* ce que je veux être, il n'y aurait plus de distance entre moi et moi. . . .
>
> *Le temps me sépare de moi-même*, de ce que j'ai été, de ce que je veux être, de ce que je veux faire, des choses et d'autrui.[15]

If successive, disconnected "après" keep the consciousness from catching up with itself in time, the consciousness' mobile, fragmented, unstable, changing vision of space is another barrier to self-perception:

> L'être spatialisant est le Pour-soi . . . ; l'espace . . . est l'instabilité du monde saisi comme totalité, en tant qu'il peut toujours se désagréger en multiplicité externe. L'espace . . . n'est ni le continu ni le discontinu, mais le passage permanent du continu au discontinu. . . .
>
> L'identification *temporelle* du mobile avec soi . . . fait se dévoiler la trajectoire, c'est-à-dire fait surgir l'espace. . . . Par le mouvement, l'espace s'engendre dans le temps.[16]

Sartre makes it clear that the coincidence of the consciousness with itself is the ultimate desire of every human being. Beckett is not so consistent in identifying the precise object of desire. Is it, as it so often seems, especially in the later works, the essential self? Or is it Molloy's mother? The Unnamable's name? Knott's house? Godot? The carafe of water in *Act Without Words I*? Krapp's past selves? A mercy-killing for Bolton? Willie's attention? The escape from perception attempted in *Film*? The "other woman" of *Play*? In spite of the apparent diversity of these aspirations, they share one important characteristic: elusiveness. The beings who desire inhabit a time and/or place separated from that of the goals they are attempting to reach, which keeps them not only from possessing what they long for, but even from clearly perceiving it: "No object prolonged in this temporal dimension tolerates possession, meaning by possession total possession, only to be achieved by the complete identification of object and subject" (*Proust*, p. 41). For only in an extratemporal, extraspatial dimension, which is not subject to the process of change, could objects remain still long enough for us to see them as they are, and not as they have been or are in the process of becoming: "La chose immobile dans le vide, voilà enfin la chose visible, l'objet pur. Je n'en vois pas d'autre."[17] Only in a state of timelessness and spacelessness could we as subjects arrest the flow of desire within us which propels our gaze from one fleeting object to another.

The condition of immobility in which a stable, unchanging subject might finally attain, see, and possess an immutable object seems to be the ultimate, and impossible, goal of Beckettian desire. Death appears to fulfill more of these prerequisites than any other state of which we can conceive, yet how can we be sure that the all-important requirement of perception of one's felicity will not be tragically lacking once life ceases, that we will have "just enough brain intact to allow you to exult" (*Molloy*, p. 140), that we will be allowed "One moment more. One last. Grace to breathe that void. Know happiness" (*Ill Seen Ill Said*, p. 59)? Hence Beckett's abiding and obsessive interest in the approach to death and its unknown and unimaginable aftermath: nearly all of his works may be read as portrayals of either the last moments of human existence on earth or of the possible states of consciousness once time as we know it has ended. In neither case are his wishes for unequivocal perception and ablation of desire fulfilled. Death is indeed the only conceivable victory over the time in which we are condemned to live, yet victory is hollow when the victor dies in battle. As Sartre writes, "C'est parce que le pour-soi est l'être qui réclame toujours un après, qu'il n'y aucune place pour la mort dans l'être qu'il est pour-soi."[18]

If, as Beckett seems to suspect, death is not the absolute end of consciousness, the alternative is even worse: we can expect, as Neary announces in *Murphy*, "At the best, nothing; at the worst, this again" (p. 228). It is impossible to conceive of a complete cessation of consciousness, because a state of nothingness is unthinkable in a universe whose only creator is human perception—such a state cannot exist if its only possible source, the mind, is extinguished. Martin Esslin summarizes the dilemma as follows: "Consciousness cannot conceive of itself as nonexisting and is therefore only conceivable as unlimited, without end."[19] Or, in Clov's words, "It'll never end, I'll never go" (*Endgame*, p. 81).

The worst, "this again," is explored by Beckett in what Cohn has labelled his "post-death plays": *Play*, *Not I*, and *Footfalls*.[20] Although Beckett's "post-death" voices may be freed from the material realities of their earthly existence, they continue to struggle with the same problems of time, space, and perception that afflicted them during their lives—death has solved nothing, liberated no one. The women and man in *Play* rehash ad nauseam the unresolved details of their adulterous existence; the mouth in *Not I* pours forth a torrent of memories of its fragmented, speechless, and incomprehensible life without being able to use the word "I"—its various selves cannot coincide in time or space even after death; and May in *Footfalls* paces obsessively back and forth on her little strip, "revolving it all" (p. 48)—all the same questions about time, place, and identity that plagued her earthly life have accompanied her across the threshold into death. The Unnamable prefigures these "post-death" theatrical voices—from its position beyond the grave, it poses the same questions they do and finds the answers equally elusive and the end to its suffering just as unforeseeable: "Where now? Who now? When now? . . . I am obliged to speak. I shall never be silent. Never" (p. 291). Though it has withdrawn from earthly time, it can speak of no other: "There are no days here, but I use the expression" (p. 292). The time it had hoped to escape by dying continues to haunt it and to invade the domain of its eternity:

> The question may be asked . . . why time doesn't pass, doesn't pass from you, why it piles up all about you . . . , why it buries you grain by grain neither dead nor alive . . . oh I know it's immaterial, time is one thing, I another, but the question may be asked, why time doesn't pass, just like that, . . . en passant, to pass the time." (P. 389)

If Beckett's "post-death" works present characters who ask questions about time in order to help pass the time of which they cannot manage to be free, Beckett's "waiting plays"—*Godot*, *Endgame*, and *Happy Days*—"yield different images of an unending present."[21] Cohn distinguishes these waiting plays from others, which she labels "the death's threshold plays"—*That Time*, *Krapp's Last Tape*, and three television dramas.[22]

This categorization seems somewhat arbitrary in view of the fact that Beckett considers all human life to be nothing more than an approach to death: "Astride of a grave and a difficult birth. Down in the hole, lingeringly, the grave-digger puts on the forceps" (*Waiting for Godot*, p. 58). The "continuous moments in the waiting plays" and the "hovering moments in the death's threshold plays" belong to the same time as does the "blend of moment and continuum in the plays wrested from the void" (the "post-death" plays).[23] For the image of time as a diminishing, but never-ending, progression of same yet different moments leading to no identifiable goal is remarkably consistent in the Beckettian oeuvre. Whether his characters speak from death's threshold, from beyond it, or from an earlier moment in their lives, their lamentations echo one another closely: they feel caught up in the movement of time that carries them from one disconnected moment to another; their present existence is negated by their compulsive attraction to a past and/or future in which they know they will never reside; any activity they may perform, however purposeful it might at first appear to be, can be reduced in the final analysis to the act of waiting. They wait for different things—Godot, a tranquilizer, the right moment to sing, the end of a story, the extinction of a torturous spotlight—and with different attitudes, yet the waiting is the same. Either the awaited object never arrives, or it arrives too late, when the thirst for it has subsided, or the "right" moment passes by unnoticed, never to be retrieved. Beckett parodies the different hopes that sustain our endless waiting in *Rough for Theatre II*, where A and B discuss the "positive elements" that keep C going in order to "make him think . . . that some day things might change": "good graces of an heirless aunt. . . . unfinished game of chess with a correspondent in Tasmania . . . hope not dead of living to see the extermination of the species . . . literary aspirations incompletely stifled . . . bottom of a dairy-woman in Waterloo Lane . . . you see the kind of thing" (pp. 88, 90). In one of his early untitled French poems, Beckett wrote this about the act of waiting: "et on attend/adverbe" (*Poèmes suivi de mirlitonnades*, p. 9). Lawrence Harvey comments perceptively on this line: " 'Adverbe' replaces any specific adverb and says, in effect, 'It makes no difference how one waits or what one does while waiting; only the necessity of waiting has any significance.' The steady passage of time, that is, cannot be objectively modified. Adverbs have negligible effect on verbs."[24] In his study of Beckett's early works, Harvey analyzes in detail the omnipresent theme of "too soon/too late" which is an essential corollary to that of waiting. When, as is so often the case in Beckett's work, the awaited object is perception of the self by the self, time bars the way. The moment is either too soon for total perception—i. e., the self has not completed its series of changes in time and is thus not yet the whole self—or the moment for perception has passed—at the instant of death, should it ever arrive, when the self would cease to change and therefore be wholly perceivable, its capacity to perceive would be eradicated. Victor, the main character of Beckett's first, and unpublished, play, *Eleutheria*, describes the problem in these terms: "Si j'étais mort je ne saurais pas que je suis mort. C'est la seule chose que j'ai contre la mort. Je veux jouir de ma mort. C'est là la liberté: se voir mort."[25]

Harvey attributes Beckett's notion of the "distressing décalage"[26] of time to the constant mobility of subject and object that precludes their convergence and thus keeps us forever separate from the goal of our fruitless, but compulsory, waiting. As Beckett states in *Proust*, this "décalage" affects relationships with other people, as well as perception of oneself:

> When it is a case of human intercourse, we are faced by the problem of an object whose mobility is not merely a function of the subject's, but independent and personal: two separate and immanent dynamisms related by no system of synchronisation. So that whatever the object, our thirst for possession is, by definition, insatiable. At the best, all that is realised in Time (all Time produce), whether in Art or Life, can only be possessed successively, by a series of partial annexations—and never integrally and at once. (Pp. 6–7)

The same process of fragmentation, nonsynchronization, and partial perspective exerts its influence both in human relationships and in art, and the mobility of time is named as the culprit.

Waiting is, by definition, a state of expectation, or desire. It is the fundamental human activity, our only mode of existing in time. Waiting destroys the present by anticipating the future, but it loses all significance if the future turns into the past the moment one reaches it, only to be replaced by another future that will suffer an identical fate. For us, as for Mercier and Camier, "past and future merge . . . in a single flood and close . . . , over a present for ever absent" (p. 32). The only time we know consists of "the irrevocable days or the unattainable days" (*Murphy*, p. 67). The present is nullified by the movement from future to past; it has no reality of its own. It is uninhabitable, unattainable, and nonexistent: "The notion of an unqualified present—the mere 'I am'—is an ideal notion."[27] Sartre defines the present as the "nothing" that separates before and after.[28] One may thus never coincide with oneself in the present moment, because the self, like the present, is either a possibility not yet realized or a memory of a being who exists no longer. In the French text of *Comment c'est*, Beckett describes the self as: "Moi suite ininterrompue d'altérations définitives" (p. 12).[29] Voice C of *That Time* calls to mind the Mouth in *Not I* when he bemoans his inability to utter the pronoun "I" because the person it is meant to designate changes continually from one instant to the next and thus defies identification:

> never the same but the same as what for God's sake did you ever say I to yourself in your life come on now (*eyes close*) could you ever say I to yourself in your life turning-point that was a great word with you before they dried up altogether always having turning-points and never but the one the first and last that time curled up worm in slime when they lugged you out and wiped you off and straightened you up never another after that. (Pp. 31–32)

How far we are here from Schopenhauer's vision of the underlying unity of the universe, where a person must strive to understand the phrase, "This thou art"! Voice C is still struggling hopelessly with the equation of "I" and "I." "Turning-point" was once a great word, for it means "a point at which a significant change occurs,"[30] yet experience has taught him the inaccuracy of that definition. Life is indeed nothing but a series of turning-points, of change, of movement from past to future to past moments and selves, but the change is devoid of significance and serves only to keep us from experiencing ourselves as stable egos existing in *this* time, rather than *that* one. C now realizes that all his turning-points have been nothing but repetitions of that first one, the moment of his birth when "they" dragged him from the womb. From that moment on, his life has been merely a series of births—no sooner has a new self begun to exist than it is replaced by another, in Beckett's "uninterrupted progression of definitive alterations," in this world "où être ne dure qu'un instant où chaque instant/verse dans le vide dans l'oubli d'avoir été" (*Poèmes suivi de mirlitonnades, p.* 23). When C questions his ability to call himself "I," he closes his eyes, as if attempting to calm the dizziness caused by the flow of time in the outside world in order to be able to perceive a self unaffected by the passage of time. This is a common procedure in Beckett's fiction and drama; his characters often speak of possessing two pairs of eyes: one which strives vainly to see forms and objects in the exterior world, and another, an "inner" pair, which when the outer eyes are closed turns inward in an equally futile attempt to escape time and achieve self-perception.

Experiencing oneself as a consistent, identifiable person residing comfortably in the present moment is thus as hopeless a prospect for Beckett as is the attainment by the consciousness of a peaceful state of immobile atemporality after death. For both the present and the timelessness of eternity share the same attributes: they are nonexistent, impossible states; they are literally nothing, a void in which there is no place for the human consciousness, which can never hope to liberate itself from the flux and change inherent in time. For Beckett, man's most unshakable certainty is that "il n'y a ni présent ni repos."[31]

Just as the right moment never arrives for Beckett's characters, neither do they ever manage to find themselves in the right place. Wherever they are, their desire transports them to another place which, once attained, becomes only another "here" from which they yearn to escape. Since all places share the same inadequacy, they become one undifferentiated space which it is futile to attempt to leave. Like the voice in *How It Is*, they ask for nothing more than to "stay for ever in the same place . . . and stir from it no more that old dream back again," yet must "go on . . . seeking that which I have lost there where I have never been" (pp. 39, 46–47). They are like the fictional founder of the nonexistent movement of Concentrism, about whom the young Beckett said in a paper he delivered as a joke to the Modern Language Society of Dublin:

> C'est bien la formule de son inquiétude, la constellation de tous ses déplacements: *va t'embêter ailleurs*, le stimulus qui finit par s'user à force de surmenage. Cette vie . . . est une de ces vies horizontales, sans sommet, toute en longueur, un phénomène de mouvement, sans possibilité d'accélération ni de ralentissement, déclenché, sans être inauguré, par l'accident d'une naissance, ter-

> miné, sans être conclu, par l'accident d'une mort. Et vide, creuse, sans contenu, abstraction faites [*sic*] des vulgarités machinales de l'épiderme, celles qui s'accomplissent sans que l'âme en prennent [sic] connaissance.[32]

This compulsive motion is akin to the ceaseless striving of Schopenhauer's Will: "As will necessarily expresses itself as a struggle, the original condition of every world that is formed into a globe cannot be rest, but motion, a striving forward in boundless space, without rest and without end."[33]

All points in time and space, by virtue of their ceaseless, meaningless fluctuations, become, in the final analysis, repetitive, interchangeable, and indistinguishable, as do the people who inhabit them. The narrator of "First Love," like Beckett, finds this concept difficult to express in words that were invented to describe another kind of time and space, but, like Beckett again, he nevertheless attempts to say the unsayable: "Some weeks later . . . I returned to the bench, for the fourth or fifth time since I had abandoned it, at roughly the same hour, I mean roughly the same sky, no, I don't mean that either, for it's always the same sky and never the same sky, what words are there for that, none I know, period" (p. 26).

The indeterminacy of time and space is a leitmotif of Act II of *Waiting for Godot*, where Vladimir and Estragon attempt to decide if they are in the same spot as they were yesterday and if the events they remember imperfectly actually took place yesterday or at another time. For every positive clue—the tree, Estragon's wound from Lucky, the boots and hat found where they had been left, the return of Pozzo, Lucky, and Godot's messenger—there is a negative indication—the bare tree is now covered with leaves, Pozzo and Lucky are much changed and do not remember "yesterday," the boots are the wrong color and do not fit, and the messenger swears he has never come before. The time and place are undeniably different, but so similar that it makes no difference at all:

> ESTRAGON: It's never the same pus from one second to the next. (P. 39)

> POZZO: . . . . one day we were born, one day we shall die, the same day, the same second, is that not enough for you? (P. 57)

> ESTRAGON: Recognize! What is there to recognize? All my lousy life I've crawled about in the mud! And you talk to me about scenery! (*Looking wildly about him.*) Look at this muckheap! I've never stirred from it! . . . I've puked my puke of a life away here, I tell you! Here! (Pp. 39–40)

The vaudeville routine that Vladimir and Estragon perform with their own and Lucky's hats affords a theatrical image of the "plus ça change, plus c'est la même chose" theme: the three hats change hands and heads in a dazzling series of mechanical movements that could be repeated infinitely, and although the result involves a change—Vladimir now wears Lucky's hat instead of his own—nothing is really different. When Vladimir inquires, "How do I look in it?" Estragon replies, "Hideous." Vladimir persists, "Yes, but not more so than usual?" and Estragon answers predictably, "Neither more nor less" (p. 46). Such permutation games occur throughout Beckett's work, and no matter how elaborately they are played and described, they always end by returning more or less to the initial situation; any resulting changes have no meaning, nor do they allow the characters or plots to "get on" in time or space. Movement is circular, repetitive, and insignificant. Change does occur, but for no reason and with no ultimate goal. In these games, as in life, we may be sure that, if we wait, we will sooner or later return to the place from which we started, for we never actually leave it. The only "other place" and the only "other time" are unimaginable, indescribable, and uninhabitable by the consciousness: they are the void where nothing dwells, the moment at which and the place from which Godot never arrives, the premises of Mr. [K]not[t].

Beckett's vision of time and space stands in direct opposition to that of Christian eschatology. For Christians, time and space as we know them will be conquered at the Last Judgment, when our souls, finally free from our bodies, will enter the timeless spacelessness of eternity—the endless torture of hell for the sinners and the ongoing bliss of heaven for the righteous. In neither case does perception cease; on the contrary, the souls in both realms are acutely aware of their condition, of the reasons for which they are experiencing it, and of its permanence and immutability. Inhabitants of the world beyond gain a clear, irrefutable perspective of their life on earth once they become distant enough from it in both time and space to view it as a whole. In addition, they enjoy an accurate, stable perspective of their "present" condition, but only because eternity shares none of the characteristics of the earthly time and space that render perspective impossible.

James Joyce offers a very clear description of the Christian conception of time in *A Portrait of the Artist as a Young Man*:

> At the last moment of consciousness the whole earthly life passed before the vision of the soul and, ere it had time to reflect, the body had died and the soul stood terrified before the judgmentseat. God had long been merciful . . . , pleading with the sinful soul, giving it time to repent. . . . But that time had gone. . . . that time was over. Now it was God's turn. . . . One single instant after the body's death, the soul had been weighed in the balance. . . .
>
> . . . The last day had come. . . . The archangel Michael . . . . blew from the archangelical trumpet the brazen death of time. . . . Time is, time was but time shall be no more.[34]

The Christian consciousness described here, like the Beckettian one, beholds a vision of its past life during its final moment. Unlike the unending jumble of fragmented moments experienced by disconnected selves in Beckett's texts, however, the earthly life is here seen, and later judged, as a whole, for which one indivisible soul is responsible. While Beckett's consciousnesses continue to contemplate "that time," since there is no other, the Christian mind has no time to reflect, because "that time" is over and has been replaced by God's "single instant" of an eternal, changeless, timeless present.

As Beckett writes in *Proust*, "we may be sure that . . . [death] is meaningless and valueless" (p. 6). The self no longer has any hope of fulfillment: the soul which was once weighed by God is now an absence: "At any given moment our total soul, in spite of its rich balance-sheet, has only a fictitious value. Its assets are never completely realisable" (*Proust*, p. 27). Malone grapples with this problem during the last days of his earthly existence, when he decides he must make an inventory of his possessions: "All my life long I have put off this reckoning, saying, Too soon, too soon. Well it is still too soon. All my life long I have dreamt of the moment when, edified at last, in so far as one can be before all is lost, I might draw the line and make the tot (*Malone Dies*, p. 181)."

These lines bring to mind Winnie's predicament in *Happy Days*, where she warns herself of the danger of putting off: putting up her umbrella, singing, and making ready for the night. She fears either that she may do these things too soon and be left with nothing to do before sleep, or that she may wait too long and never accomplish them. Her acts, like Malone's inventory and the judgment of the soul, will never be completely realized in the endless, meaningless time and space to which she is condemned.

Escape from earthly time and space is possible only if one believes in the existence of another temporal/spatial dimension. Christianity clearly posits two distinct domains in which all souls and consciousnesses exist. The linear, progressive time and space of earthly life culminate definitively at the moment of death. This endpoint, which is also the beginning of the circle of eternity, endows the moments that have gone before with meaning and integrity, bringing them into perspective. In the Christian view, life is clearly a movement towards an inevitable and attainable goal, in contrast with Beckett's formless series of disconnected instants and places in which we move and change constantly, without coming any closer to the timeless, spaceless stasis that we nevertheless continue to desire: "So on to this second day and get it over and out of the way and on to the next. . . . But let me get up now and on and get this awful day over and on to the next. But what is the sense of going on with all this, there is none. Day after unremembered day" ("From an Abandoned Work," pp. 46, 47–48).

If Christian earthly time and space are a linear progression, their goal is a realm where movement is circular, never more fully and beautifully described than by Beckett's beloved Dante in the *Paradiso*. Dante's conception of a linear earthly existence and circular eternity is overwhelmingly present in the Beckettian oeuvre, even though it is no longer believed possible, and is often referred to nostalgically as belonging to a happier era.

In the final canto of the *Paradiso*, Dante's pilgrimage ends in rapture before the sight of God in the Empyrean sphere, which lies outside of time and space, and around whose divine light revolve all the spheres of heaven. Here time is not measured in earthly terms; Dante marvels at the power of a single moment in this realm compared to that of centuries on earth: "A single moment makes for me deeper oblivion than five and twenty centuries."[35] Space is just as different: the choirs of heaven sing "to the fixed point, which holds and shall ever hold them in the place where they have ever been."[36] The last sphere "is not in space and does not turn on poles" like the earth; "this heaven has no other *where* but the Divine Mind."[37]

Dante compares the Eternal Light to a book which "contained, bound by one volume, that which is scattered in leaves throughout the universe."[38] Leaves are also an image of time, since we read in them the passage of the seasons. In canto xxvi, Dante had heard Adam compare the inconstancy of humans to the leaves of a tree: "The usage of mortals is like a leaf on a branch, which goes and another comes."[39] Only in paradise are the leaves of time, which are scattered throughout the space of the universe, "fused together in such a way that what I tell of is a simple light."[40]

When the narrator of "From an Abandoned Work" dreams of a Dantean paradise where an unbroken, changeless time and space would conquer both life and death, he too compares the leaves of books and trees to the disparate, inconstant moments of earthly existence:

> But let us get on and leave these old scenes and come to these, and my reward. Then it will not be as now, day after day, out, on, round, back, in, like leaves turning, or torn out and thrown crumpled away, but a long unbroken time without before or after, light or dark, from or towards or at, the old half knowledge of when and where gone, and of what, but kinds of things still, all at once, all going, until nothing, there never was anything, never can be, life and death all nothing, that kind of thing, only a voice dreaming and droning on all around, that is something, the voice that once was in your mouth. (Pp. 48–49)

This longed-for victory over time and space seems less certain in the following lyric passage from *Waiting for Godot*, where the image of leaves is juxtaposed to that of the sands of time, but where neither union nor harmony is foreseeable for the scattering leaves:

> Estragon: All the dead voices.
> Vladimir: They make a noise like wings.

ESTRAGON: Like leaves.
VLADIMIR: Like sand.
ESTRAGON: Like leaves.
Silence.
VLADIMIR: They all speak at once.
ESTRAGON: Each one to itself.
Silence.
VLADIMIR: Rather they whisper.
ESTRAGON: They rustle.
VLADIMIR: They murmur.
ESTRAGON: They rustle.
Silence.
VLADIMIR: What do they say?
ESTRAGON: They talk about their lives.
VLADIMIR: To have lived is not enough for them.
ESTRAGON: They have to talk about it.
VLADIMIR: To be dead is not enough for them.
ESTRAGON: It is not sufficient.
Silence.
VLADIMIR: They make a noise like feathers.
ESTRAGON: Like leaves.
VLADIMIR: Like ashes.
ESTRAGON: Like leaves.
Long silence.

(P. 40)

Unlike Dante's souls, which unite in the perfect harmony of Paradise to gaze upon and sing praises to the vision that fulfills all desire and liberates them from the scattered moments of earthly life, Beckett's dead continue to contemplate their pasts, each one speaking only to itself about the time which was "not enough" because even death brought it to no end, to no alternate state where its desire to see and to partake of a whole would be granted.

When in the *Paradiso* the divine vision is finally revealed to the eyes of the enraptured pilgrim, liberation from earthly time and space at last permits him to see the object for which he has been thirsting from the moment of his birth—"the Infinite Goodness," "the Eternal Light," "the Love that moves the sun and the other stars."[41] Just as Beckett concentrates his attention upon the state his characters desire to reach rather than upon the precise object that they might find there, Dante devotes much more time to describing the effects of the heavenly vision than its actual appearance. He tells us that when

> I reached with my gaze the Infinite Goodness. . . . my mind, all rapt, was gazing, fixed, still and intent, and ever enkindled with gazing. At that light one becomes such that it is impossible for him ever to consent that he should turn from it to another sight; for the good which is the object of the will is all gathered in it. . . .
>
> . . . . Not that the living light at which I gazed had more than a single aspect—for it is ever the same as it was before. . . . O Light Eternal, that alone abidest in Thyself, alone knowest Thyself, and, known to Thyself and knowing, lovest and smilest on Thyself. . . . now my desire and will, like a wheel that spins with even motion, were revolved by the Love that moves the sun and the other stars.[42]

The traveler's eyes finally come to rest upon an object that fulfills all their desire to see; never again need they seek another sight, for in the single moment of eternity, desire is instantaneously fulfilled and rekindled by the even, circular motion of God's love. The object from which Dante cannot, and would not, turn his intent gaze is complete unto itself. Its existence, which is entirely independent of human perception, presents only one single aspect, not a multitude of fragmented facets, to the believer who learns to see it. It is unchanging because it abides outside of time, "ever the same as it was before." It is both subject and object, three persons in one, which can perceive and know itself rather than constantly pursue an elusive "me" with a human "I" (or "eye"); it is, in Dante's words, "one Essence, so one and so three-fold that it admits agreement both with *are* and *is*."[43] Beckett might add that it also admits agreement with *I* and *Not I*.

Beckettian man also raises his eyes and prayers upward, but the divinity has long since vanished from the misty grey skies, and the thirst for vision remains unsatisfied: "In vain I raised without hope my eyes to the sky to look for the Bears. For the light I steeped in put out the stars, assuming they were there, which I doubted, remembering the clouds" ("The Calmative," p. 46). The other time and place of Paradise, which allowed earthly existence both to end and to have a purpose, no longer shape his life, which has become "a veritable calvary, with no limit to its stations and no hope of crucifixion" (*Molloy*, p. 78). He must return his disappointed gaze to the confused spectacle of the only world available to him, with no hope of an end to his earthly torment:

> All this business of a labour to accomplish, before I can end, of words to say, a truth to recover, in order to say it, before I can end, of an imposed task . . . to perform, before I can be done . . . , I invented it all, in the hope it would console me, help me to go on, allow me to think of myself as somewhere on a road, moving, between a beginning and an end, gaining ground, losing ground, getting lost, but somehow in the long run making headway. All lies. I have nothing to do, that is to say nothing in particular. . . . Having nothing to say, no words but the words of others, I have to speak. . . . Nothing can ever exempt me from it, there is nothing, nothing to discover, nothing to recover, nothing that can lessen what remains to say, I have the ocean to drink. (*The Unnamable*, p. 314)

Dante both opens and closes the *Paradiso* with a complaint about his inability to describe adequately the vision he was accorded in the highest realm:

> The passing beyond humanity cannot be set forth in words . . . .[44]

> O how scant is speech and how feeble to my conception![45]

Centuries later, Beckett echoes the Florentine's laments about the insufficiency of words in text after text. However, where Dante found language lacking in the ability to express a vision which had nevertheless been totally clear and comprehensible to his eyes, Beckett bemoans not only the fact that there is "nothing with which to express," but, indeed, "nothing to express." The domains of literature and painting share the same shortage, not only of means, but also of object: "There is nothing to paint and nothing to paint with."[46]

Beckett's admiration for Dante is a well-documented fact, and he borrows heavily from Dante's language, imagery, and ideas in his treatment of time and space as well as many other concepts, even though he shares none of the religious beliefs that provided the foundation for Dante's great poem. Christianity is a frequent source of both formal and thematic inspiration for

Beckett, due in part to his traditional Irish Protestant upbringing, just as it was for his compatriot and friend, James Joyce, who wrote the following lines about the lingering effects of religion in the mind of his disbelieving hero:

> —It is a curious thing, do you know, Cranly said dispassionately, how your mind is supersaturated with the religion in which you say you disbelieve. Did you believe in it when you were at school? I bet you did.
>
> —I did, Stephen answered.
>
> —And were you happier then? . . .
>
> —Often happy, Stephen said, and often unhappy. I was someone else then.
>
> —How someone else? . . . .
>
> —I mean, said Stephen, that I was not myself as I am now, as I had to become.[47]

Beckett's nostalgia for the happy days, the old style, "the blessed days of blue" ("Lessness," p. 557), is a longing for a time and place when the self was not "someone else." Like Stephen Dedalus, who no longer believes in the Christianity which made such being in the "here and now" possible, Beckett finds himself incapable of returning to a conception of time and space that permitted vision, for the blessed days of blue were "never but imagined the blue in a wild imagining the blue celeste of poesy . . . Never was but grey air timeless" ("Lessness," p. 559). Recognizing the impossibility of recapturing the old vision, however, in no way diminishes Beckett's yearning for it.

Joyce's priest, in commenting upon Saint Thomas's characterization of damnation as man's turning away from divine light, describes the terrible loss that is so keenly felt by Beckett:

> God, remember, is a being infinitely good and therefore the loss of such a being must be a loss infinitely painful. . . . At the very instant of death the bonds of the flesh are broken asunder and the soul at once flies towards God. The soul tends towards God as towards the centre of her existence.[48]

Beckett's Watt is brought to tears by the sight of a picture in Knott's house which gave "the illusion of movement in space, and it almost seemed in time," representing, perhaps, "a circle and a centre not its centre in search of a centre and its circle respectively, in boundless space, in endless time" (pp. 128–29). The center towards which Dante's and Saint Thomas's souls fly at the instant of death and around which they form an unbroken circle of wholly satisfied perception can exist only in a time and space whose dimensions are radically different from Beckett's earthly space and time, where constant but unsynchronized movement precludes the possibility of a circle and its center, or a subject and its object, uniting in a reciprocal, harmonious, eternal relationship: "To every man his orbit, that's obvious" (*The Unnamable*, p. 398).

The discussion of Beckett's writing in this chapter has been achronological and has remained purposely rather general, a procedure justified by the fact that it has dealt solely with the conceptual content of the works, which has remained quite consistent over the many years of Beckett's career. This is not to imply that the oeuvre is static and repetitious. On the contrary, Beckett's writing has evolved considerably from his earlier to his most recent works, and this evolution will be analyzed in the chapters to come. The evolution has been formal rather than thematic, and the remainder of this study will trace chronologically the development of the dramatic forms used by Beckett to portray the time, space, and movement that act as barriers to vision in the modern universe. Six plays, spanning the years from 1957 to 1981, have been chosen for detailed analysis, in an attempt to support the hypothesis that Beckett's drama has broken with the Western theatrical tradition which preceded it, creating a rupture in dramatic perspective akin to that which has occurred in other domains of thought and expression during this century. The six plays—*Endgame*, *Cascando*, *Film*, *Eh Joe*, *A Piece of Monologue*, and *Rockaby*—will be discussed in terms of the dramatic techniques used to convey this loss of perspective.

While the theme of perception and Beckett's new dramatic perspective are ubiquitous in his works, the plays chosen here for analysis lend themselves particularly well to a comparative study. Their common setting is a room, usually with a window, with the exception of *Cascando*, where the images of room and window are nevertheless present. Most of them present a single character involved in listening to, and/or looking at, himself. Two of them—*Film* and *Eh Joe*—use the camera eye as an agent of self-perception, while another pair—*Eh Joe* and *Rockaby*—show a character on stage listening to a voice that represents his or her consciousness. Images that recur in all or several of the works include eyes, pictures, chairs, the seashore, and cameras. Comparison and contrast of the plays are facilitated by the dramatic images and techniques that carry over from one to the next.

Endgame was selected as a representative of Beckett's early, and most widely appreciated, theater because it contains, in expanded and more traditional form, the germs of all Beckett's later dramatizations of characters enclosed in rooms, condemned to making up stories about themselves and their existence, yearning for an end that will most likely never come. *Cascando* is a complex and little-known drama representative of Beckett's brilliant exploitation of radio's capacity to portray mental landscapes, to dramatize the invisible. *Film*, Beckett's first and only experiment with the medium of film, is an obvious choice for a study of the theme and technique of perspective in Beckett's work, since its central thesis is that of the inevitability of self-perception. *Eh Joe*, Beckett's first work for television, uses many of the same camera techniques and images as *Film* for its portrayal of another man who cannot escape the eye and voice of self. Analyses of two quite recent works for the stage—*A Piece of Monologue* and *Rockaby*—conclude the discussions of individual dramas. Both portray single characters in boundless rooms engaged in the act of listening to their own voices recount all their failed past and present attempts at vision in an unperceivable world.

In spite of all they have in common, the plays chosen for analysis are all unique works that represent a great diversity of methods of approach to dramatization of the problem of perspective in the twentieth century. They have been selected as much for the ways in which they differ as for what they share. In addition to diverse characters, dramatic techniques, language, and form, they represent not only a number of different periods in Beckett's writing career, but also the variety of dramatic media—stage, radio, film, and television—in which Beckett has pursued his formal experimentation.

Chapter 2

ENDGAME:

"How are your eyes?"

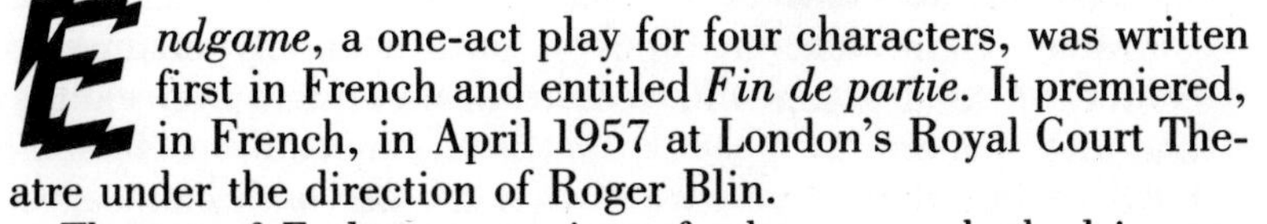

Endgame, a one-act play for four characters, was written first in French and entitled *Fin de partie*. It premiered, in French, in April 1957 at London's Royal Court Theatre under the direction of Roger Blin.

The set of *Endgame* consists of a bare room bathed in grey light, with two small windows set high on the rear wall, one giving out onto the ocean and one onto land. There is a door to the right through which Clov, the servant, enters and leaves his kitchen; a picture hanging near the door with its face to the wall; two ashbins to the left which contain the legless couple, Nell and Nagg; and in the center, an armchair on castors in which sits the blind and imperious Hamm—pitiless master of Clov, ungrateful son of Nell and Nagg, compulsive storyteller, and former tyrannical lord of an ill-defined, but now defunct, domain.

Hamm is blind; Clov manages, with some difficulty, to look out the windows to report back to his master, and to the spectators, what he sees: Zero. Both men live in an enclosed shelter outside of which, in the words of Hamm, "it's death" (p. 9). Both speak of leaving this space, Hamm through his death and Clov through abandonment of his master, yet the play leaves us with much doubt as to whether either will attain his goal.

Movement is a fundamental characteristic of the time and space of *Endgame*. Time passes; the characters "get on"; yesterday and the future continually contaminate the present.

Hamm, though confined to his wheelchair, insists upon being wheeled around to the utmost limits of his room; Clov walks stiffly from window to window, in and out of his kitchen, and back to his master's side. Nell and Nagg, though maimed and confined to their ashbins, pop up and down so long as they are thought to be alive. There is indeed a great deal of movement in *Endgame*, yet nothing and nobody can actually be said ever to get anywhere, except perhaps a bit closer to an end whose very existence is uncertain.

The time and space of *Endgame*, as announced by its title, are those of an ending; the form and content of the play convey the impression of a world that is in gradual decline, where everything and everybody are weakening, winding down, running out. In spite of this progressive diminishment, however, the end toward which all seems to be moving is uncertain, unknown because unknowable, and perhaps unattainable. *Endgame* portrays a universe which is nearing its end but which seems likely to continue repeating itself, in an increasingly contracted form, forever. Beckett uses a variety of dramatic techniques to structure this picture of an ending, yet endless, time and space.

All of the characters suffer, to a greater or lesser degree, some physical deterioration: Hamm is blind and cannot use his legs; Clov sees, but his eyes are bad, walks, though with great difficulty, and cannot sit; Nell and Nagg have long ago lost their legs and Nell probably dies during the play. References are made to other people who once existed but have now died, some perhaps as a result of Hamm's abuse or neglect: Hamm's "paupers," an old doctor, the navigators, Mother Pegg, a painter, a man who begged Hamm for food for his child one Christmas Eve. Life itself is defined in terms of degeneration: Hamm refutes Clov's assertion that "there's no more nature" with the proof, "But we breathe, we change! We lose our hair, our teeth! Our bloom! Our ideals!" and Clov is forced to admit, "Then she hasn't forgotten us" (p. 11).

The décor of *Endgame* also contributes to the impression of a world coming to its end. Hamm refers to the room on stage as a "shelter" (p. 3), and its bareness, grey light, and the grey nothingness of the barren, uninhabited world outside the windows all point to the distinct possibility that Hamm, Clov, Nell, and Nagg may be the last survivors of some dreadful catastrophe. (It is worth noting that, at the time Beckett wrote *Endgame*, the many hours spent in air-raid shelters during World War II were still vivid memories to most Europeans, and the horrors of impending nuclear war were becoming a matter of widespread concern.) Even though a picture remains on the wall of the room, it is turned over so its decorative function is no longer served, and towards the end of the play Clov takes it down to replace it with an alarm clock which, Hamm fears, is also nearing its end. Hamm offers a possible clue to the origin of this enigmatic picture when he tells Clov about a mad painter he once used to visit in an asylum:

> I'd take him by the hand and drag him to the window. Look! There! All that rising corn! And there! Look! The sails of the herring fleet! All that loveliness!
> (*Pause.*)
> He'd snatch away his hand and go back into his corner. Appalled. All he had seen was ashes. (P. 44)

The situation Hamm describes contains some striking parallels with his own present existence in the shelter with Clov, who also takes his companion to the windows of the room and describes what he sees on the earth and in the sea. Hamm's correction of the tenses he uses in summing up his narration of these visits suggests the extent to which he identifies with the mad artist: "It appears the case is . . . was not so . . . so unusual" (p. 44). However, where Hamm had described a landscape of color and beauty to his friend, who could perceive nothing but the undifferentiated greyness of ashes, Clov and Hamm have each moved one step further away from traditional vision in perspective: Hamm is totally blind, and the person who serves as his visual interpreter of the world reports that earth and sea have turned grey. Visions like the one Hamm describes here from memory are mentioned throughout *Endgame*, and they always belong either to a distant past, like this one and like the old folks' memory of their romantic boat ride on Lake Como, or to a dream, as when Hamm speaks of going into the woods in his sleep, where "My eyes would see . . . the sky, the earth . . . Nature!" (p. 18). If such visions were once possible, they are clearly so no longer. It is thus fitting that the painting should be turned to the wall, and finally removed, in a universe where colored landscapes seen through the imaginary window of a painting in perspective have turned to a flat, barren, uncertain greyness that offers only fleeting, fragmentary, indistinct images to the eye of the observer. Clov's replacing of the picture with an alarm clock late in the play underscores the relationship between painting and time: the mobile, endless, aimless, repetitious time of *Endgame*'s universe renders obsolete a form of art that grew out of a different conception of time (and space).

If the characters' physical appearance and the décor of *Endgame* convey the visual impression of an ending, its text fills our ears with references to the end. From the very first line of the play, when Clov announces, "Finished, it's finished, nearly finished, it must be nearly finished" (p. 1), we hear allusion after allusion to the end of time, of people, of stories, of food, of objects, of nature, of color, of sight, of fleas and rats, of light, of the day, of love, of the meaning of words, of the earth and sea, of laughter, of weather, of the sun, of kisses, of clocks, of spring, of God, of sound, of motion, of song, of beauty, of order, of the game played by Hamm and Clov, of all "This . . . this . . . thing" (p. 45). Just as time is running out, so are all the people, attributes, and objects that once composed the universe. Clov and Hamm engage over and over again in a comically repetitive exchange where Hamm asks Clov to observe or give him something, and Clov responds, "There are no more." Over the course of the play, there are, successively, "no more": bicycle-wheels, pap, nature, sugar-plums, tides, navigators, rugs, pain-killer, and coffins.

This diminution of the elements of the universe, as well as the impression conveyed that the world surrounding Hamm's and Clov's shelter is in ruins, suggest a possible interpretation of *Endgame* as a perverted parody of the Noah's ark myth.[1] While in Genesis the Lord commanded Noah, father of Ham, to build an ark with a window and a door and to furnish it with representatives of all living species in order to insure the continuance of his creation after the great flood, Beckett's Hamm makes every effort to see that his refuge, which, like Noah's ark, contains the last supply of food in the world, will engender no further life, not even so much as a future generation of fleas or rats. The many references to animals in *Endgame* add credence to the Noah's ark analogy. The names of the characters all suggest various animals: Hamm, the flesh of the pig; Clov, the spice used to cure ham; Nell, a common name for a horse; and Nagg, a word used to describe an old, worn-out horse.[2] At one point,

Nagg sucks on a dog biscuit called "Spratt's medium" (p. 10), and Clov later presents Hamm with a toy dog he has been making for his master. The nobility of Noah's mission to save human and animal life is savagely parodied in Beckett's version of the story, where the animals chosen to inhabit the refuge represent the lowest, dirtiest, most useless, annoying, or comical forms of life: a rat, a flea, and an artificial dog with three legs and no sex. The people are likewise far removed from the righteousness and fertility of Noah's family. Physically and spiritually sterile, they present a bleak outlook for the future of humanity. The death of Nell, the last female of the group, seems to confirm the impossibility of the reproduction of the species, although even in life she had for some time been unable to have any form of physical contact with her husband.

Charles Lyons sees in *Endgame* an ironic reversal of another biblical account, that of the creation of the world. In his provocative essay, "Beckett's *Endgame*: An Anti-Myth of Creation,"[3] he presents a fascinating and coherent reading of the play as a depiction of the disintegration of the universe as perceived by a dying consciousness. While God created the world by separating the earth from the waters and by creating light, Beckett shows us a universe where the earth and waters, as perceived by Clov from the two windows of the set, come to resemble each other more and more, as they are reduced to "grey" and "zero," and where people like Mother Pegg die for lack of light.

Even though time, space, and life are winding down in *Endgame*, they are not certain ever to die out altogether. Just when Hamm, Clov, and the audience are convinced that outside the room shown on stage all is indeed zero, grey, and death, Clov reports the sighting of a small boy whom he identifies as a "potential procreator" (p. 78). Clov has gone to great pains during the play attempting to destroy a rat he found in his kitchen and to kill a flea which invaded his pants, in order to please Hamm, who fears that "humanity might start from there all over again!" (p. 33). It therefore comes as somewhat of a surprise to him, and to us, when Hamm forbids Clov to go after the boy with a gaff, explaining, "If he exists he'll die there or he'll come here. And if he doesn't . . . " (p. 78). Whether he dies there, comes into the shelter (perhaps to replace Clov if he leaves or Hamm if he dies), or doesn't exist, the regenerative potential suggested by this boy calls the possibility of there being an end to "this . . . thing" (p. 45) into question. The original French play devotes many more lines than the English to this episode and describes the boy in greater detail: immobile, seated on the ground leaning against a rock, he contemplates his navel. The French text also shows a change in Hamm's attitude, from an initial desire to exterminate the boy to a philosophical resignation to his possible existence. In addition, it alludes both to the stone that was rolled away from Christ's tomb and to Moses' dying vision of the promised land. Martin Esslin has suggested that, when Clov contradicts Hamm's comparison of the boy to the dying Moses, but not the image of the lifted stone connected with the resurrection, he reinforces the idea of birth and reproduction suggested by the boy's fetal position.[4] In both versions, the incident with the little boy strongly suggests that the outside world may not be as dead as we might have believed, and that the ending so long awaited with both fear and eagerness by Hamm and Clov may be yet a while, perhaps forever, in coming.

Another aspect of *Endgame* that serves to cast doubt upon the possibility of any ending to the game being played out before our eyes is Hamm's persistent effort at storytelling, and especially his seemingly futile desire to bring his story to a close. The tale he relates to his captive audience—his parents, his servant, and the spectators in the theater—may well be autobiographical. We know that Hamm, like the rich gentleman in his first-person narrative, was once the master of a large domain who took pleasure in refusing aid to the less fortunate creatures that depended upon him. The child whom his character was asked to take in against his wishes may well be Clov, and the ending to his story that keeps eluding him may coincide with the equally elusive ending of his own life. Clov makes evident the coincidence between Hamm's story and his life in the following exchange: "Hamm: What story? Clov: The one you've been telling yourself all your days" (p. 58). Hamm describes the progress he is making on his story in the same terms he uses to evaluate his life with Clov and his parents: "I've got on with it" (p. 59). Though Hamm feels compelled to continue his chronicle, he fears its end, but Clov reassures him that, should the conclusion be reached, "You'll make up another" (p. 61). Hamm would prefer to put a definitive end to "the prolonged creative effort" that has been draining him, to drag himself down to the sea where "I'd make a pillow of sand for my head and the tide would come" (p. 61), for the only way he can imagine an end to his storytelling is to imagine an end to his life. However, even though the idea of ending has obsessed Hamm throughout his existence, just as it has been a constant theme and image of *Endgame* from the first moment of the play, the end may never be reached. As Hamm concludes, in an ironic recasting of a biblical verse, "The end is in the beginning and yet you go on" (p. 69).

When Hamm speaks of ending his tale, he foresees, like Clov, that another will come to take its place: "Perhaps I could go on with my story, end it and begin another" (p. 69). He dreams of "the end," which has been "so long coming," when he will be "in the old shelter, alone against the silence and . . . the stillness," where, "'if I can hold my peace, and sit quiet, it will all be over with sound, and motion, all over and done with" (p. 69). The "if" is of cardinal importance here, for it postulates a state of immobility as the precondition for the end. Since immobility is impossible in the Beckettian scheme of existence, so, it would seem, is the end. Hamm's words recall an earlier statement made by Clov to explain why he was straightening up the objects in the room on stage: "I love order. It's my dream. A world where all would be silent and still and each thing in its last place, under the last dust." Here again, stillness is the prerequisite for the end, and it is once more impossible, a mere dream. Realizing this, Clov does not object when Hamm orders him to drop the things he has picked up, and he remarks with resignation, "After all, there or elsewhere" (p. 57). For in the world in which he lives, each thing does not have its place, since order, silence, and stillness are impossible, and the last dust may therefore never come to fulfill his dream. Hamm, too, acknowledges the futility of his desire for the stillness which would allow "it [to] . . . be all over and done with." As he serenely envisions his solitude in the old shelter where he would wait for his end, he suddenly becomes agitated when he realizes that the peace he longs for will be withheld even there. For, though he may succeed in withdrawing from the world outside his shelter, and in driving away the last companions he has within it, he will be unable to put an end to the process of self-perception, which he describes as "All kinds of fantasies! That I'm being watched! A rat! Steps! . . . Then babble, babble, words, like the solitary child who turns himself into children, two, three, so as to be together, and whisper together, in the dark" (p. 70). It is indeed entirely possible that this is the situation in which we now see Hamm: alone at last in the old shelter, he may be merely imagining the watchful presence of Clov, Nell, and Nagg, splitting himself into the various characters of *Endgame* in order to maintain the condition necessary for the continuation of the human consciousness—the subject/object dichotomy.

Hamm comments upon his story's progress with the same self-consciousness he displays when he critiques the game in which he and Clov are engaged; his life in the shelter is in many respects a living proof that "all the world's a stage." His name recalls both the main character of *Hamlet*, Shakespeare's greatest "play-within-a-play," and his role as a "ham actor" in the drama of human existence. Hamm's "chronicle" is a story-within-a-story-within-a-story, in a seemingly endless procession of characters and dialogue. His relationship and verbal exchanges with Clov are no less contrived and self-consciously dramatic than the story he "makes up." Indeed, all the characters of *Endgame* reflect upon their speech and actions using the vocabulary and cynical objectivity of experienced drama critics: "We're getting on" (p. 9); "This is slow work" (p. 12); "Why this farce, day after day?" (p. 14); "What does that mean?" (p. 20); "Will this never finish?" (p. 23); "This is deadly" (p. 28); "Things are livening up" (p. 29); "I see . . . a multitude [the audience] . . . in transports . . . of joy" (p. 29); "What's happening?" (p. 32); "Do you not think this has gone on long enough?" (p. 45); "Got him that time!" (p. 49); "Our revels now are ended" (p. 56—cf. Shakespeare's *The Tempest*, IV:i); "What is there to keep me here? . . . The dialogue" (p. 58); "Ah let's get it over!" (p. 70); "I'm tired of our goings on" (p. 76); "Let's stop playing!" (p. 77); "Let it end!" (p. 77); "An aside, ape! Did you never hear an aside before? . . . I'm warming up for my last soliloquy" (pp. 77–78); "Not an underplot, I trust" (p. 78); "Articulate!" (p. 80); "This is what we call making an exit" (p. 81); "Nicely put, that" (p. 83); "Since that's the way we're playing it . . . let's play it that way" (p. 84).

The technique of presenting a play-within-a-play, or a story-within-a-play-within-a-play, gives the spectator an impression of being led into a hall of mirrors, where images and situations lose their identity and precise contours as they are reflected in an endless labyrinth of change and flux. We have no way of knowing for certain where Hamm's story ends and the saga of

Hamm and Clov begins, or if Hamm and Clov might suddenly decide to bring the game they are playing to an end only to recommence another in this, or a different, place with these, or other, characters.

The cessation of the consciousness, the end of existence, immobility and silence—all are merely impossible dreams for Hamm. The only solution to the endless game of perception in which he feels trapped is equally impossible: "Breath held and then . . . " (p. 70). Hamm seems to be speaking here of suicide by apnoea, which Beckett described in the following manner in *Murphy*: "Suicide by apnoea has often been tried, notably by the condemned to death. In vain. It is a physiological impossibility" (p. 185). Earlier in the same novel, birth is defined as "the moment of . . . being strangled into a state of respiration" (p. 71). Thus, existence, which is characterized by breathing and which is savagely forced upon our unwilling bodies at the beginning, is equally implacable at the end: our breath will not stop, no matter how much we might will it to do so, and the end so longed for by Hamm continues to elude him. Hamm sums up his reflections on the problem of not being able to end either his story or his life with a poignant reference to one of Zeno's paradoxes: "Moment upon moment, pattering down, like the millet grains of . . . that old Greek, and all life long you wait for that to mount up to a life" (p. 70). These words echo Clov's from the beginning of the play: "Grain upon grain, one by one, and one day, suddenly, there's a heap, a little heap, the impossible heap" (p. 1). The moments of existence, which can never add up to make a life because they are endless and in constant motion, are like the pile of millet grains which Zeno proposed splitting in half, then in half again, and again, and again, ad infinitum, in a process that could come to an end only in a time and space unknown to, and unperceivable by, the human consciousness. It is characteristic of Beckett's fine sense of irony that he chose a paradox created by a philosopher whose goal was to prove the impossibility of movement in order to illustrate his own conception of the impossibility of immobility.

Describing time in terms of grains "pattering down" into a heap also brings to mind a common image of time: that of an hourglass filled with grains of sand. Although the flow of sand in an hourglass does come to an end, the process can be renewed continuously by turning over the glass to set the grains in motion again. In much the same way, the action, time, space, and speech of *Endgame* come to rest after Hamm's final soliloquy, yet we know that all will recommence when the play is repeated for a subsequent audience. The silent tableau at the end of the play may thus be nothing more than the moment Hamm describes when he says "Breath held and then . . . "; the "fantasies" of perception, animals, motion, babbling voices, and moment piling upon moment as he waits to "get it over" which are the substance of *Endgame* are likely to flow on forever, subject to brief pauses, and slight changes in their order of occurrence, just like the sands of time in an hourglass.

If Hamm's inability to finish his story, or his life, underscores the endless nature of Beckettian time, the question of Clov's departure, a constant theme from the beginning of the play, presents a similar conception of space. He clearly desires to leave and often announces his intention to do so to Hamm; at the end of the play he appears dressed for travel and remains impassive and motionless as Hamm delivers his final speech. We will never know for certain if he succeeds in leaving, since he is still standing at the door when the curtain falls. Clov's very name underlines the ambiguity of his situation, since *clove* is the past participle of the verb *to cleave*, a word which means, oddly enough, both *to separate* and *to adhere*. Clov's position at the end of the play recalls that of Didi and Gogo at the end of *Waiting for Godot*, when the exchange, "Vladimir: Well? Shall we go? Estragon: Yes, let's go," is followed by the indication, "*They do not move. Curtain*" (p. 60). In both cases, Beckett creates doubts in our minds as to the future actions of his characters by juxtaposing contradictory dialogue and stage directions. We cannot be sure if Clov will leave, but we do know that he hasn't done it yet, and we have had several indications over the course of the play that such a departure would be impossible, e.g., "Hamm: You can't leave us. Clov: Then I won't leave you" (p. 37). In two separate passages, Clov sums up his predicament and makes clear the reason he will never be able to leave: "There's nowhere else" (p. 6); "I say to myself—sometimes, Clov, you must be there better than that if you want them to let you go—one day. But I feel too old, and too far, to form new habits. Good, it'll never end, I'll never go" (p. 81). What prevents Clov from going is the indeterminacy of space: there is nowhere else than the endless, formless, inescapable space he has always inhabited because a "there" can exist only by contrast with a well-defined "here"; he would have to "be there," i.e., experience a sense of place, better than he knows how, in order to be able to conceive of a different space to which he might escape. Hamm had earlier expressed the same idea when he announced to Clov, "Do you know what it is? . . . I was never there . . . Absent, always" (p. 74). For both the characters in the play and its spectators, the only time and space of *Endgame*'s universe exist on the stage; outside all is grey, zero, and death. Just after Hamm tells Clov that he "was never there," he poses a question which many spectators of *Endgame* must have asked their fellow theatergoers: "Do you know what's happened?" Clov's response takes the form of two essential questions: "When? Where?" (p. 75). In order for a definable "something" to happen, it must occur in an identifiable, discrete, time and place. When any one of these elements breaks down, so must the others, and their dissolution puts an end to the linear perspective of post-Renaissance drama, with its well-made plots and unities of time (when?), place (where?), and action (what's happened?). Beckett's response to the question of "what happens" in *Endgame* is adamant in its refusal to define the undefinable: "Hamm as stated, and Clov as stated, together as stated, nec tecum nec sine te, in such a place, and in such a world, that's all I can manage, more than I could."[5]

At one point in *Endgame*, Hamm announces to Clov, "Gone from me you'd be dead" (p. 70). It does indeed seem that though Clov cannot stand to live with his difficult master, he would not be able to exist without him. This "*nec tecum nec sine te*" relationship, which is similar to that of Didi and Gogo in *Waiting for Godot*, has been used, like the one between the two tramps, to support a reading of *Endgame* as a representation of a human consciousness.[6] The scene may be taken to suggest the interior of a human skull, a privileged image for Beckett, especially in his novels. The two windows would be the eyes; the grey light would evoke the grey matter of the brain. The four characters might represent diverse elements of a single human personality: Hamm would be the inner "me," irrational and emotional (this would explain his sudden, savage mood changes); Clov would be the rational "me" who maintains contact with the external world; Nell and Nagg could be simply memories that are weakening and disappearing—the act of putting the lids on the ashbins would thus represent an attempt to repress painful memories. Hamm and Clov live in a symbiotic state; the blind Hamm depends upon Clov's sight, and since he is paralyzed, he could not survive were Clov not there to feed him; since Clov does not know the combination of the cupboard where the food is kept, he would die of hunger without his master. According to this interpretation, *Endgame* would thus present an image of the dissociation of a human consciousness in the last minutes before death: the death of the exterior world resembles the dissolution of ties with outer reality that occurs in a dying mind. The final stalemate of this endgame portrays the paradox of human consciousness which is omnipresent in Beckett's work: the consciousness can never attain a definitive end, because it would be unable to perceive the nothingness that it would meet there. At the end of *Endgame*, or of his life, Hamm will not know for certain if Clov has left, for if Clov leaves, Hamm will die and thus be incapable of perceiving Clov's absence.

Beckett leads the spectators to understand Hamm's perceptual dilemma by producing similar uncertainties in our minds regarding both Clov's departure and Hamm's death. When the final curtain is drawn, Clov is preparing to go, and Hamm has delivered his "last soliloquy" (p. 78), called his father and his servant, with no response, and covered his face with his handkerchief. It would indeed seem that Hamm has finally been able to reach his end, yet when we remember the beginning of the play, the ending seems less certain. Just as Clov opened *Endgame* with the word "finished," Hamm has closed by repeating one of his first lines—"Old stancher!"—and by replacing the handkerchief that he had removed from his face at the beginning of the play. It is entirely possible that Clov will proceed to cover the ashbins and Hamm with sheets and then retire to his kitchen while Hamm sleeps, only to return to his master's side the following morning when he will remove the sheets, announce once more that "it's finished, nearly finished," and recommence his game with Hamm. Once again, the existence we are witnessing upon the stage finds a parallel in the nature of the theater: *Endgame* will indeed begin again tomorrow, before a different audience, with slight variations in its performance and reception, taking as its point of departure the announcement of its ending. We thus become aware of yet another level in the series of plays-within-plays in which we have become embroiled: from Hamm's chronicle to his self-conscious ham acting for his family and for the larger audience in the theater, we are led to consider the single performance of *Endgame* that we have viewed as merely one repetition in a potentially infinite series of productions which begin at the end, and end at the beginning, and yet go on. Beckett has succeeded in creating a dramatic form for *Endgame* that corresponds to our contemporary notions of time and space. More traditional forms of drama, which present linear plot developments with clear-cut beginnings, climaxes, and conclusions, were appropriate for audiences who believed that human life and history were organized in the same manner. At one point in the play, Clov attempts to bring the action to a close by borrowing one of the traditional forms of a theatrical finale: song (p. 72). Hamm stops him with the command, "Don't sing," and when Clov inquires, "One hasn't the right to sing any more?", Hamm's response is "No." Clov's next question, "Then how can it end?", goes unanswered, for the days when lives and plays could end may be gone forever. Thus, the most optimistic reply we can offer to Hamm's exasperated and furious question, "Will this never finish?" (p. 23), is Clov's unconvincing "It may end" (p. 5).

If *Endgame* may end, it may not, either. Hamm may be a king in stalemate position when the curtain closes, not yet in check, but unable to move into any other position, approaching his end, yet never attaining it. Many critics have pointed out the relationships between *Endgame* and the game of chess, which inspired its title. Hamm's first words, "Me . . . to play" (p. 2), are repeated in his final speech, after which he refers to the "old endgame lost of old" (p. 82), and says, "Since that's the way we're playing it . . . let's play it that way" (p. 84). Like the game of chess, *Endgame* is rigidly structured and both the game and the play take the form of a progressive stripping away of elements from an enclosed space. Like pieces on a chessboard, the characters of *Endgame* are severely restricted in their movements, each obeying a different rule of motion (e.g., Hamm can sit but cannot stand, while Clov can stand but cannot sit). The frequent "pause," which is by far the most common stage direction in *Endgame*, helps to structure the play like a chess game where each player reflects silently before proceeding with his next move. Beckett's affinity for the game of chess is a well-known fact, perhaps most evident in his novel *Murphy*, but present throughout his work. The colors of chess, white and black, have become the predominant colors of his latest works, and he has long been fascinated with experiments in permutation, the fundamental principle of the game of chess.

In *Homo ludens*, a study of the social function of games and play, J. Huizinga defines the characteristics of games in terms that help us to understand the motivation underlying all the games played by the characters of *Endgame*. A game, he says, is played to create order, to lend a temporary, limited perfection to a confused and imperfect world. It takes place in an expressly circumscribed, clearly limited time and place, beginning at a given moment and continuing until its end, which is easily recognizable. It follows a specific and absolute order created by an arbitrary set of rules that are freely consented to by all players. Situated outside the sphere of utility and material necessity, it is experienced as "fictitious" by the participants, who nevertheless become completely absorbed by it. A game is conducted in an atmosphere of enthusiasm, accompanied by the tension created by elements of uncertainty and chance, and its end is characterized by feelings of joy, relaxation, and release.[7] It is no wonder, then, that Hamm and Clov seize upon every possible opportunity to play games in a universe that is without order, imperfect, and in which time and space are unlimited, undefinable, and unperceivable.

B. S. Hammond has pointed out the importance of the game theme in *Endgame* as a means of imposing structure upon a world which has none:

> In a world no longer rendered purposeful by Christian conceptions of eschatology, time is experienced not as a linear development towards a goal, but as a yawning vacuum, a black hole without structure. Structure has to be imposed from without through routine and, for Beckett's characters, through the playing of games. The games Hamm and Clov play are futile, but they are all there is.[8]

Beckett's choice of a chessboard to structure *Endgame*'s universe brings to mind another instance in which chessboards were used to structure art: painting in linear perspective. Time and time again in these paintings a floor is laid out in a checkered pattern whose receding lines organize the entire picture space. Beckett borrows this longstanding esthetic tradition and adapts it to his new dramatic perspective; his characters attempt to play out their lives according to rules formulated in and for another era, and they seem doomed to an endless, repetitious, meaningless series of movements in a space that is no longer rational, measurable, and comprehensible like the one of the paintings whose checkered floors led the observer's eye to their central vanishing point. Instead of succeeding in bringing their game to an orderly end, they move blindly and confusedly on a chessboard that seems to exist only as a nostalgic relic of an era when vision was possible.

Beckett employs several other traditional images of vision and perspective in similar fashion—the objects remain although they no longer fulfill their former functions. Eyes, for example, are prevalent in *Endgame*. Hamm's blind eyes have "gone all white" (p. 4), and he can see only through the eyes of Clov, which are "bad" (p. 7), and which, he prophesies, will continue to get worse until "one day you'll be blind, like me. . . . Infinite emptiness will be all around you" (p. 36). Although Hamm wears glasses and Clov uses a telescope to assist his exploration of the world beyond the window, these optical aids seem to have outlived their usefulness and exist only as vestiges of an earlier time when people believed in the possibility of perfecting vision by using instruments of their own invention.[9] Likewise, the set of *Endgame* contains two windows, the conventional frame through which spectators view a scene in perspective, yet the windows no longer function as before—they offer a vista which Clov sums up as "Corpsed," "All gone," "Lead," "Zero," and "Gray" (pp. 30–31). The picture hanging beside the windows is similarly obsolete—it is merely a reminder of the bygone days when one could see, and paint, fields of corn and fleets of ships, when nature was visible and comprehensible to human eyes.

Hamm has retreated to an enclosed shelter, perhaps in an effort to define a space for himself that would permit vision by affording a definable and stable point of view upon the world around him: he insists upon Clov's wheeling him around to the limits of his room, then back to its exact center, so that he can perceive and comprehend the space in which he exists. Yet the effort is futile, for the walls are boundaries between Hamm's universe and the nothingness that lies beyond, merely "hollow bricks" dividing this place from "the . . . other hell" (p. 26). Since there is nothing on the other side, they are unattainable, in spite of Hamm's violent urgings to "hug the walls" and go "Closer! Closer! Up against!" (pp. 25–26). His desire to be replaced in the exact center of the room is just as vain, since a center can be defined only in relation to precise boundaries, and boundaries can exist only if they delimit one space from another. So Hamm's attempt to separate his own space from the one he wishes to observe is a failure, since the only space available for observation is that in which he exists. In spite of his glasses, the windows of his room, and all his efforts to perceive the ends of the time and space of his life, he can put nothing in perspective, since he can attain no stable, exterior, definable point of observation, and admits to having lost the game he has been playing: "Old endgame lost of old, play and lose and have done with losing" (p. 82). He realizes that his story, like the play in which he stars, will end in darkness, with no conclusion: "Moments for nothing, now as always, time was never and time is over, reckoning closed and story ended" (p. 83).

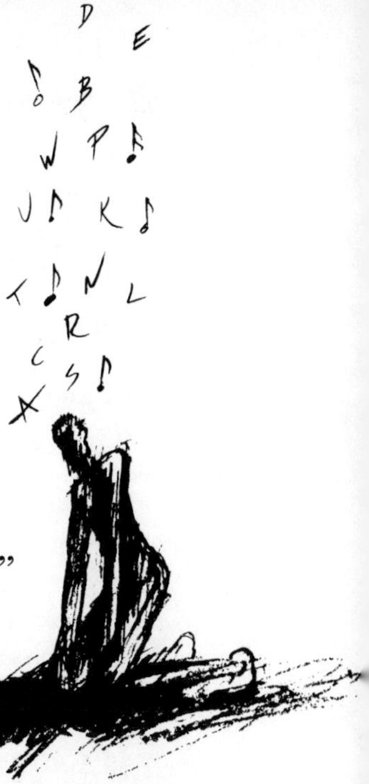

Chapter 3

CASCANDO:

". . . see him . . . say him . . . to the end . . ."

Cascando, a radio play written originally in French in 1961,[1] with music by Marcel Mihalovici, was first broadcast in Paris by ORTF on October 13, 1963, under the direction of Roger Blin. Beckett had written several radio dramas before *Cascando*, the most recent of which was *Words and Music*, a work that has much in common with *Cascando*, in terms of both form and content.[2]

It may seem a bit odd to choose to study a purely aural work in a discussion of Beckett's dramatic perspective. The selection is justified, however, both by this play's role in the evolution of Beckett's dramatic oeuvre, and by Beckett's interest in exploiting the capacity of radio to dramatize the same perceptual issues with which he deals in his visual drama. The radio medium is capable to a much greater extent than theater, film, or television of portraying the inner stage of consciousness that is so dear to Beckett. As Irving Wardle points out, "Radio's natural range correspond[s] . . . to one of the main upheavals in modern European literature: the emergence of individual consciousness as the only certain reality." He compares modern radio drama to the theater of the absurd and concludes, "The dramatic idiom that has taken shape in the past fifteen years has considerably narrowed the gap between radio and the theatre."[3] Charles Hampton asserts that Beckett's first radio drama, *All That Fall*, attacks traditional dramatic conventions in a way that not even his earlier stage plays had done:

> I am convinced that Beckett's appeal to contemporary theater people, at least in part, lies in their realization that his plays are revolutionary in the strictest sense; that is, that they represent a destruction of the efficacy of traditional dramatic forms and assumptions, that, amid the giggles and gloom of *Godot* and *Endgame* there emerges a glorious freedom for the playwright and director, that someone, finally, has taken an axe to Strindberg's superannuated trees. But neither *Godot* nor *Endgame*, while they do destroy many of the larger structural assumptions of post-Renaissance drama, is able to attack verisimilitude. *All That Fall* does.[4]

If even a rather naturalistic radio drama like *All That Fall* can be seen to have had such a tremendous impact upon theatrical assumptions, the above assessment of Beckett's originality must apply tenfold to the later, much more innovative *Cascando*.

In *Cascando*, a character named Opener calls forth, listens to, and comments upon streams of words and music provided by Voice and Music, who perform both separately and together. What we hear are fragments of obviously ongoing, continuous monologues of Voice and Music, and Opener's control of their manifestations to his (and our) consciousness diminishes as the play progresses. Opener begins by directing Voice's and Music's "entrances" and "exits" with the commands "I open" and "I close," but as the work evolves, Voice and Music often begin and end their parts at will. Voice recounts, in fragments, the story of a man named Woburn, who leaves his shelter one night to go down to the sea where he falls face down in the mud, picks himself up, falls and rises again and again, and winds up afloat on the water. Voice and Music are in desperate pursuit of Woburn, and "nearly" catch up with him at the end. Voice not only tries to tell the story of Woburn, but also offers commentaries upon its progress. For example, it announces the reason for the chase at the beginning of *Cascando*: "—story . . . if you could finish it . . . you could rest . . . you could sleep. . . .no more stories . . . no more words . . . " (p. 9), as well as near the end: "Woburn . . . . see him . . . say him . . . to the end . . . " (p. 18).[5]

While Cohn views *Cascando* as another in the long series of Beckett's works where the fictional authors' struggles to create are "metaphors for Everyman seeking definition through words,"[6] Esslin interprets this play more specifically as an image of the process of artistic creation.[7] Beckett's own words support this latter reading: "It [*Cascando*] is an unimportant work, but the best I have to offer. It does I suppose show in a way what passes for my mind and what passes for its work."[8] Opener would thus be the artist, who is making a conscious effort to orchestrate and express the formless voices and emotions that emanate from the depths of his being. In his essay on Proust, Beckett described the artistic process in terms that correspond very closely to the structure and content of *Cascando*: "the work of art . . . [is] neither created nor chosen, but discovered, uncovered, excavated, pre-existing within the artist, a law of his nature. The only reality is provided by the hieroglyphics traced by inspired perception (identification of subject and object)" (p. 64).

Opener attends to the streams of Voice and Music, now separately, now together, as he struggles unsuccessfully to find the form that would make of them a work of art. This process takes place within the mind of the artist, who is thus, unlike the traditional omniscient creator, inserted into the field of his own creation and incapable of observing it as an intelligible, ordered whole. The listeners reproduce his partial perspective, and if *Cascando* is a difficult work to comprehend, this is due in part to Beckett's success at dramatizing the obscure, fluctuating vision of the modern artist at work at his impossible task.

Whether *Cascando* is seen as a dramatization of the artistic process or as an image of the self seeking to perceive and define itself through words (and Beckett might very well equate these two interpretations), this play vividly illustrates the problem of perception in the Beckettian universe:

> The Opener, it might be argued, is the perceiving part of the self, while the voice and the wordless stream of emotion that is the music in *Cascando* are the part of the self that the perceiving part perceives. But the perceived portion of the self, by its very nature, is in constant flux. The voice tells a different story at any given moment, and so the artist's being itself is in constant flux; he can do no more than be true to each momentary atom of self-perception, of *Being*.[9]

The extremely important place accorded to Music in *Cascando* can be analyzed in terms of Schopenhauer's assertion that music is the only art form which completely embodies the Will. As a universal language, music expresses not the phenomenon, but the in-itself of all phenomena, and it is "the language of feeling and of passion, as words are the language of reason."[10] Schopenhauer states that the "deep relation which music has to the true nature of all things . . . explains the fact that suitable music played to any scene, action, event or surrounding seems to disclose to us its most secret meaning, and appears as the most accurate and distinct commentary upon it."[11] The esthetic experience, of which music is the highest form, is for Schopenhauer a way in which one can, temporarily, escape individuality, or the feeling of separation from the essence of being which lies, for him as for Beckett, at the source of all human suffering. By splitting the self, in *Cascando*, into its verbal and musical aspects, and then attempting to bring them together, Beckett is portraying the striving to be, the quest to reunite self with self and thus self with the underlying unity of the universe, or with what Schopenhauer calls the Will. Of course, since Beckett has no faith in the underlying unity of either the self or the universe, such a striving can never achieve its goal, but knowledge of the futility of his desires has never kept Beckett from attempting to express them.

As a purely aural drama, *Cascando* presents a disembodied Voice that nevertheless speaks of its mission "to see" (p. 14). Just as the words "to see him" are followed immediately by "to say him" (p. 14) in *Cascando*, the process of perception, for Beckett, "leads to the obligation to express what he perceives."[12] Hannah Copeland notes the close relationship between the images of eye and voice in Beckett's work:

> The two principal images for the compelling force have similar though clearly distinct roles in the creative experience: the inner eye perceives and the inner voice communicates that perception. The vision takes on the form of works as it is transmitted to the writer. . . .
>
> The babbling voice depends upon the perceiving eye; bereft of perception it would be stilled. As long as one is conscious, however, a steady stream of words fills the mind; and one is compelled to give utterance to them.[13]

Opener is thus compelled to pay heed to Voice and Music and to attempt to give their babblings form. If it is true that perception precedes creative expression, then so long as Woburn is unseeable he will remain unsayable, and the work of art will continue to be a failure because it is attempting to express what cannot even be perceived.

While in *Endgame* the spectators both see and hear the blind Hamm struggling to find the right words with which to define his undefinable self so he can put an end to his endless story, in *Cascando* we hear, but do not see, a person's compulsive attempt to see and express his elusive self. While the interpretation of *Endgame* as a monodrama portraying different parts of the self is merely one possible reading among many, *Cascando* makes it clear that its subject is one person engaged in the process of self-perception and/or expression. The nature of theatrical space, and certainly the history of stage plays and theatrical conventions up till the time of *Endgame*'s creation, made it necessary for Beckett to use four separate actors to play the parts in that work. Even had his sole intention in *Endgame* been to dramatize the mental processes of a single character, and this is certainly open to debate, he had not yet developed the dramatic techniques that would enable him to do so in his later stage plays. As if attempting to liberate his craft from the traditional spatial constraints of theater in order to define a new type of dramatic space that carries with it none of the "realistic" connotations of the room of *Endgame*, Beckett explored in several works the possibilities of the only dramatic medium not anchored in space: radio. When listening to a radio play, we create images of what we hear upon the stage of our minds, so it was natural for Beckett to be attracted to a form of drama whose space corresponded precisely to the space of the consciousness he wished to portray. After *Cascando* he returned to visual drama, writing and helping with the production of *Film*, and writing and directing plays for both television and, once again, the stage. He brought many of the lessons he learned from radio back to the theater, where in his later years he has created monodramas that have redefined the entire concept of theatrical space. But this is a story to be continued in later chapters.

The word *cascando* is an Italian present participle that means "falling." Once more then, as in *Endgame*, the title indicates the general form and direction the play will take: a gradual diminishing, winding down, movement towards an end.[14] This end, however, never comes, and the choice for the title of a present participle signifying progression rather than termination is thus particularly significant. The play opens with Opener's dry announcement that "It is the month of May . . . for me" (p. 9).[15] May, a month traditionally associated with rebirth and renewal, ("You know, the reawakening" [p. 15]), may seem an unusual season for a story focused so single-mindedly upon an end. Yet, as Beckett tells and shows us time and time again, births and deaths, beginnings and endings, contain and imply one another and can never be clearly separated. The ending sought by Opener in this month of May, and identified by Voice's first words as "—story . . . if you could finish it . . . ," is precluded by the continual rebirths of Woburn, the changing self who never remains the same long enough to allow for its unequivocal perception and expression by Voice, Music, and Opener.

The line "It is the month of May . . . for me" serves also to call to mind the style with which the omniscient authors of a bygone age opened their stories and novels, which they then proceeded to develop methodically, logically, self-assuredly, in complete, syntactical sentences through a climax and right up to the conclusion they had envisioned from the start. Balzac, for example, often began his works by situating them in a specific month of a specific year. Elsewhere, Beckett has called Balzac's style "plane psychology,"[16] and written of it:

> To read Balzac is to receive the impression of a chloroformed world. He is absolute master of his material, he can do what he likes with it, he can foresee and calculate its least vicissitude, he can write the end of his book before he has finished the first paragraph, because he has turned all his creatures into clockwork cabbages and can rely on their staying put wherever needed or staying going at whatever speed in whatever direction he chooses.[17]

Beckett is not the first modern author writing in French to parody Balzac's technique of "writing in perspective" in a work that shows how the condition of humanity, and therefore of the artist, has changed since the nineteenth century. In *La Peste*, Camus' character Grand, a petty bureaucrat whose life ambition is to write a great piece of literature, cannot get past the first sentence, upon which he has been working for years, and which begins, "Par une belle matinée du mois de mai,"[18] because the old style is no longer appropriate for an artist who lives in a universe bereft of meaning and perspective and where the omniscient, rational, organizing eye of the demiurgic writer has become blind and anachronistic. Grand's description of his artistic goal is quite similar to the process attempted by the protagonist(s) of *Cascando*: "Quand je serai arrivé à rendre parfaitement le tableau que j'ai dans l'imagination, . . . alors le reste sera plus facile et . . . il sera possible de dire: 'Chapeau bas.' "[19] Opener opens and closes the channels of his imagination to try to perceive the picture that lies therein so he can render it perfectly in words and music, yet the day when he, or anyone else, will say "Hats off!" to a final product seems unlikely to arrive. After his attempt to begin his story in the Balzacian mode, and his approval of the traditional first line, "Yes, that's right," he "opens" and Voice takes over in quite a different fashion.

While Opener's voice was "dry as dust" and spoke in complete, punctuated sentences, Voice breaks in, "low, panting," with choppy, unconnected phrases punctuated only by three dots. Voice's paratactical utterances are a series of speech fragments that often repeat words, groups of words, sounds, or images we have heard before, without any of the coordinating or subordinating linguistic elements that characterize Opener's more traditional syntactical language. The fact that Woburn, the pursued object, cannot be seen or captured by the pursuing subjects, Voice and Music, is reflected in the form of language Beckett uses to describe the chase: in parataxis, as opposed to syntax, subject and object are not fixed in a logical, permanent, linear, and analyzable relationship, but follow each other in a circular, repetitious, endless "series subject object subject object quick succession" (*How It Is*, p. 11).

So, in its own special language, whose form corresponds to its content, Voice begins its first speech with a description of its goal: "—story . . . if you could finish it . . . you could rest . . . you could sleep . . ." Like *Endgame*, *Cascando* begins with an allusion to a longed-for end that may never come. Like Hamm, Voice equates the ending with the completion of a story, "the right one," but, like Hamm again, it has been telling its stories forever, "all I ever did . . . in my life . . . ," without ever being able to bring them to a successful close so it can "sleep . . . no more stories . . . no more words . . ." Mouth in *Not I* uses words and a style similar to those of *Cascando* to recount a similar desperate, and futile, quest for the "right" story: "something she had to tell . . . . nothing she could tell . . . try something else . . . . not that either . . . all right . . . something else again . . . so on . . . hit on it in the end" (pp. 21–22). In a similar vein, the Animator of *Rough for Radio II* urges Fox to continue talking in the hopes that some day he will succeed in telling his story: "You might prattle away to your latest breath and still the one . . . thing remain unsaid that can give you back your darling solitudes, we know" (p. 125).

In spite of the "thousands and one"[20] stories Voice has already finished without finding "the right one," it has not resigned itself to failure and expresses the conviction that "this one . . . it's different . . . . it's the right one . . ." even though it has just told us that all the times before it had also said to itself, "this time it's the right one . . . this time you have it . . . and finished it . . . and not the right one . . ."

Thus, after warning us, through repetition of words from the past which had proven false, that we may be embarking upon another fruitless journey, Voice "begins" its story as it began this first speech—in the middle, or rather, somewhere near the end. Its first word in *Cascando*, "—story," was preceded by a dash, as if to make it clear that we were breaking in upon an endless internal monologue that knows no beginning and can therefore know no end, and the story of Woburn likewise commences at an indeterminate point in the life of its equally indeterminate character: "Woburn . . . I resume . . . a long life . . . already . . . say what you like . . . a few misfortunes . . . that's enough . . . five years later . . . ten years . . . I don't know . . . Woburn . . ." The contrast between Voice's paratactical language and Opener's traditional syntax corresponds to the very different ways in which they express time. Opener situates the drama in a rational, measurable, conventional time: the month of May. But he hastens to add, "for me," as if to warn us that the voice we will be hearing has no use for words that describe the linear time of a bygone era. "[F]ive years later . . . ten years . . . I don't know . . ." is as close as Voice can come to giving his story a "when"; this information places the character in no temporal perspective whatsoever, since we do not know *what* it is now five or ten years later *than*. All we know is that we are not beginning at the beginning, which should serve as a clue not to expect the story to end at its end.

Voice's statement, which will be repeated in a later speech, that "Woburn . . . he's changed . . . not enough . . . recognizable . . . " defines the dilemma of self-perception: due to its mobility in time and space, the self we pursue is always different each time we attempt to see it, yet never quite different enough from what it was before to enable us to distinguish it as a discrete being, separated from past and future "me's" by precise contours. Voice encounters this avatar of Woburn in an enclosed space, "in the shed . . . yet another . . . ," another in the succession of sheds, shelters, and rooms in which Beckett's characters so often seek refuge. Woburn will reverse Hamm's trajectory, since we first come upon him in his shelter and then follow him into the world outside. He is "waiting for night . . . night to fall . . . to go out . . . go on . . . elsewhere . . ." and "lifts his head . . . . his eyes . . . to the window . . ." to see if it is dark enough outside to begin his journey. Thus, even though he leaves his refuge to wander in the external world which Hamm has fled, the space outside his window is dark, barren, and uninhabited, and he will pass blindly through it on his way to another shelter, the inside of his head. But we are getting ahead of ourselves, and of Woburn. In Voice's first speech, Woburn "slips out" of his shed and has to choose his direction: "right the sea . . . left the hills . . ." (p. 10), a geographical division recalling the space outside the windows of *Endgame*. Before Voice can announce Woburn's decision, Opener cuts him off with, "And I close." Even when Voice and Music begin to open and close "at will" (p. 12), their segments begin and end, as here, in the middle of phrases, a procedure emphasized in the written text by the use of dashes before the first and after the last words of each of Voice's utterances. This technique conveys to the listeners the impression that we are merely eavesdropping from time to time upon arbitrarily selected passages of Opener's inner voices and emotions, which continue to babble on even when we, and Opener, do not focus our attention upon them. Once again, the beginnings are not clear-cut beginnings, and the segments end in the middle; such is the form of both individual passages and the complete script of *Cascando*, and such is the form of the Beckettian space and time that the play embodies.

Opener next opens and closes Music, then opens both Voice and Music together. Voice comments upon the progress of the Woburn story using the same words Hamm employs in *Endgame* to describe both his story and his life: "It's getting on." Repeating many of the same phrases from its first speech, a technique that conveys to the listener the repetitive, non-progressive nature of the pursuit of Woburn, Voice urgently encourages the chase to continue, optimistically predicting its imminent success.

In its next speech, unaccompanied by Music, Voice continues to describe Woburn's voyage in the outside world, coming upon him as he is roaming through a landscape described in traditional poetic terms: "—down . . . gentle slope . . . boreen . . . giant aspens . . . wind in the boughs . . . faint sea . . ." (p. 11). But for Woburn the "night [is] too bright," so he "hugs the bank" (just as Hamm hugs the walls of his room in order to define the spatial limits of his being), and "falls . . . . face in the mud . . . ," an image that recalls the primeval setting of *How It Is.* At this point Voice thinks "we're there already," at Woburn's end and at the end of the story, a belief shared by Hamm at the end of *Endgame.* But Woburn's "ending" is no more conclusive than that of Hamm, for "he gets up" and "he goes on." Now "he goes down . . . . in his head . . ." to find "a hole . . . a shelter . . . a hollow . . . . a cave . . ." Thus, from the enclosed shelter he left in order to seek a place "elsewhere . . . sleep elsewhere . . ." (p. 9), he has traveled through the open countryside and now reached the ultimate destination of the Beckettian character: the inside of his head. The landscape of the external world disappears, just as it had in *Endgame*: "no more trees . . . no more bank . . ." But the barren night is still "too bright" for Woburn to sleep, since the light of consciousness remains when all else has been eliminated, and the story continues. Woburn's situation parallels the end Hamm envisions for himself in *Endgame*: "There I'll be, in the old shelter, alone against the silence" (p. 69). Woburn, in the shelter of his head, encounters "not a soul." However, like Hamm, whose desire to have it "all over and done with" (p. 69) is precluded by "All kinds of fantasies! That I'm being watched! . . . Steps!" (p. 70), Woburn is hindered in his pursuit of the dark sleep of non-being by the Voice and Music of self-perception which, in their turn, pursue him.

Voice and Music, for their part, ask for nothing more than to be allowed to end their work, to "—rest . . . sleep . . . no more stories . . . no more words . . . ," but they can do so only if Woburn reaches his end. They are doomed to "follow him . . . to the end . . ." because they *are* him, an identity rendered explicit in the passage "we're there . . . nearly . . . I'm there . . . somewhere . . . Woburn. . ." The perceiving and perceived self, though they belong to the same indivisible individual, can never coincide, and therefore never reach their goal, which is perfect perception and expression of the self. Voice and Music will never see and describe "the right one" because he is always just out of their grasp: each time they think they've "got him . . . seen him . . . said him . . ." (p. 15), "he's changed" (pp. 9, 11, 17) and requires catching, seeing, and saying all over again.

Opener next intervenes with a comment upon the fact that Voice and Music are now opening and closing on their own: "So, at will" (p. 12). His inner feelings and perceptions seem to be gaining the upper hand and exerting more and more control over the telling of Woburn's story, a phenomenon which Beckett himself claims to have experienced at the turning point of his career as a writer, and which he recorded in *Krapp's Last Tape* in the following words: "Spiritually a year of profound gloom and indigence until that memorable night in March, at the end of the jetty, in the howling wind, never to be forgotten, when suddenly I saw the whole thing. The vision, at last. . . . clear to me at last that the dark I have always struggled to keep under is in reality my most—"(pp. 20–21). Beckett's comments in a 1961 interview with Tom Driver concerning the tension between his chaotic inner voices and the formal requirements of artistic expression shed further light upon the relationship between Opener and the channels of perception that gradually take control of the creative process in *Cascando*:

> Then he [Beckett] began to speak about the tension in art between the mess and the form. Until recently, art has withstood the pressure of chaotic things. It has held them at bay. It realized that to admit them was to jeopardize form. . . . But now we can keep it [chaos] out no longer, because we have come into a time when "it invades our experience at every moment. It is there and it must be allowed in. . . .
>
> "What I [Beckett] am saying does not mean that there will henceforth be no form in art. It only means that there will be new form, and that this form will be of such a type that it admits the chaos and does not try to say that the chaos is really something else. . . . To find a form that accommodates the mess, that is the task of the artist now."[21]

Cascando clearly represents one of Beckett's efforts "to find a form that accommodates the mess," to give dramatic shape to the formless chaos that confronts the modern artist when he attempts to perceive and express in a universe where perception and expression are impossible.

After remarking that Voice and Music are slipping out of his control, Opener offers a commentary upon his critics: "They say, It's in his head. It's not." It would be difficult not to hear Samuel Beckett speaking here to his own critics through the words of his character. Opener enlarges upon this theme a bit further on: "They say, He opens nothing, he has nothing to open, it's in his head. . . . I don't protest any more, I don't say any more, There is nothing in my head. I don't answer any more. I open and close" (p. 13). Opener's assertion that "it's" not in his head does not disprove the interpretation of *Cascando* as a presentation of the workings of the artistic consciousness. It is rather a rephrasing of Beckett's early statement about the dilemma of the modern artist: "that there is nothing to express, nothing with which to express, nothing from which to express, no power to express, no desire to express, together with the obligation to express."[22] The "nothing" that is in Opener's head is nevertheless the only thing left to express once all that is outside his head has been done away with. Woburn, the pursued self, is simply not there, and this fact renders the search for him endless. Yet the obligation to see and express the ineffable, nonexistent Woburn remains, so the search goes on. Resigned to the hopelessness of his endeavor, Opener continues, like Sisyphus, to perform the endless task he has been assigned: "I open and close" (p. 13). These words, so often repeated in *Cascando*, refer literally to the calling forth of the strands of words and music from the depths of Opener's consciousness, but also evoke the act of opening and closing one's eyes. To be expressed, Woburn must first be seen, and when Opener opens his inner eyes, the organs of self-perception, he is attempting to conjure up the image of the nothing that is in his head. Since nothingness, like Woburn, is unperceivable, each of Opener's attempts to see and say it end in silence, and he closes the channels of perception from which Voice and Music issue forth, as if to rest and regain strength for his next attempt to see the unseeable and name the unnamable. Later in *Cascando*, Opener will admit that he is "afraid to open," yet "must open. So I open" (pp. 16–17), echoing the lament with which Beckett closes

The Unnamable: "You must go on, I can't go on, I'll go on" (p. 414).

Voice describes Woburn as fallen down, "face in the sand" (p. 12), an image that recalls Hamm's longing to "drag myself down to the sea! I'd make a pillow of sand for my head and the tide would come" (p. 61). But in the dying universe of *Endgame*, as Clov announces, there is no more tide to come and put an end to Hamm; similarly, in *Cascando*, Woburn is not allowed to stay on the sand to wait for his end, the moment when Voice and Music would finally catch up with him, but must "get . . . up . . . . on his feet . . . . he's off again . . ." only to fall back down in the sand a little further on. If Woburn would lift his eyes, he could see the "—lights . . . of the land . . . the island . . . the sky . . . . but no . . ." (p. 13). The external world still exists, as evidenced by its lights, but Woburn has chosen to turn his eyes from it and to keep his face in the sand. However, like the blind Hamm, Woburn continues to go on being, changing, and moving because the light of self-perception will not go out. Voice and Music join together to announce their goal "to find him . . . in the dark . . . to see him . . . to say him . . ." and believe that success is near at hand: "this time . . . it's right . . . we're there . . . nearly . . . finish—" (p. 14). Opener takes heart from their words and echoes their optimism: "We have not much further to go. Good" (p. 15). Voice's and Music's union in the preceding passage, as well as their assertion that the search for Woburn is nearly over, cause Opener to believe that all is at last coming together in the unity that would allow his work to cease: "From one world to another, it's as though they drew together." "They" may be Voice, Music, and Woburn, or subject and object, or perceived and perceiving self, or artistic expression and the thing expressed, and are probably all of the above.

Voice and Music continue to announce that the end is in sight: "—nearly . . . I've got him . . . . we're there. . . nearly . . . no more stories . . . . this time . . . it's the right one . . . . I've got him . . . follow him . . . . to—." Since Opener responds "Good," it seems that he believes Woburn is finally about to be followed to his end, yet when he opens again, Voice and Music are no longer together, and Woburn has slipped away from them to yet another scene. Voice describes him floating on some unnamed object out to sea, back to land, out again, heading for an island, "then no more . . .

elsewhere . . . anywhere . . . heading anywhere . . . lights—" (p. 16). The lights of consciousness will not go out so Voice and Music can encounter Woburn "in the dark" (p. 14), where they could at last see and say him; the ending where the pursued object would be at last immobile and therefore perceivable seems more and more unlikely as Woburn keeps drifting "elsewhere" (p. 16).

Opener's remark about the image of Woburn upon the waters is, "No resemblance." Woburn keeps changing places and appearances so much that Opener begins to realize he will never be visible enough to be expressed by his inner voices. The comment "No resemblance" applies equally to Opener's previous line, "They said, It's his, it's his voice, it's in his head." The voice in Opener's head bears no resemblance to the voice "they" hear because adequate expression of one's inner voices is as impossible as the seeing of Woburn, one's inner self; in fact, as *Cascando* shows, these two tasks are different aspects of the same unrealizable process.

Opener then listens to a brief passage of Music and asks, "Is that mine too?", emphasizing the disparity between what he is trying to express and the insufficient form which that expression takes. His next words are, "But I don't answer any more. And they don't say anything any more. They have quit. Good." "They" are both the critics who accuse Opener of seeing, saying, and expressing nothing and the strands of Voice and Music that have ceased momentarily. Opener pauses to enjoy the peace of this silence and valiantly attempts once more to tell a traditional story, the kind possible in the days when authors saw their characters from an external, omniscient point of view instead of pursuing them, like Opener, through the dark, twisted labyrinth of their inner being. So Opener begins again, as he has twice before, "Yes, the month of May, that's right, the end of May. The long days," and he "opens," although he admits, "I'm afraid to open," as if he knows that his story will again go out of his control and prove unfinishable.

Voice resumes its description of Woburn adrift on the "vast deep," but this time there is "no more land . . . his head . . ." (p. 17). Encouraged by this development—the liberation of Woburn from the earthly space in which he was continually changing places, thus eluding his pursuers—Opener joins Voice in urging the chase on to its end: "Come on! Come on!" Voice is more than ever assured that the end is at hand, that Woburn will be caught, that there will be "no more coming . . . no more going . . . seeking elsewhere . . . always elsewhere . . ." "Nearly" all the lights of the land are gone, though Woburn could still see the lights of the sky if he'd "only. . . turn over . . ." Voice announces that Woburn has "changed . . . nearly enough . . . ," in contrast to the "he's changed . . . not enough . . ." of earlier passages (pp. 9, 11). Does this mean that he has nearly died, i.e., nearly become separate enough from the part of his consciousness that pursues him to be perceivable? If this is the case, the change will always be either not enough, or too much, for if the moment of separation and, therefore, possible perception, ever arrives, Voice and Music will have died along with the object of their pursuit and their story will remain unfinished.

Opener reacts to Voice's and Music's closing of the gap between themselves and Woburn with a "Good God . . . . Good God good God," and then attempts to distance himself from the unthinkable, unexpressible confrontation of the different parts of the self by recalling "an image" (p. 18) from his past failed creations: "Two outings, then at last the return, to the village, to the inn, by the only road that leads there." This image evokes many episodes from Beckett's previous works, e.g., the early poem "Dieppe," *Watt*, *Molloy*, and *Malone Dies*. It may also be an effort to express Voice's and Music's pursuit of Woburn in traditional poetic terms. Unsatisfied with the results, Opener "opens" the channels of his consciousness once more and Voice and Music have come together again, announcing that "this time . . . we're there . . . Woburn . . . nearly—." Opener joins them in celebrating the coming union: "As though they had joined arms." From now on, Voice and Music remain united as they approach their goal, which is described variously as "Woburn . . . . finish . . . no more stories . . . sleep . . . . Woburn . . ." (pp. 18–19), and Opener cheers them on with two "Good's" (p. 18). Yet *Cascando* ends, like almost all other Beckettian works, without achieving its end, for Woburn "clings on" (p. 19), and the last words of the play command the search for vision of self and expression thereof to continue: "come on . . . come on—."

Although *Cascando* is "over" for its listeners at this point, since Opener, Voice, and Music are no longer heard, the play's form and content leave the impression that the mental processes which have just been presented will continue to operate in our absence, just as they had obviously been going on for quite a long time before the opening lines of *Cascando*. In spite of the assertion that "we're there . . . nearly . . ." (p. 19) with which the play closes, if we were able to listen in to Voice's next speech, it might closely resemble the text from the beginning, relegating the version of Woburn's story that we have just heard to the pile of all "the ones I've finished . . ." which turned out never to be "the right one" (p. 9).

The form of *Cascando* corresponds closely to its content: the search for an end that may never come. Like *Endgame*, it ends without really ending, just as it began somewhere in the middle of its character's desperate pursuit of vision, expression, and, finally, sleep. And, again like *Endgame*, *Cascando*'s pursuit of this elusive end takes the form of escape from travel and failures at perception in the outside world into the equally unperceivable, yet somehow preferable, inner realms of consciousness. Beckett exploits the literal blindness of his radio audience to free his drama from the space of the world outside the mind and to draw us deeper inside the self of a character than he had ever yet been able to do on stage.

Chapter 4

FILM:

"Esse est percipi"

Film is a twenty-four minute black and white film written by Beckett in 1963, made in New York in the summer of 1964, first shown at the Venice Film Festival in September 1965, directed by Alan Schneider and starring Buster Keaton. Its main character is a man who, like Hamm in *Endgame*, has fled to the "illusory sanctuary" (p. 58)[1] of a chair in a room in an attempt to reach an end. The impossible end sought by the character of *Film* is, like the final sleep desired by the Voice of *Cascando*, much more explicitly defined than the end to "this . . . this . . . thing" (p. 45) for which Hamm longs: while in *Cascando*, Voice wishes to finish its story by expressing perception of an unseeable self, *Film*'s protagonist seeks only to end the process of perception. In his unusually illuminating notes to *Film*'s script, Beckett explains first that "*esse est percipi*"[2] (to be is to be perceived), and then that his character is fleeing from perception in "search of non-being" (p. 11).

Beckett summarizes the idea of *Film* at the beginning of the comments that precede the script: "All extraneous perception suppressed, animal, human, divine, self-perception maintains in being" (p. 11). The story of *Film* is quite simple: a man hastens blindly through a street, avoiding, insofar as possible, seeing or being seen by passersby, although at one point he collides with an elderly couple. He turns into an open doorway and starts to mount a stairway when he hears the footsteps of an old flower lady who is coming down and hides from her. He finally goes up the stairs and into a shabby, sparsely furnished room where he proceeds to remove all possible sources of "extraneous perception": he covers a window and a mirror, ejects a dog and cat, takes from the wall and destroys a print of "the face of God the Father" (p. 32), covers a parrot cage and goldfish bowl, and sits down in a rocking chair to inspect a series of photographs before tearing them up. Then he nods off to sleep, awakens with a start, goes to sleep again, and reawakens suddenly to confront his own image staring intently at him. He reacts with horror and anguish to this perception, and the film ends with his sitting in the rocker, bowed forward, his head in his hands, before cutting to a close-up of an eye, the same image used to open the film.

Film's director Alan Schneider asserts that the "audacity" of Beckett's concept in his first, and only, film script lies in the "highly disciplined use of two specific camera viewpoints."[3] Beckett uses the camera eye in *Film* not merely as a means of recording a story, but as an integral player in the drama. The camera conveys two separate perceptions of reality: that of E, the perceiving eye, and that of O, the perceived object. Both visions belong to the protagonist, although this is not meant to be clear to the spectators until the end of the film. O's vision is distinguished from E's by being blurred through a lens gauze. In a production conference for *Film*, Beckett explained: "We're trying to find a technical equivalent . . . a visual, technical, cinematic equivalent for visual appetite and visual distaste . . . a reluctant . . . a disgusted vision [O's] and a ferociously . . . voracious one [E's]."[4] In parts one and two (the street and stairway scenes), most of the vision is E's, i.e., the clear-cut images representing the perception of the pursuing eye. O's blurred perceptions are recorded in these scenes only twice: when he jostles the elderly couple and briefly sees their faces and when he observes the flower lady who has collapsed on the floor of the vestibule. O's perceptions play a larger role in part three (the scene in the room), where the camera switches back and forth between the two points of view: "We see O in the room thanks to E's perceiving and the room itself thanks to O's perceiving" (p. 58). By alternating between camera shots of O's and E's visions, and even showing two images of E at the end of the film, Beckett gives dramatic form to the problem that has revolutionized so many domains of modern thought and expression: the injection of the eye of the observer into the field of observation.

Beckett establishes a convention in his introductory notes that O becomes aware of being perceived only when the camera angle from which he is viewed by E exceeds forty-five degrees. When E exceeds this "angle of immunity," O experiences the "anguish of perceivedness" (p. 11), and this happens only three times: when E first sights O in the street, when E follows O into the vestibule at the foot of the stairs, and at the end of the final scene in the room "when O is cornered" (p. 11). Beckett also has the other characters of *Film*—the couple in the street and the flower lady on the stairway—register shocked and terrified expressions when they become aware of being perceived by E; he explains in his notes that the purpose of both these episodes, which are "undefendable except as a dramatic convenience, is to suggest as soon as possible [the] unbearable quality of E's scrutiny" (p. 57). The anguish caused by perception of E, i.e., the realization of one's "perceivedness," or percipi, is the anguish of being, or esse, since *Film* defines being as being perceived. One may elude, as O almost does, the perception of others,[5] yet perception by the self remains so long as one exists, and this inescapable truth forms the basic dilemma of the human condition. This idea is present, in many forms, throughout Beckett's oeuvre, yet nowhere is it so clearly and succinctly stated as in *Film*.

The following comments by Raymond Federman upon the originality of Beckett's use of a limited camera angle and the dual perceptions registered by the camera eye of *Film* point out the important place this work must occupy in a study of dramatic perspective and the question of vision in Beckett's drama:

> Conventionally, the viewer of a film sees more than the characters in the film. One might say that the spectator has a total perception of the action whereas the characters have a partial perception. In "Film," however, since the field of vision of the camera-eye never exceeds that of the protagonist, the viewer is denied total perception. . . .
>
> While the camera and the spectator have a clear and distinct view, though limited by its angle, the total inner vision of the protagonist is blurred and unprecise. What Beckett suggests here, and what

> Boris Kaufman achieves through his excellent photography, is a visual ambivalence which stresses and exposes the tragic limitations of external and internal vision.[6]

Like *Cascando*, *Film* is much briefer and more condensed than *Endgame*. Where much of the impact of *Endgame*, and the total effect of *Cascando*, are aural, *Film* is silent, with the exception of a single "ssh!" uttered by the woman in the street to her companion. *Film* is therefore completely visual, as befits a cinematic study of the problem of perception. Its central image is that of the eye, an image which was present in *Endgame* and *Cascando*, but only as one element among many. Although there are four (human) characters in *Film*, as in *Endgame*, the protagonist played by Keaton clearly dominates his work to a much greater degree than does Hamm. The elderly couple encountered briefly in the street may be a reincarnation of Nell and Nagg, but the Clov/Hamm pair has been reduced to a single person who is split into O and E. We encountered a similar division of one person into separate characters in *Cascando*, where Opener, Voice, Music, and Woburn represent diverse aspects of a single personality.

The concentration of dramatic elements in *Film* is characteristic of the direction in which Beckett's work has evolved over the years. While Beckett clearly intended most of the aspects of *Film* that contribute to this dramatic condensation, one of them grew out of a technical accident: the initial street scene was written to be much longer and more complex than the short scene we see in the film. Before the incident where O runs into the elderly couple, there were to be shots of people going to work in pairs, bicycles, a horse-drawn cab, with all the people "shown in some way perceiving—one another, an object, a shop window, a poster, etc., i.e., all contentedly in *percipere* and *percipi*," and O "hastening blindly along sidewalk, hugging the wall on his left, in opposite direction to all the others" (p. 12). While all of this activity was shot by the makers of *Film*, the footage was discarded because the results were technically unsatisfactory and the film's budget did not allow for the scene to be redone.[7]

The dominant idea of *Film*, that esse est percipi, was clearly present in *Endgame* and in *Cascando*, though it was not so unequivocally stated and methodically developed. All of the agents of "extraneous perception" which the protagonist of *Film* successively suppresses—animal, human, divine—are also done away with in *Endgame*: rats and fleas are mercilessly destroyed; people are dying off, both outside Hamm's shelter and in it; and Hamm concludes a collective prayer to God with the bitterly hilarious remark, "The bastard! He doesn't exist!" (p. 55). Perception of Woburn by animals or other people is not mentioned in *Cascando*, although two passages allude to his refusal, or inability, to perceive the lights of the sky shine upon him (pp. 13, 17). The section of *Endgame* where Hamm imagines his end might be seen as a preliminary outline for the script of *Film*:

> There I'll be, in the old shelter, alone against the silence. . . . If I can hold my peace, and sit quiet, it will be all over . . . and done with. . . . And then? . . . All kinds of fantasies! That I'm being watched! A rat! . . . Then babble, babble, words, like the solitary child who turns himself into children, two, three, so as to be together, and whisper together, in the dark. (Pp. 69–70)

Just like the future self envisioned by Hamm, the man in *Film*, alone in his refuge, attempting to sit quietly so that it may all be over at last, cannot attain his goal of non-being because of the perception he cannot escape: first, that of the animals and of God, and finally, his own, as he realizes that he has split himself into E and O, pursuer and pursued, an incompatible couple who, like Hamm and Clov, cannot stand to be together but could not exist separately. Woburn faces a similar situation in *Cascando*, although he has fled from the refuge that shelters Hamm and O: chased relentlessly by Opener, Voice, and Music, "he clings on" (p. 19) to life—motion, perception, and perceivedness—by constantly eluding his pursuers' grasp, thus barring the peaceful, silent ending toward which all the play's characters strive.

If certain elements of character and theme can be traced from *Endgame* and *Cascando* to *Film*, the three pieces also share many common images. Both *Film* and *Endgame* take place in a bare room to which their main character has retreated from the external world, while *Cascando* begins with Woburn leaving his "shed" to wander in the dark night outside. *Film* is shot entirely in black and white, creating a color scheme similar to both the grey light that bathes the room of *Endgame* and the nocturnal landscape of *Cascando*. Whereas in *Endgame* we see only the room, and in *Cascando* we see, literally, nothing, the exterior world is shown at the beginning of *Film*. Our vision of the outer world in *Endgame* and *Cascando* comes only through Clov's and Voice's descriptions of it as dark, barren, and deserted, while in *Film* we see it with our own eyes as alive and populated, in spite of its lack of color. The three cases, however, may not be so dissimilar after all: it is entirely possible that the external world of *Endgame* has turned to ashes only for the dying consciousness of its protagonist(s), and where Clov perceives only "zero," others may still see visions of rising corn and herring fleets. Voice's descriptions of the land and sea through which Woburn travels grow progressively barer and darker, and we have no reason not to believe that this change is taking place only inside Opener's head, where, as he suggests, the entire scene is located. The street scene in *Film*, although clear and animated to our eyes as seen by the camera viewpoint representing E, is virtually nonexistent to O, who, as Beckett states four times, hastens "blindly" through it. In his notes, Beckett explains that we see so few of O's perceptions in the initial scenes because they "must in fact have been negligible" (p. 58). It is thus much clearer in *Film* than in *Endgame* or *Cascando* that the death of the outer world is a product of its character's voluntary flight from it.

Beckett's brief note at the beginning of *Film*, "Unreality of street scene" (p. 12), deserves comment here. The *reality* of street scenes was an important goal for early painters in perspective. In the late fifteenth century, Italian artists perfected the technique of painting "an open street with very strong perspective lines vanishing to one point near the center of the picture," a scenic organization that was to have a strong influence upon theatrical décor in the years to come.[8] By calling for a street scene to give the illusion of unreality, and by quickly withdrawing his dramatic action from it into the room of *Film*, which also has an "unreal quality" (p. 23), Beckett is, consciously or unconsciously, turning his back upon a major convention of linear perspective. Where painting and theatrical décor in perspective draw the eye to a geographical vanishing point in order to create the impression of physical distance, Beckett renounces this effect of depth in space in favor of a descent into the depths of consciousness. The protagonist of *Film*, having fled the unreality of the street and suppressed, to an even greater extent than Hamm, all extraneous perception, would thus seem, like Woburn, to be one step further along than his predecessor in this solitary voyage. In spite of his failure to achieve his goal of uniting the self by overcoming the duality of percipere and percipi in a blessed state of non-being, the inner pathway he is following, however endless it may be, is the preferred trajectory of the Beckettian character.

The shed of *Cascando* is described as "yet another" (p. 9) of the series of sheds and rooms in Beckett's work, and we learn only that it has a window through which Woburn peers at the beginning to assure himself that it is dark enough to leave on his voyage. The sparse décors of the rooms in *Film* and *Endgame* are more important dramatic elements, and they are remarkably similar. Both are furnished with a door, a curtained window (two in *Endgame*), a picture on the wall, and a chair. The windows in both works are means of visual contact with the outside world, but they function differently. In *Endgame*, Hamm keeps insisting that Clov look out the windows to report back what he sees, while the character in *Film* takes care to draw the curtain on his window the moment he enters the room. O is much more clearly resigned to the suppression of the outside world, and more obviously the cause of it, than Hamm, who alternates between ordering the extinction of everything that might bring it to life again and wishing to feel the sunlight and hear the sea through the windows of his room. Similarly, though both characters sit in chairs, Hamm's confinement is involuntary and he demands to be moved around the room in his wheelchair, while O seeks out his rocker and asks nothing more than to be allowed to sleep there peacefully until the end.

The picture on the wall plays a much less ambiguous role in *Film* than in *Endgame*. We never know for certain what the picture of *Endgame* represents, since it is turned to the wall from the beginning, and when it is silently removed by Clov, it is simply stood on the floor, face still against the wall. In *Film*, on the other hand, we see the picture: it is a bearded caricature of "the face of God the Father" (p. 32) whose eyes stare severely down at O. When O rips the picture from the wall, "tears it in four, throws down the pieces and grinds them underfoot" (pp. 32–33), he is clearly carrying out his project of suppressing all extraneous perception—in this case, divine.

Walls enclose the refuges of both Hamm and O, separating their sanctuaries from the outside world. In both works, the characters "hug" their walls: Hamm when he asks Clov to wheel him to the limits of his domain, "Closer! Closer! Up against!"

(p. 26), and O when he "approaches mirror from side and covers it with rug" (twice—pp. 26–27 and p. 31). Although Woburn has left the confines of his walls, as he traverses the countryside, "he hugs the bank" (p. 11). In their searches for an end—to time, to perception, to their lives—Hamm, Woburn, and O seek also to define the spatial boundaries of their existence. All of the Beckettian journeys can be, and have been, interpreted as explorations of the limits of the self,[9] and just as the precise contours of the self can never be delineated or perceived, so the walls of Beckett's stage décors are ineffectual in aiding his characters to establish the perimeters of a domain in which they might finally attain a sense of unity of self. Walls disappear altogether from the sets of Beckett's later plays; while they are alluded to in the texts, the spectators no longer see them upon the stage, but see instead the characters suspended, like Woburn at the end of *Cascando*, in a space which is as undefined and endless as is the time whose boundaries they also seek in vain. Although we still see the walls of *Endgame* and *Film*, and hear of the bank to which Woburn clings in *Cascando*, the characters' attempts to use them to enclose, define, limit, and end the space of their existence are fruitless, for the awareness of percipi, be it that of the "potential procreator" of *Endgame*, of the pursuing Voice and Music in *Cascando*, or of E's perception in *Film*, continues to invade the consciousness of the protagonists and keeps them from achieving the peace, stillness, and state of non-perceivedness that would allow them to reach their longed-for end. Before *Film*'s protagonist retreats to the illusory comfort of his four walls, we see him "hugging the wall" that lines the sidewalk down which he hastens blindly as he flees the perception of others on the open street (p. 12), and "cringing aside towards [the] wall" of both the sidewalk and the vestibule he enters (pp. 12 and 18) each time he becomes aware of being perceived by E. Here, too, the wall seems to be a defense against invasion from the eye of the perceiver, since O turns to it in his vain attempts to escape the "anguish of perceivedness."

If the walls of *Endgame* and *Film* represent attempts to fix the spatial limits of the self, these two plays share another image that may perform the same function. Both Hamm and O wear hats, a frequent accoutrement for the Beckettian character that serves to define the upper limit of his body, as Beckett makes clear in his early story, "The Calmative": "Up aloft, my hat, the same as always, I reached no further" (p. 31). The resemblance between Hamm and O goes even further: both men use handkerchiefs to cover their faces—Hamm, completely, at the beginning and end of *Endgame*, and O only partially, with the handkerchief he wears inside his hat and which he uses to hide his face from E and other people on the street in the opening sequences of *Film*. Just as Hamm removes his handkerchief at the beginning of *Endgame*, O removes his at the beginning of his sojourn in the room of *Film*. The hat-and-handkerchief routine is not indicated in Beckett's original script for *Film*, since it resulted from Buster Keaton's desire to use his trademark, a flattened Stetson, instead of the hat that Beckett had envisioned O pulling down over his eyes. Beckett's ready acceptance of Keaton's suggestion as "more interesting than what was originally called for"[10] may have stemmed from his recollection of the success of a similar image in *Endgame*.

In addition to the handkerchief with which he hides his face, O wears a black patch over his left eye, which is seen for the first time near the end of *Film* (the camera scrupulously avoids O's face until this point). The patch may be another means by which O attempts, like an ostrich, to escape awareness of being perceived, by blocking his vision of the agents of perception. It may also be another indication of Beckett's desire to represent in drama the loss of perspective characteristic of the current human condition, for vision in only one eye precludes perception of depth, the illusion of which is a major goal of painting in perspective. The black patch on O's eye calls to mind Hamm's black glasses, just as his "blind haste" (p. 15) on the street, upon which Beckett insists, corresponds to Hamm's more literal blindness. In *Cascando*, not only does Voice have difficulty seeing Woburn, but Woburn often "can't see" (pp. 11, 12, 14) because he is lying face down in mud and bilge. In none of these plays, however, do the objects covering the characters' eyes or their states of blindness enable them to put an end to the process of perception, which continues inside the mind even when all "extraneous perception" has been successfully eliminated.

Handkerchiefs cover the faces of Hamm and O; glasses and patches cover their eyes; sheets, curtains, rugs, and coats cover the windows and furnishings of their rooms. While *Endgame* begins with an uncovering of the windows, ashbins, and Hamm's chair so the play can begin, the room sequence in *Film* consists of a progressive covering up of the window, mirror, birdcage, and fishbowl in an effort to abolish all external means of perception. This variation in the use of the same dramatic technique from one play to another shows Beckett's fondness for experimenting with permutations of similar elements. It also supports a reading of *Film* as a sequel to *Endgame*: the man we see in the chair in the final tableau of *Endgame*, who has once again covered his face with his handkerchief, is in many respects the dramatic forerunner of the man with a handkerchief covering his head whom we meet at the beginning of *Film*. O's covering of the set of *Film* is a counterpart to Clov's uncovering of the set of *Endgame*: in the later work, we may be witnessing the continuation of *Endgame*'s preparation for that impossible moment when "all would be silent and still and each thing in its last place, under the last dust" (p. 57). However, since time in the Beckettian universe is diminishing, yet circular and repetitive, so can *Film* be seen as both a later moment of the story begun in *Endgame* and a possible introduction to it: it is conceivable that O's Clov, his pursuing eye (E), may proceed, after the final scene we see, to uncover all the furnishings of the room and engage in a game with O which is similar to the one played out by Hamm and Clov with respect to both its absurdity and its endlessness. Similarly, it is entirely possible to consider Opener, from the chronologically earlier play *Cascando*, as a later manifestation of O from *Film*: he would have gone from O's awareness of the inescapability of self-perception to acceptance of same and determination to carry the pursuit of self by self to its logical, if unattainable, conclusion—union of perceiver and perceived in perfect perception. Or *Film* might be simply a retelling of the story of *Cascando*, this time emphasizing the anguish of the perceived rather than that of the perceiver. Woburn could thus be another O, fleeing the pursuing eyes of Opener, Voice, and Music. Although *Film* ends by showing Eye confronting its Object head on, there is no indication that these two parts of the protagonist will not recommence their game of flight and pursuit after the final frame recorded by the camera, in the never-ending cycle of "I'm there . . . nearly . . . . I've got him . . . nearly—" (p. 18) that characterizes *Cascando*.

Endgame, *Cascando*, and *Film*, then, are all about ends that never come. *Endgame* opens with the announcement that "it must be nearly finished" (p. 1), yet closes before we can be certain that the game is really over, presenting a final tableau much like the one at the beginning of the play. In *Cascando*, Voice begins its text by stating its desire to finish its story and finally be allowed to sleep, and at the end the story is only "nearly" (p. 19) complete, leaving much doubt as to whether what we have just heard might not be merely another in a series of "thousands and one" (p. 9) false starts. *Film* is characterized by a similar blurring of the boundaries between beginning and end. At the beginning of *Film*, the camera comes upon O as he is hurrying down the street; the "story" of the film obviously had its beginning elsewhere, and the spectators plunge, unprepared and almost certainly bewildered, right into the middle of O's frantic flight from perception and search for an end. At the end of the film, in spite of all his attempts to reach the ending defined as absence of percipi, he is as far from his unattainable goal as ever. As if to underscore the hopeless circularity of O's predicament, *Film* opens and closes with the same image: close-ups of Buster Keaton's eye, with its "beautifully creased and reptilian" lid.[11] William Van Wert proposes that this use of a framing eye "suggests that the whole film takes place in the time between eyes closed and eyes opened, that is, the time between blinks."[12]

Eye imagery links not only the beginning and end of *Film*, but all that comes in between. *Film*'s concentration upon the single theme of the inescapability of self-perception is paralleled by its insistent exploitation of this single, age-old image of perception. Other images are certainly present in the work, yet the eye is clearly dominant. Indeed, as Schneider tells us, the original title of the script was *The Eye*,[13] and the perceiving half of the protagonist is named E, for "eye." After the close-up of the eye with which the film begins, the camera eye shifts to O on the street. O hides his eyes, and his whole face, from our view until the final sequence of *Film*, but we are bombarded with images of other eyes throughout the production. Close-ups of the face of the old couple on the street show them putting on and taking off (her) lorgnon and (his) pince-nez as they observe O and E, and closing their eyes at the end of this episode. Similarly, the camera shows us a close-up of the terror-stricken face of the flower lady in the vestibule, whose expressive eyes register her "agony of perceivedness" before closing, as she sinks to the ground.

When O finally manages to escape to his room, where he will be safely hidden from the eyes of other people, he finds that his self-imposed task of eliminating extraneous perception has only half begun, for the room is full of eyes, real and symbolic, which he methodically suppresses. First he covers his window, the room's "eye," which both looks out onto the external world and permits vision of the interior from the outside. Next he covers the mirror with a rug, so his own eyes will not catch their image in its reflection. He then inspects the headrest of the rocker, which, by a "happy accident" discovered during filming, has two holes resembling eyes carved into it.[14] At this point he ejects the dog and cat from the room, in a highly comic sequence, because their eyes have been staring at him since he entered. When the rug falls from the mirror, he replaces it, again approaching the mirror from the side in order to avoid being perceived by its eye. He sits down in the rocking chair, but only briefly, because he is disturbed by the picture of "the face of God the Father, the eyes staring at him severely" (p. 32). After ripping it up and grinding it underfoot, he sits down again and takes a folder from his briefcase. Another pair of eyes was discovered here during the filming: the two eyelets that make up the folder's clasp seem to be staring up at O, forcing him to turn the folder ninety degrees in order to avert them.[15] The parrot and goldfish are the next observers to bother him, so after close-up shots of their eyes, we see him cover cage and bowl with his coat.

Sitting down again (each time he sits, we see a shot of the "curious headrest" [p. 33] with its "eyes"), O takes a series of photographs from the folder and inspects them carefully before tearing them up. The photos are being observed not only by O's eye, but by E as he watches O, by the camera's eye as it records both E's and O's perceptions, and by the eyes of the spectators as we follow the camera's roving eye. These multiple levels of perception are further complicated by the nature of the photographs themselves: in all but the last picture, we see the same male figure, at different points of his life, in the process of being looked at by one or more people or by an animal. Beckett's description of the photos in his notes to *Film* (p. 61) insists upon the state of percipi in which we see their subject: as an infant, his mother's "severe eyes devour . . . him"; at four years old, he prays with closed eyes, while his mother bows her head toward him, again with "severe eyes"; as a boy of fifteen, he is shown teaching a dog to beg, and the dog is "on its hind legs looking up at him"; when he graduates at age twenty, a "section of the public [is] watching"; a year later, he has his arm around his fiancée while "a young man takes a snap of them"; a soldier at age twenty-five, he holds a little girl in his arms as "she looks into his face." Only in the last picture is the man shown alone: he is thirty, but looks over forty, wears a hat and overcoat, and has a patch over his left eye. This is obviously the likeness of *Film*'s protagonist, so the photographs must be shots of him at earlier periods of his life. Although he is alone in the last photo, as he is in his room, he is still being perceived by multiple sets of eyes. A photographer took the picture using the eye of his camera, and many eyes, including O's, are now upon it as it is displayed in *Film*. The biography recounted by the set of photographs corresponds in many respects to the story recorded by *Film*: a man has successively suppressed much extraneous perception in his life—animal (the dog), human (mother, public, young photographer, little girl), and divine (the prayers of the second pose)—yet his self-perception remains. The patch over one of his eyes, in both the photo and the room, may indicate an effort to reduce his ability to perceive, and thus his ability to be perceived, yet we, and he, know that such a hope is in vain: even were he to cover up his other eye, the inner vision effected by his "eyes not the blue the others at the back" (*How It Is*, p. 8), whose object is the self, would continue its relentless efforts at perception. The major difference between the story we see in *Film* and the one told by the photographs is the pace of the action. The photos present a slow-motion review of the process of perception that is the subject of *Film*. Conversely, just as a motion picture is a series of still photographs speeded up in order to produce the effect of continuous motion, *Film* can be regarded as a fast-paced résumé of the life of O recorded in the still photos. The scene with the photographs is thus a (slow-motion) film-within-a-film, as well as a dramatist's self-conscious commentary upon the medium in which he is working.

In an essay entitled "The Cinematographic View of Becoming," Henri Bergson asserts that the "*mechanism of our ordinary knowledge is of a cinematographical kind*,"[16] i.e., that we view the process of becoming artificially, as a series of still snapshots taken at various stages of the process, which is in constant motion and can therefore never be adequately represented by an immobile image. *Film*'s protagonist, whose eye of self-perception is identified with the eye of the camera, and who reviews his life by looking at a series of photographs, certainly takes a cinematographic view of his own becoming. Bergson's description of the results of such a method of perception could very well be a summary of the perceptual dilemma suffered by all of Beckett's characters:

> The application of the cinematographical method . . . leads to a perpetual recommencement, during which the mind, never able to satisfy itself and never finding where to rest, persuades itself, no doubt, that it imitates by its instability the very movement of the real. But though, by straining itself to the point of giddiness, it may end by giving itself the illusion of mobility, its operation has not advanced it a step, since it remains as far as ever from its goal.[17]

O is indeed as far as ever from his goal of escaping self-perception after he views his life through the photographs. After closely inspecting each of the photos twice, he rips them up and drops the pieces on the floor. Like the man in the last picture, he now seems to have freed himself from all the eyes that have been trained upon him. Yet his escape from percipi is as illusory as was that of the man in the photo: he will doze off twice, only to be awakened suddenly each time by an awareness of perceivedness. The camera eye that continued to observe the man in the final photo, even when he had managed to remove all other observers from his picture, corresponds to the motion picture camera eye of *Film* when it reports E's perception of O to the spectators. After O starts awake for the first time, experiences the anguish of perceivedness by E, and nods off to sleep again, E makes a wide circle of the room, showing images of "curtained window," "shrouded mirror," and "shrouded bowl and cage," before coming to rest again upon O's face "against ground of headrest" (pp. 40–41). E seems to be taking inventory of the eyes that O has occluded before his final confrontation with O, which shows that all O's previous efforts to escape percipi have been in vain. Now that the eyes representing "extraneous perception" have all been covered, ejected, or destroyed by O, his own eye will be shown for the first time in *Film* (with the exception of the initial image), and will dominate the remaining footage. The camera, doubling E's vision, confronts O head on and records his terrified expression as he awakens to find E staring at him. After registering "that look" (p. 44), the camera cuts briefly to E's face, which we see for the first time: "It is O's face (with patch) but with very different expression" (p. 47). E is standing in front of the spot where the face of the divinity has been ripped from the wall, as evidenced by the empty nail visible near his left temple. The eye of self-perception has thus literally replaced the eye of God. After a "long image of the unblinking gaze" of E (pp. 47–48), the camera returns to O, still showing "that look" (p. 48), who closes his eyes and covers his face with his hands. E's eyes are then shown in close-up before the camera returns to O, who is rocking gently, bowed forward in the chair, his head in his hands. The film closes with a huge close-up of the only eye that O will never be able to escape: his own.

If the image of the eye is omnipresent in *Film*, it undergoes a clear evolution over the course of the work which parallels O's story. The eyes of passersby in the street that O escapes by fleeing to his room are replaced by the animate and inanimate eyes he confronts, and eliminates, inside the room. This done, he proceeds to deal with the eyes in his photo collection, which represent memories of the past. Having suppressed the external agents of perception in both his present and his past, he closes his eyes in an attempt to reach the state of "non-being" (p. 11) that is possible only if one can completely escape the experience of perceivedness. He learns, to his horror, that "self-perception maintains in being" (p. 11) even when all other eyes have been avoided, and the eye that closes *Film* is larger, more menacing, and more powerful than all the rest.

In a production conference during filming, Beckett described the camera progression in *Film* as follows: "moving from the maximum of exposed exterior or man completely exposed and . . . at the other extreme the maximum of protected interior, enclosure, seclusion . . . a maximum of exterior quality, a transitional quality and a maximum of interior quality."[18] O's voyage from the external world to the shelter of his room to the depths of his consciousness, which is given form and continuity by the image of the eye that accompanies it, follows the same direction as Beckett's work in general: while many of his early characters travel in geographical space in search of either vision and self or a clear-cut end to both, their later counterparts inhabit the undefinable space of their consciousnesses. Of the "two pairs" of eyes which Beckett so often asserts we all possess—the outer pair of flesh, and the inner eyes which are trained upon the self, it is the latter that comes to dominate his work.

Film is not regarded as one of Beckett's most successful works, by either its author, director, or critics. Alan Schneider admits that "half of it was a failure and the other half successful."[19] Its shortcomings are due partly to well-documented technical problems involved in Beckett's and Schneider's experimentation with an unfamiliar medium. *Film* is a difficult work for even the most sophisticated spectator to understand, since Beckett's idea of using two different camera viewpoints to represent the perceptions of E and 0 becomes clear to most viewers only after they have read the author's remarks which accompany the script. This problem leads to the other major difficulty with *Film*, which is Beckett's uncharacteristic attempt to illustrate a philosophical "truth" in this work. He tries to forestall such a criticism by his disclaimer to his introductory remarks: "No truth value attaches to above, regarded as of merely structural and dramatic convenience" (p. 11). However, his attempt to illustrate a single, specific theme—esse est percipi—whether "true" or not, renders *Film* less evocative and therefore less rich than much of his other work. Beckett's drama is at its best when it attempts to give shape to certain universal aspects of human existence, e.g., the act of waiting in *Waiting for Godot*, or the experience of ending in *Endgame*. After *Film*, Beckett abandoned the use of drama to illustrate a point, returning to his old habit of refusing to explain the meaning of his works, insisting instead that they mean nothing other than what they show, i.e., that their form is their content. *Film* is not, however, a total incongruity in the Beckettian oeuvre. Many of its images and other dramatic elements reappear in Beckett's later plays, just as *Film* borrows much from earlier works. The theme of perception and its equation with being also underlie nearly every piece of Beckettian fiction or drama, but never again will they be so methodically and even didactically developed, both within the play and through the author's commentaries, as they are in *Film*. Beckett did not stop writing copious notes to accompany his scripts after *Film*; in fact, in some of his later works the notes outnumber the lines of text. However, future notes deal solely with technical issues and instruct directors and actors how to execute the drama according to the author's formal intent; no more explanations of theme or meaning will be offered. Beckett will henceforth follow his earlier advice to leave the task of interpretation up to the critics (and "let them. . . . provide their own aspirin").[20] They will nonetheless find his comments upon *Film* to be of great value in understanding the concept of perception that is central to all his work.

Chapter 5

EH JOE:

"No one can see you now"

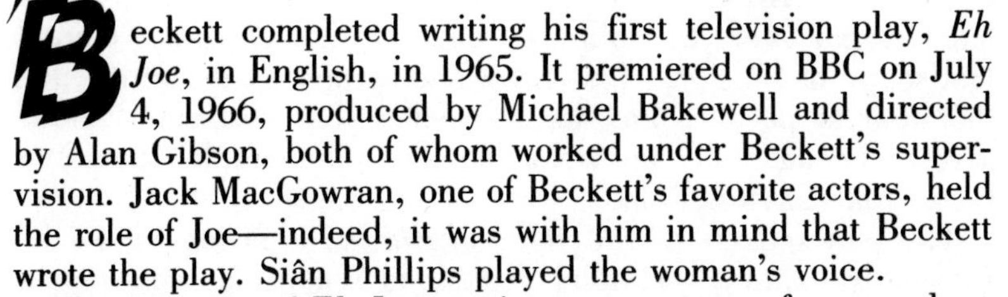

Beckett completed writing his first television play, *Eh Joe*, in English, in 1965. It premiered on BBC on July 4, 1966, produced by Michael Bakewell and directed by Alan Gibson, both of whom worked under Beckett's supervision. Jack MacGowran, one of Beckett's favorite actors, held the role of Joe—indeed, it was with him in mind that Beckett wrote the play. Siân Phillips played the woman's voice.

The situation of *Eh Joe* consists, once more, of a man alone in a sparsely furnished room. At the beginning, the camera shows Joe, a man in his late fifties with grey hair, going from his bed to his window, opening the window to look out, closing it, and drawing its curtain. He performs similar business with the door and cupboard of his room and then inspects underneath the bed. He finally relaxes on the edge of the bed, with his eyes closed. The camera starts to move in upon his face, but its approach is halted by the first word of a woman's voice, emanating from an unseen source. The voice is described as "low, distinct, remote, little colour, absolutely steady rhythm, slightly slower than normal" (p. 36).[1] During the rest of the play, the camera makes "nine slight moves in towards face," being stopped each time "by voice resuming, never camera move and voice together" (p. 35). The play ends with a "maximum close-up of face" (p. 35), with voice and image going out together.

When the voice begins to speak, Joe opens his eyes and listens intently. He relaxes briefly between speeches, "when perhaps voice has relented for the evening," but comes to attention again each time the voice resumes, his face reflecting the "mounting tension of *listening*" (p. 36). The voice comments first upon Joe's preparation of the room, then identifies itself as the voice of an abandoned lover from Joe's past, and proceeds to narrate the story of a woman spurned by Joe who committed suicide for love of him.

The alternating voice and camera eye are clearly different parts of Joe, although the spectators perceive them as physically external to the actor. The narrowing field of the camera parallels the direction of Joe's perception: he switches his attention from the outer world—the universe beyond his window and door, and then the space enclosed by the walls of his room—to the inner scene of his consciousness. The voice makes the mental setting of *Eh Joe* explicit in its third speech: "You know that penny farthing hell you call your mind . . . That's where you think this is coming from, don't you? . . . . And look at him now . . . Throttling the dead in his head" (p. 37). Jack MacGowran offers the following characterization of the mental landscape of *Eh Joe*: "It's really photographing the mind. It's the nearest perfect play for television that you could come across, because the television camera photographs the mind better than anything else."[2]

The text spoken by the voice of *Eh Joe* is accompanied by extremely explicit technical directions regarding Joe's movements and facial expression, the camera moves, the length of pauses between voice and camera moves, and the rhythm and tone of the voice's phrases. Beckett's attention to these nonverbal components of the play is much more than simply an indication of his growing interest in the technological capabilities of the electronic media or of his experience with directing his own plays. His emphasis upon the nontextual dramatic elements of *Eh Joe* corresponds to the way in which his dramatic work has evolved: towards an integration of visual and sound effects—light, images, camera moves, voice texture, tone, and rhythm, the sound and shape of words—with the "content" conveyed by the spoken text.

Beckett has returned, with *Eh Joe*, to the combination of visual and aural dramatic expression he used in *Endgame*, yet the effects he achieves in this television drama are quite different from those of his early stage plays, which seem somewhat traditional in retrospect. In *Eh Joe*, he has combined the unseen voices of *Cascando* with the mute protagonist of *Film* to create a striking image of a man looking at, and hearing, himself.

Eh Joe tells much the same "story" as the previous works in this study, and it uses many of the same images and dramatic techniques. Beckett's longstanding fascination with the mathematical concept of permutation carries over into his work with both narrative fiction and drama: time and time again, a limited number of formal and thematic elements are reworked, repeated, varied, and experimented with in different contexts. In *Eh Joe*, Beckett uses a new medium—television—and a different combination of words, images, and technical procedures to illustrate the problem of perception, which is summed up by the opening words of the woman's voice: "Thought of everything? . . . Forgotten nothing? . . . You're all right now, eh? . . . No one can see you now . . . No one can get at you now . . . Why don't you put out that light? . . . There might be a louse watching you" (p. 36). This brief passage is rich with resonances from all of Beckett's work and thus announces, at the play's beginning, that nothing is really beginning, that we are, instead, about to witness a continuation, in somewhat different form, of the same endless, beginningless, impossible, yet inevitable process of perception explored in previous writings. The woman's voice could just as well be speaking to O, or to Woburn, or even to Hamm (during the final moments he envisions alone "in the old shelter" [p. 69]), as to Joe, for all of these characters have attempted to think of everything necessary to insure their safety from the perception of others and their solitude in the dark, only to become excruciatingly conscious of the ineluctable light of self-perception. The "louse" which might be watching Joe recalls the flea and rat of *Endgame* as well as Hamm's fantasy that, at the end, he would be watched by a rat, not to speak of the many animal eyes that besiege O in *Film*. The louse may also very well be Joe himself—the cruel son and lover who rejected parents and mistresses one by one and is now murdering their memories in his mind. At any rate, it is obvious that we are watching yet another attempt by a Beckettian character to achieve the peace that comes from absence of percipi, an end barred by the omnipresent eye of the self.

Like Hamm and O, Joe has fled to the confines of a bare room with a window. Another room is later evoked by the woman's voice in *Eh Joe*—the house from which the woman who died heard the "sea through open window" (p. 40), a line that reminds us of Hamm's desire "to hear the sea" (p. 64) through the window of his room. This second, unseen room in *Eh Joe* seems very close to the invisible shed evoked by Voice in *Cascando*: in both plays, a person leaves the shelter at night, traversing a briefly described landscape in order to lie face down at the water's edge in search of sleep, peace, and an end. Such repetition of images is accompanied by intra- and intertextual repetition of words here, as throughout Beckett's work. For example, the woman of *Eh Joe*, who is first described as "sitting on the edge of her bed in her lavender slip," "slips out" (p. 40) of her room, just as Woburn "slips out" when he begins his travels in *Cascando* (pp. 9–10). The "house" of *Eh Joe* is called a "shed" in *Cascando*, yet the description of the woman's journey from shelter to sea in *Eh Joe* repeats the word "shed" in a totally different context: "The pale eyes . . . The look they shed before" (p. 41).

When Joe covers his window, door, and cupboard at the beginning of the play, we might think of Clov uncovering the set of *Endgame* at its outset, or of O closing his door, drawing the curtain over his window, and covering mirror, birdcage, and goldfish bowl in *Film*. While in *Endgame* the windows are often used to try to establish contact with the outside world, yet in *Film* the window is occluded to shut out the exterior, Joe first looks out his window and door and into his cupboard, and then covers them. The exterior he rejects by so doing is never seen by the spectators, as it is at the beginning of *Film*. It is, however, evoked in words, as in *Endgame* and *Cascando*.

The world outside the room in *Eh Joe* exists only in memories described by the woman's voice. She speaks first of the idyllic setting of her love affair with Joe: "Those summer evenings in the Green . . . . When we sat watching the ducks" (p. 38). The next outdoor scene occurs in the final passage of *Eh Joe* (pp. 40–41), where the voice describes the suicide of the woman who died for love of Joe. It is, once more, a "warm summer night." The woman is first seen "sitting on the edge of her bed in her lavender slip" and next as she goes "down the garden and under the viaduct . . . Sees from the seaweed the tide is flowing." Our mental image of this scene is richly colored, in lavender and greens, at the beginning. The colors fade when the voice tells of the "moon going off the shore behind the hill," as the woman "stands a bit looking at the beaten silver," and the moon's silver turns to the grey of the rock, shingle, and stones on which the woman dies. Color reappears briefly as the voice repeats the words used to introduce this woman in an earlier passage: "The green one . . . The narrow one," but fades again in the following phrase: "Always pale . . . The pale eyes." Our mindscape becomes progressively colorless, as Beckett multiplies his use of the word "stone," italicizing it for emphasis several times near the end: "Lips on a *stone*," "To the *stones*," "The *solitaire* [another colorless stone] . . . Against a *stone*," "*Breasts* in the stones," "In the *stones*." This striking, rhythmic repetition of a single word serves not only to imitate the sound and motion of waves washing over rocks, or to evoke the visual image of the stones on which the woman is dying, but also to overlay the final scene of *Eh Joe* with a coat of grey paint, causing the color of Joe's memory of the woman to blend with the black and white of the television setting in which he, and we, perceive it. Her memory—turned from lavender and green to grey—the black, white, and grey television image before our eyes, and the voice of "little colour" (p. 36) are all extinguished simultaneously at the end of *Eh Joe*. Here, as elsewhere in Beckett, color belongs to the past, and the dying universe of his dying character turns to a uniform grey before we lose sight of it. The same loss of color is evident in *Endgame*, where the world outside the windows is grey and where color exists primarily in memories of days gone by, and in *Film*, shot in black and white. The setting of *Cascando* is likewise dark, and ever darkening, and it also describes a character who lies with his "—face . . . in the stones . . . . all stones . . . . in the stones . . ." (p. 14). *Eh Joe* represents one of the most ingenious, effective, and sustained uses of color, and the lack thereof, in the entire Beckettian oeuvre.[3] In it, Beckett presents a grey-haired man in a black and white room who is throttling the colored memories of his past, of the days when he lived outside his mind. Although we continue to perceive the television image in black and white, the woman's voice evokes colored images in Joe's, and our, mental landscapes, only to turn them to stone grey at the end. At the close of the play, the grey outside world and grey inner consciousness of *Eh Joe* seem about to meet in the blackness of non-perception, in the final close-up of Joe's face, to which "the next step can only be the blackness of a blank screen."[4]

The final image of *Eh Joe*—Joe's face in close-up—brings

to mind the last shot of *Film*—the close-up of Buster Keaton's eye. Eye imagery is prevalent in *Eh Joe*, even if its manifestations are not quite so frequent nor so dominant as in *Film*. When Joe relaxes on his bed at the beginning of the play, he closes his eyes, and opens them again when he hears the woman's voice. When this voice speaks of the mental setting of the drama—"your mind . . . That's where you think this is coming from, don't you?"—it locates it "behind the eyes" (p. 37). Thus, while Joe's eyes may be open, they are trained inward, upon himself and his memories. The most vivid of these memories—that of the woman who killed herself—concentrates heavily upon her eyes: "The pale eyes . . . Spirit made light . . . To borrow your expression . . . The way they opened after . . . Unique" (p. 39). Towards the end of the play, a similar description is offered: "The pale eyes . . . The look they shed before . . . The way they opened after . . . Spirit made light . . . Wasn't that your description, Joe?" (p. 41). This image of a woman's eyes, open after lovemaking, in which spiritual beauty may be read, strikes a deep chord of recognition within us, not only because it is offered for the second time in the play, or even because it is a simple, clear, beautifully written description of a nearly universal experience, but also because the same image has occurred in previous works of Beckett, recorded in different, yet similar, terms. For example, in *Krapp's Last Tape*, the old Krapp's clearest and most persistent memory is of a woman's face during a love scene in a boat: "The eyes she had! . . . . Everything there, everything on this old muckball, all the light and dark and famine and feasting of . . . . the ages!" (p. 24). The description of a woman's face in *Words and Music* comes even closer to the one in *Eh Joe*: "Seen from above at such close quarters in that radiance so cold and faint with eyes so dimmed by . . . what had passed, its quite . . . piercing beauty is a little . . ." (p. 29).

Joe, like many another Beckettian character, seems to have begun his efforts at perception by seeking to see another person, to enter her soul and mind through her eyes, those windows that separate each person's inner being from the outside world. While such communion of souls was once believed possible, in the days when phrases like "spirit made light" were invented, it is so no longer. Each time the woman's voice says "spirit made light," it attributes the words to Joe: "To borrow your expression" (p. 39); "Wasn't that your description, Joe?" (p. 41). These passages echo another portion of the text where the woman whose voice we hear recalls her love affair with Joe: "How you admired my elocution! . . . Among other charms . . . Voice like flint glass . . . To borrow your expression . . . Powerful grasp of language you had" (p. 38). The days when Joe had a powerful grasp of language—when he believed in the potency of artistic expression—are thus linked to the days when he believed in the possibility of seeing and hearing other people. Today, when he has renounced vision and hearing in the outer world and is perceiving only fragmentary mental images and phrases, which he tries to destroy one after another, language has also begun to fail him. His powers of hearing and expression have been "squeezed down to this" (p. 38)—the slow, remote voice he hears droning in his head—and the voice predicts even further degeneration: "How much longer would you say? . . . Till the whisper . . . You know . . . When you can't hear the words . . . Just the odd one here and there" (p. 38). These lines recall the passage of *Not I* where the woman is described "straining to hear . . . the odd word . . . make some sense of it" (p. 21). This is, in fact, just what happens at the end of *Eh Joe*, as the phrases become uniformly short, and the "voice drops to whisper, almost inaudible except words in italics" (p. 41). Soon after this stage direction, the phrase "spirit made light" is compressed into "spiritlight" and followed immediately by "month of June . . . What year of your Lord?" (p. 41). Thus, Beckett subtly links vision of other people, love, language, measurable time, and religion. All of these concepts are useless, fading vestiges of another age, referred to in fragmentary language, perceived only by nostalgic glances into the depths of Joe's memory.

While we listen to the voice telling us, and Joe, of the dead woman's eyes, and asking us to "imagine the eyes . . . Spiritlight" (p. 41), the camera is showing Joe's own eyes, behind which, we have been told, is the source of all we are seeing and hearing. The eye of the camera in *Eh Joe* is, as in *Film*, used as a representative of self-perception, to record for the spectators' eyes the inward motion of Joe's thoughts and vision and to convey concretely the way in which the eye of the self pursues its object, getting closer and closer to the inner essence it is seeking, without ever being able to reach it. Just as, for Joe, the light of consciousness would have to be extinguished in order for his inner eye to meet, see, and remain fixed upon his inner self, the only way in which the camera could perfectly capture the union of self with self would be to show a blank, dark, silent television screen. Even Beckett has not yet found a way to dramatize literal nothingness—absence of sight, sound, movement—although his drama has, like the eye of the camera in *Eh Joe*, moved consistently in that direction over the years.

Both *Film* and *Eh Joe* end with the eye of the camera trained intently upon their protagonists' eyes (although the last shot of *Eh Joe* does include the rest of Joe's face). This image dramatizes the inevitability of the eye of self-perception that has pursued O and Joe throughout the plays. Both works begin with camera shots that encompass larger fields of vision than do the shots of their final scenes. In *Film*, the camera's vision shrinks progressively from street to vestibule to room, to O's face and eyes. *Eh Joe* begins with the camera viewing Joe "from behind," following "Joe's opening movements . . . at constant remove, Joe full length in frame throughout" (p. 35), before progressive close-ups of Joe are shown. When the camera shoots Joe from behind, he is preoccupied with the task of preparing his room for the evening's session with himself and with his memories; only when the camera confronts him face-to-face (or eye-to-eye) does Joe enter into a state of self-perception. Such a use of two different camera angles to represent separate states of percipere and percipi calls to mind the convention of *Film*, where O entered into perceivedness only when the camera angle exceeded forty-five degrees. In *Beckett and Broadcasting*, Clas Zilliacus compares the use of the camera in each of these works and concludes that the technical solution of *Eh Joe* is superior to that of *Film*:

> Both works deal with the struggle between perceiver and perceived, an old Beckett theme now subjected to camera treatment. But if *Film* was a kind of illustrated theorem, *Eh Joe* is first and foremost an illustration, an image. It does not depend, in order to be fully grasped, on the proper decoding of more or less arbitrary conventions: there is no 45 degree immunity threshold, and there is none of the important but highly puzzling distinction, in *Film*, between O's and E's respective modes of perception.[5]

Another difference between the camera techniques of the two works resides in the treatment of the final scenes. In *Film*, although the camera concentrates more and more upon O's face and eyes at the end, even in the final sequence of shots, we see portions of the room and rocking chair as background for E and O, and the camera moves back and forth from E to O. It does not, as in *Eh Joe*, zoom relentlessly inward upon Keaton's face and eyes. This difference in the use of the camera in *Film* and *Eh Joe* may be explained in two ways. First, Beckett wished the camera of *Film* to record two separate visions at the end—E's an O's—precluding the possibility of a consistent zeroing-in upon one image to the exclusion of any other. In *Eh Joe*, on the other hand, the camera comes to represent a single vision—the eye of the self—which moves jerkily, but in one direction only, closing in upon its object, Joe. Another, more technological consideration lies behind the way the camera is used in each work. Beckett possesses a particular genius for understanding and exploiting the specific capabilities of each dramatic medium for which he writes, and *Eh Joe*, although his first play for television, exhibits a masterful grasp of the expressive possibilities of the television screen. In "Beckett and the Art of Broadcasting," Martin Esslin comments upon the impact of the image Beckett offers in *Eh Joe*, asserting that such an effect would be unachievable upon the cinema screen, which was the medium of *Film*: "Only in television can this technique of a camera approaching a human face in gradual steps have the desired impact. The cinema screen would be far too large, so that the ever larger close-ups of Joe's features would become disproportionate and lose all human scale." He goes on to note that the intimacy of the television medium enables Beckett to create, in *Eh Joe*, a face and voice that have the same scale as other faces and voices in the room where the spectators are sitting, thus enhancing their psychological force. He sums up his discussion of the play with high words of praise for Beckett's understanding of television, an authoritative tribute from a man so widely experienced and highly regarded in the field of broadcasting: "It is almost impossible to find, in the vast literature of television drama, another play which is as totally conceived in terms of the small television screen and its intimate audience psychology as *Eh Joe*. . . . As a demonstration of what is specifically televisual *Eh Joe* is unique and a masterpiece."[6]

The originality of *Eh Joe* resides then primarily in the new form and technology in which Beckett envelops his character's perceptual processes. As we see and hear of Joe remembering, and then "throttling," images of others—parents and lovers—

in his head, the woman's voice warns him that he is headed down the now-familiar Beckettian pathway towards self-perception, which has no end and from which there is no escape. The voice admonishes Joe to "Watch yourself you don't run short, Joe . . . Ever think of that? . . . Eh Joe? . . . What it'd be if you ran out of us . . . Not another soul to still . . . Sit there in his stinking old wrapper hearing himself" (p. 37). Attempts at perception in *Eh Joe* thus follow the same direction as in *Endgame*, *Cascando*, and *Film*: perception of the outside world→ hearing and seeing voices and images of others in one's mind→ the inevitable awareness of self-perception. The Hamm/Clov couple of *Endgame* exists, at least on one level, as separate people in a recognizable, "realistic" space, although the play might well be taking place within one man's mind, and Hamm at one point envisions his final moment, when self will confront self. In *Cascando*, we come across Woburn after he has given up contact with other people, but still in the world outside his shed, before he "goes down . . . . in his head . . ." where he first discovers a "vague memory" but "soon . . . . not a soul . . ." (p. 11). In *Film*, we see only a brief glimpse of O's dealings with other people in the street, and a longer sequence as he eliminates animal and divine perception in his room, before he sits down to tear up the photos which are his memories, in preparation for the final encounter with his perceiving self. *Eh Joe* begins at yet a later point in the perceptual journey: when we encounter Joe, he is inside (though we see him cast a last intent look at the exterior) and alone. All of the other people and places mentioned in the play clearly exist only as Joe's memories, and the voice foresees the time when Joe will be done with all the others, and have only himself to listen to. It goes even one step further in its predictions, imagining what would happen if Joe could ever put a stop to his self-perception: "How's your Lord these days? . . . . Wait till He starts talking to you . . . When you're done with yourself . . . All your dead dead . . . . Ever think of that? . . . When He starts in on you . . . When you're done with yourself . . . If you ever are" (p. 39). Divine perception, which is absent in *Endgame* ("The bastard! He doesn't exist!" [p. 55]), not mentioned in *Cascando*, and destroyed in *Film* before self-perception commences (when O tears up the picture of God), is, in *Eh Joe*, a purely hypothetical process whose condition, the cessation of self-perception, is impossible. The woman's voice makes this clear when it tells Joe that he will never attain the silent paradise of which he dreams because his own voice will never be silent: "Sit there in his stinking old wrapper hearing himself . . . . Weaker and weaker till not a gasp left there either . . . Is it that you want? . . . Well preserved for his age and the silence of the grave . . . That old paradise you were always harping on . . . No Joe . . . Not for the likes of you" (pp. 37–38). The eye of God, which was the perceiver Berkeley had in mind when he said "esse est percipi," is thus eliminated in Beckett's visual scheme, replaced by the impotent, yet everlasting, eye and voice of the self.

Like most of Beckett's other works, and certainly like *Endgame*, *Cascando*, and *Film*, *Eh Joe* may be read as a portrayal of the last moments of a dying man, as an image of the time when all ties with the exterior are being broken, when all is gone but self-perception, and the only light remaining is the flickering half-light of self-consciousness whose extinction will never be perceived by the mind it both inhabits and observes.

In three of the four plays studied so far, including *Eh Joe*, Beckett evokes an image that corresponds perfectly to the indeterminacy characteristic of the perceptions of his dying characters: a person lying face-down on the beach, waiting for his or her final peace. In *Endgame*, Hamm describes his idea of the perfect way to end his story, his life, and the play: "If I could drag myself down to the sea! I'd make a pillow of sand for my head and the tide would come." But Clov denounces the desire as impossible, since "there's no more tide" (pp. 61–62). In *Cascando*, Woburn seeks his unattainable end "face in the sand . . . arms spread . . . bare dunes . . . ," then "face . . . in the stones . . . no more sand . . ." (pp. 12, 14), before he drifts off to sea. And *Eh Joe* closes with a description of a woman dying at the water's edge, "her face in the stones" (p. 41). The frequency of beach imagery in Beckett's works is attributable partially to his origins in the island country of Ireland, but also to the appropriateness of such a setting for the moods and situations he is trying to convey. The seashore is a space that is real but undefinable; due to the constant motion of the tide, one can never perceive the exact place where the sand ends and the water begins. Boundless, endless, characterized by rhythmic, ceaseless, back-and-forth motion, a space where two things meet but in an indeterminate and unperceivable fashion, the water's edge is the ideal setting for the dramatization of the last moments of consciousness. The sound and rhythm of the waves hold a special attraction for an ear as finely tuned to poetry and music as Beckett's, and he uses this natural phenomenon to give form and rhythm to many of his most poetic passages, most notably, perhaps, in the closing phrases of *Eh Joe*, where the words wash like waves over our mental image of the woman expiring by the sea. The two elements of the seashore—sand and water—also evoke images that carry great meaning for both Beckett and his spectators. The sands of time are shifting, separate yet alike, infinitely divisible, yet always running out, as Beckett's characters approach union with the waters of nothingness, waiting for the waves to pick them up, carry them out to sea, and envelop them in the mobile, liquid environment in which they began their endless lives. Birth and death, beginning and ending, sand and water, all meet in a space that is perceivable at any given instant, though never the same from one glance to the next, ever changing because of the constant motion to which it is subject. It is no wonder that Beckett's inner eyes and pen dwell so often upon the seashore, whose time, space, and movement correspond so precisely to his own perspective on the world.

Beckett's use of such images as the beach, rooms, and eyes accounts for much of the esthetic novelty and power of *Eh Joe*, as well as of his other plays. He does not, however, pay any less attention to the language of his dramas as his work becomes ever more imagistic. He rather uses the texts of the plays to enhance the effect of the images, as well as to create images in his audiences' minds that are not present in the concrete stage space. For example, in *Eh Joe*, we both see Joe in his room and hear the woman's voice speak to him of his situation in it; the other room of the play—the house the woman leaves to die on the beach—is evoked only in words. We see Joe's eyes, as well as the inward motion of the eye of the camera, while we are listening to a description of the eyes of the dead woman. We do not see the beach upon which she expires, yet we hear its rhythm in the passage that describes it. The words of *Eh Joe* create as many different types of effects—visual, aural, emotional, intellectual—as the other dramatic elements of the play. Instead of simply conveying a story, or an idea, the spoken text of *Eh Joe* is conceived in such a manner that its form is an integral part of the work. Its power lies in the fact that it does not merely explain the sounds, sights, and movements of *Eh*

Joe, but exists as a dramatic element in its own right that is intricately woven into the fabric of the play.

While the syntax of *Eh Joe* is more traditional than that of *Cascando*, causing the individual phrases to seem more separate one from another and thus less ambiguous than those of the radio play, the text once again takes the form of an internal monologue. Complete sentences are mixed with sentence fragments, and each phrase is separated by an ellipsis that represents "a beat of one second at least" (p. 36). This constant repetition of a uniform pause, the extensive repetition of sounds, words, phrases, and images in the text, the monotonous tone and "absolutely steady rhythm" (p. 36) of the voice, and the progressive concentration of the camera eye upon a single image, all combine to produce a hypnotic effect upon the spectators, similar to the one Joe himself must feel as he shuts out all external stimuli and focuses his attention more and more upon his inner vision and voices. The voice comments upon this narrowing of the perceptual field in the passage where it speaks of Joe's once "powerful grasp of language" which has been "squeezed down to this" (p. 38). Beckett has composed the voice's text to correspond exactly to this "squeezing down" of linguistic ability. For example, when it evokes the memory of the dead woman, it begins with long, rather traditionally written phrases: "Sitting on the edge of her bed in her lavender slip . . . You know the one . . . Ah she knew you, heavenly powers! . . . Faint lap of sea through open window" (p. 40). It ends the description with shorter, more repetitious, less colorful, starker words appropriate to the moment when we perceive the death of both the woman and Joe's memory of her: "*Breasts* in the stones . . . And the *hands* . . . Before they go . . . *Imagine* the hands . . . What are they at? . . . In the *stones* . . . (*Image fades, voice as before.*) What are they fondling? . . . Till they go" (p. 41). By now, according to Beckett's stage directions, the low voice has dropped to a whisper, and is almost inaudible save for the italicized words. Voice, image, and words have been compressed in order to portray the situation the text had earlier announced: "You stop it in the end . . . Imagine if you couldn't . . . Ever think of that? . . . If it went on . . . The whisper in your head . . . Me whispering at you in your head . . . Things you can't catch . . . On and off . . . Till you join us . . . Eh Joe?" (p. 38). Although we do not see what happens to Joe after the voice and image go out together—

indeed, we could not since we are duplicating the eye of Joe's self-perception through the camera—there is no reason not to believe the prediction of the voice, which has proven so accurate in all other respects. Instead of being able to stop the whispering in his head and the eye and ear of the self, Joe has most likely joined the voice to which he has been listening, inside somebody else's head, where he drones endlessly on, like the dead voices of *Waiting for Godot*: "All the dead voices. . . . They all speak at once. . . . Each one to itself. . . . They talk about their lives. . . . To have lived is not enough for them" (p. 40). Joe will thus probably never cease, "it" will never stop, and *Eh Joe* succeeds no more than any of Beckett's previous dramas in bringing its character to an ending that he, and therefore we, might perceive.

Joe's uncertainty that he will ever attain the silence, rest, and absence of percipi that he so earnestly seeks is communicated to our ears both by the content of the text and by the interrogative form so frequently employed in it. In *Cascando* the same effect is achieved by the widespread use of negatives and of statements that refute previous assertions. Questions are prevalent in *Endgame*, where they also help to convey the characters' uncertainty about the ending that preoccupies them. In *Endgame*, however, the presence of two (and occasionally four) characters who engage in rapid-fire question-and-answer routines creates a comic effect reminiscent of old vaudeville and music-hall sketches. The answers, facetious as they may be in *Endgame*, are totally absent from *Eh Joe* where the voice assails the character with question after question, making us feel that we are witnessing a merciless interrogatory of a helpless victim who can neither stop the voice that tortures him since it is his own, nor supply the answers to the problems of perception that it poses. The question which is most frequently repeated in the play, and with which it closes, is also its title: "Eh Joe?" The semantic content of this bisyllabic question is as important as its familiar tone and rhythmic effect. "Eh" is both a rhetorical question asked by a speaker who in no way expects a meaningful answer, or even any answer at all from his interlocutor, and a word used by a listener who has not clearly heard something he desires to have repeated. It is thus a most fitting refrain for a play in which a voice asks unanswerable questions that become less and less audible to the ears of the self to which it belongs.

By ending the play with words which have been repeated

throughout and which have always been followed by other streams of words, Beckett suggests the possibility that the extinction of voice and image after the last "Eh Joe?" is merely a respite for the man on stage who is destined to continue hearing and imagining his inner voices and visions long after the spectators turn off their television sets. Even in an answerless universe, our ears are still accustomed to expect something to follow a question mark; old forms of speaking, writing, and listening often survive long after they have lost their relevance. What follows the final question of *Eh Joe* is left open to speculation, just as neither Beckett, Joe, nor we can presume to know what, if anything, follows the final moment of a person's perception, or, indeed, if this final moment ever arrives. It is entirely possible to imagine that the ending of *Eh Joe* is not an ending at all, but merely a pause in a cycle. For the voice of *Eh Joe* has already stopped briefly many times between phrases, and for longer periods between paragraphs, just before and during the camera moves. The play's ending may thus be yet a longer pause between all that we have witnessed so far and another set of phrases, pauses, and paragraphs. We have just seen and heard Joe throttle a memory in his head, so the disappearance of voice and image may merely represent the death of the dead woman's memory, not the cessation of Joe's process of perception, of which this memory is only a small part. The voice has already told us that Joe had previously killed off memories of many other "mental thuggee[s]" (p. 37); since we joined the play after these throttlings, it is logical to assume that future ones will occur in our absence. The next murder may well be that of the woman whose voice Joe is hearing, since she is still alive in Joe's mind after the narration of the other woman's suicide on the beach. She seems, in fact, to have been the initially intended victim of the evening's throttling, since her voice was summoned at the beginning, and her story told before the tale of the other woman's death. By having the first woman introduce both her story and that of the other woman with similar words and circumstances—"The best's to come, you said, that last time . . . Hurrying me into my coat" (p. 36)/"The best's to come, you said . . . Bundling her into her Avoca sack" (p. 39)—Beckett enmeshes their memories one within the other in the text, just as they must be in Joe's mind. He also thereby raises the possibility that the woman who committed suicide may in fact be the same woman whose voice we are hearing. This interweaving of memories and characters indicates that Joe's throttlings may not be definitive; he may have killed the memory of the woman on the beach, and/or of the woman whose voice he is hearing, many times over, only to be reminded later of her by the voice of his consciousness (or conscience) which asks him: "Ever know what happened? . . . She didn't say? . . . Will I tell you?" (p. 40). Similarly, although he has done away with his father, mother, and countless others in his mind, their memories are evoked, however briefly, by the woman's voice, and nothing indicates that their tales may not be recalled and expanded at some future point. The next session with his inner eyes and ears may conjure up any one of these supposedly dead voices, or another, to speak to Joe of themselves, others, and himself and of their respective endings, which, though ardently desired, seem more and more doubtful. Furthermore, if we believe the voice, once all the memories of others are gone, if indeed they ever could be, Joe would probably never be done with listening to and trying to see himself in his own mind. One of Beckett's stage directions at the beginning of *Eh Joe* strongly suggests the interminable structure of the play: "Brief zones of relaxation between paragraphs when perhaps voice has relented for the evening" (p. 36). Perhaps, indeed, the voice has, at the end of the play, finally relented for the evening. And perhaps it will begin again tomorrow evening, after Joe isolates himself in his room and allows the eye of his mind to move from the space without to the space within, closing in upon and finally destroying, if only temporarily, another of the endless circle of perceivers who inhabit his consciousness.

If Joe does resume his introspection after the final black-out, the result is likely to be similar to the part of the process recorded in *Eh Joe*, yet somewhat different. Another room may be prepared, another memory recalled, and/or another voice heard. The object of all his efforts is to strip his mind bare till he reaches the silent, still, unchanging, unperceived core of himself, but the ceaseless whispering in his head and the unstoppable motion of the eye of the camera/self bar the way to "that old paradise" (p. 38). His self is as changeable, labyrinthine, unstable, fragmented, and unstoppable as the memories to which he listens, which are, in fact, parts of the Joe he is attempting to perceive. If the memories recur in different forms, under different names, in different circumstances, so do the many selves that Joe successively pursues. Just because we lose sight of his inner eye and voice at the end of the play called *Eh Joe* is no reason to assume that we will not meet him again. If *Endgame* shows a world and its inhabitants that are only "nearly finished" (p. 1), *Cascando* a pursued self who is only "nearly" (p. 19) caught at the end, and *Film* a man caught up in the inescapable cycle of self-perception, *Eh Joe* portrays another unsuccessful attempt at bringing a consciousness' perception of itself to an end. When the woman's voice predicts that the whispers in Joe's head may never stop "till you join us" (p. 38), it may be referring to the way in which all of Beckett's characters end without ending, as they join the company of past voices that continues to murmur throughout his work, just as each person's company of past selves remains with him as he progresses from past to future, changing composition and appearance with the constant addition of each successive "me." Joe's future appearances on the Beckettian stage and screen take the form of such diverse, yet similar, characters as: the pacing woman of *Footfalls*, who converses with the voice of her unseen mother; the face of the old man in *That Time*, who listens to his own voice speaking to him of different moments of his past; the Male Figure in a room that is very similar to Joe's in *Ghost Trio*, whose actions are narrated by another woman's voice; the old man who passes through a circle of light on the television stage of *. . . but the clouds . . .* speaking of the memory of a woman, whose face appears intermittently on the screen; the Listener of *Ohio Impromptu*, whose story is read to him by a Reader who resembles him closely; the Speaker of *A Piece of Monologue*, who stands in a room narrating the tale of a man remembering his loved ones in a room; and the woman of *Rockaby*, who sits listening to her recorded voice recounting her own past and that of her mother.

Chapter 6

A PIECE OF MONOLOGUE:

"No such thing as no light"

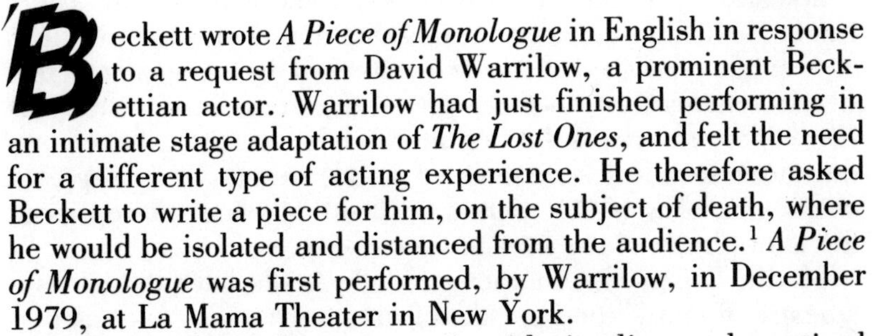

Beckett wrote *A Piece of Monologue* in English in response to a request from David Warrilow, a prominent Beckettian actor. Warrilow had just finished performing in an intimate stage adaptation of *The Lost Ones*, and felt the need for a different type of acting experience. He therefore asked Beckett to write a piece for him, on the subject of death, where he would be isolated and distanced from the audience.[1] *A Piece of Monologue* was first performed, by Warrilow, in December 1979, at La Mama Theater in New York.

A Piece of Monologue is, as its title implies, a dramatized fragment of internal monologue delivered by a single character, the Speaker. Although the text is only ten pages in length, Warrilow delivered it slowly, and the performance lasted fifty-five minutes. During the monologue, he remained practically motionless in a standing position downstage to the left of the audience, and his face was not clearly seen.

A Piece of Monologue presents, once more, a man alone in a room. Unlike the sets of *Endgame*, *Film*, and *Eh Joe*, however, that of *A Piece of Monologue* does not define the room by the contours of its walls, which are not seen, but by costume, furnishings, and text. The white-haired Speaker is dressed in a white nightgown and white socks, and the white foot of a bed, an image that we encountered for the first time in *Eh Joe*, is visible on the extreme audience right. The stage is bathed in a "faint diffuse light" of unseen origin and to the left of the Speaker is a "standard lamp, skull-sized white globe, faintly lit," which is the same height as he is (p. 69).[2] By virtue of staring at the Speaker and the lamp while hearing a ceaseless monologue delivered in a low, monotonous voice for nearly an hour, some spectators experience visual and auditory hallucinations, perceiving movement, change in light intensity, and volume and tempo changes in the sound, where none actually take place. Warrilow is conscious of these effects and is persuaded that Beckett knew about and intended them when he composed the play. Beckett has thus, paradoxically, succeeded in creating a fixed, static, precisely defined dramatic image which nevertheless has the effect of inducing perceptual disorientation and flux in the consciousness of his spectators.

In *A Piece of Monologue*, Beckett subtly blurs the contours between the man before our eyes and the visions within that man's mind, to the point where the Speaker becomes not only the chronicler, but also the actor, director, and spectator of the character he presents to our eyes, ears, and imagination. There can be no doubt that we are witnessing in this play the workings of a single man's consciousness. Beckett has dramatized this situation many times before, yet, of the works in this study, *A Piece of Monologue* is the first in which he successfully conveys the inner scene of a character's mind without using separate characters, or at least separate or recorded voices, to represent the multiplicity of the human personality.[3]

Martin Esslin has characterized Beckett's later drama as a "theatre of stasis" and speaks of his most recent plays as "visually fixed poems."[4] These terms certainly apply to *A Piece of Monologue*, which presents a single, immobile visual image accompanied by a meticulously crafted text whose skillful use of a variety of linguistic techniques clearly places it within the category of dramatic poetry. The following discussion of the perspective and dramatic techniques of *A Piece of Monologue* will therefore center largely upon the text of the drama, analyzing both the content and form of the words Beckett has chosen to paint yet another voyage into the unfathomable depths of a human mind.

The Speaker opens with a paradoxical statement about time: "Birth was the death of him" (p. 70).[5] Words and images associated with birth and death permeate the text, and the structure of the play, which treats of the end from the very beginning, as do all the plays analyzed in this study, corresponds closely to the idea that birth is the beginning of dying. Kristin Morrison notes the incongruity of the use of the words "ghastly grinning" in this context: this would be said more appropriately of a skull than of a child. The phrase is followed by "up at the lid to come. In cradle and crib," implying that, even as a baby, the man anticipated his death (represented by the lid of the coffin that will become a prominent image in the monologue).[6]

After his opening remark, the Speaker says, "Again. Words are few. Dying too. Birth was the death of him." The command "again" calls for repetition, which is the conceptual and linguistic mainstay of the text, as well as of the Speaker's perceptual experiences. The two following sentences contain the same number of syllables and rhyme with each other, thus repeating both rhythm and sound. They record the second instance of dying in the monologue; words are also in the process of expiring, from the very moment they commence in the play. Beckett thus links repetition to the process of entropy, whereby both the protagonist's statements and his moments of existence echo one another, while each one seems somehow less than all that have come before.

Beckett makes widespread use of alliteration, another repetitive poetic technique, in *A Piece of Monologue.* The first nine lines of text contain these striking examples: "*G*hastly *gr*inning ever since," "In *cr*adle and *cr*ib," "At suck *f*irst *f*iasco," "*Ba*ndied *ba*ck and forth," "So *g*hastly *g*rinning on," "*F*rom *f*uneral to *f*uneral," "To *n*ow. This *n*ight." These alliterative lines are enclosed within two passages of similar structure: phrases that are repeated exactly, in response to the order, "Again." To the "birth was the death of him. Again. . . . Birth was the death of him" of the beginning corresponds the "two and a half billion seconds. Again. Two and a half billion seconds" that follows "this night." Next comes the remark, "Hard to believe so few," which shocks us momentarily, since it follows the naming of an extremely large number. Both the initial /f/ and final /yü/ sounds of "few" are repeated in the next phrase, which offers another commentary upon the repetitive yet diminishing structure of time: "From funeral to funeral. Funerals of . . . he all but said of loved ones." Time is then counted in another fashion—"Thirty thousand nights"[7]—and the results evaluated by repeating the earlier formula, "Hard to believe so few," which also repeats the /yü/ sound of "funeral." The following statement, "Born dead of night," echoes, in sound and meaning, the first sentence of the play, "Birth was the death of him." The grammatical economy of "born dead of night" renders its meaning ambiguous: was "he" born in the dead of the night, or was "he" born dead, of the night?[8] At any rate, birth and death are once again linked, both conceptually and linguistically.

The only mention of color in the entire text comes in a description of the night of birth: "Sun long sunk behind the larches. New needles turning green." Here, as so often in Beckett, a black, white, and grey image is on the stage before our eyes while a color from the past is evoked. The green of the larch needles is soon canceled, however, by the dark night that surrounds them, and by the evocation of a colorless interior: "In the room dark gaining. Till faint light from standard lamp. Wick turned low." This could just as well be the situation of the beginning of the Speaker's life as his present one: the light of consciousness, emanating from a "skull-sized white globe" (p. 69), has faintly illuminated the world around him since the very first moment when darkness began to gain upon him—the moment of birth. But, just as the stage is lit by both the white globe of the lamp and another "faint diffuse light" (p. 69), a second light source is now mentioned in the text: "Faint light in room. Whence unknown." This unextinguishable light from an unidentifiable source, which calls to mind the relentless, mysterious spotlight of *Play*, seems to be another manifestation of the light of consciousness. If consciousness is split into perceiver and perceived, it is appropriate that the dramatic embodiment of that consciousness be dual also. And if consciousness, by its very definition as an endless interplay between subject and object, can never come to a final rest, the light that represents it can never be completely extinguished.

A window, not seen on the stage, is now introduced into our mental image: "None [no light] from window. No. Next to none. No such thing as none. Gropes to window and stares out. Stands there staring out. Stock still staring out. Nothing stirring in that black vast" (pp. 70–71). This man staring out a window into next-to-nothingness calls to mind Clov's description of the world outside *Endgame*'s windows as grey and zero, Woburn's waiting for the earth outside his window to darken before embarking upon his voyage in *Cascando*, and Joe's staring outside his room's window at the beginning of *Eh Joe*. From the window through which he sees no light, no color, no movement, or next to none, the man "gropes back in the end to where the lamp is standing" and lights it. Here, as elsewhere in the monologue, the lamplighting process is described in precise detail, as if the Speaker were reading stage directions from a Beckettian script. Just as such directions help an actor or director to translate a dramatist's intentions into action and visual images, they animate and guide the scene we are creating in our own minds.

After lighting the lamp, the man backs away from it to face a blank wall. The Speaker then sums up his nightly movements in a few terse phrases—"So nightly. Up. Socks. Nightgown. Window. Lamp"—before describing the wall that he is facing. If, as seems likely, the Speaker is now referring to the position in which we see him on the stage, the wall he mentions can be none other than the conventional invisible fourth wall of the theater which the spectators' eyes penetrate as we gaze upon the scene. Here, as he so often does, Beckett is alluding to, and using, a time-honored esthetic tradition and at the same time breaking away from it, for the wall we look through to see the Speaker is no longer completely transparent, since we are soon asked to conjure it up in our minds quite precisely. What begins as a "blank wall" is remembered by the man, described by the Speaker, and thus visualized by us, in vivid detail:

> Covered with pictures once. Pictures of . . . he all but said of loved ones. Unframed. Unglazed. Pinned to wall with drawing-pins. All shapes and sizes. Down one after another. . . . Ripped from the wall and torn to shreds one by one. Over the years. Years of night. Nothing on the wall now but the pins. Not all. Some out with the wrench. Some still pinning a shred. (Pp. 71–72)

This wall resembles the walls seen by the spectators of *Endgame* and *Film*: Hamm's wall first has on it a picture, turned face to the wall, and then an alarm clock hung from the same nail when the picture is removed; O tears the picture of God from his wall and rips it up, leaving a large nail visible in its place. The pictures of loved ones that have been shredded in *A Piece of Monologue* remind us of the photographs of family, friends, and self that O rips up in *Film*. Furthermore, the life recounted by the Speaker is described both in terms of movement from funeral to funeral and of years of night spent destroying the memories embodied by pictures, just as the man in *Eh Joe* has lived through a succession of deaths of family and lovers after which he attempts to throttle their memories in his mind.

The lines following the description of the wall contain one of Beckett's finest expressions of the process of entropy that pervades his work: "Dying on. No more no less. No. Less. Less to die. Ever less. Like light at nightfall." Repetition of words associated with ending and nothingness ("no," "less," "dying—die") and of sounds (/l/, /n/, /ī/, /īt/) gives verbal shape to this life that is running out, dying on, each night a bit less, yet continuing. The dying of light at nightfall is Beckett's favorite dramatic time of day. As every twilight minute passes, the light fades a bit more, is ever less, yet no human eye can identify the precise point at which it crosses the threshold into night. The faint diffuse light of *A Piece of Monologue* corresponds not only to the waning light of dusk, but also to the nature of the dying consciousness that it both portrays and illuminates to our eyes.

The dying light of nightfall introduces a series of grey images: the "blank pinpocked surface once white in shadow" which is the wall; the "grey void[s]" that stand where the man's family pictures once hung; the dust under the bed where the shreds of pictures lie; and the "faint smoke issuing through vent in globe. Low ceiling stained by night after night of this" (pp. 72–73). The words "once white" recur constantly in the text from this point on. Whiteness and light turn to grey and approaching darkness in a movement towards black and total darkness. However, the faint light which remains after the lamp goes out at the end of the play reminds us that there is "no such thing as no light" (p. 74), or total blackness, just as the only void attainable by the human consciousness is a "grey void." The Speaker continues to remind us throughout the monologue that there is "no such thing as none." The "blest dark" (p. 76) sought by the man of *A Piece of Monologue* is as impossible a goal as the silence and stillness longed for by Hamm, the sleep that will come in *Cascando* if Woburn's story can ever be finished, the end to self-perception desired by O, and the silence of the grave which represents paradise to Joe.

Since there is "no such thing" as no sound, one of the faint sounds heard in the room is that of "rain some nights still slant against the panes. Or dropping gentle on the place beneath."[9] This rain, and the place beneath, will be mentioned again later in the monologue when the Speaker evokes a rainy funeral. But now the text moves quickly back inside the grey room, and the man's nightly movements are described once more: "Up at nightfall and into gown and socks. No. In them already. In them all night. All day. All day and night." Just as the "various motions" performed by the man are progressively reduced in the text, it is likely that the Speaker before us represents simply another stage in the repetitive, yet diminishing, life we are hearing about: already up, already in his socks and nightgown, window no longer in sight, and lamp already on, he has but to stare at the blank wall and speak of the many nights, from his birth to this night, when he has confronted himself, and of the dying that has been the sole direction of his life.

We next hear of the man groping back to the window where he again "stands stock still staring out. Into black vast." He "dwells thus as if unable to move again. Or no will left to move again. Not enough will left to move again" (pp. 73–74). Yet, subject as he is to the inexorable movement which is the fundamental characteristic of all that dwells in Beckettian time and space, he "turns in the end and gropes to where he knows the lamp is standing," and backs away from it to face the wall. The description of the gown, socks, hair, and foot of pallet as "once white to take faint light" brings the text we hear and the scene we are looking at closer together, since it explains the color of the verbal image in terms of a technical, visual reality of the theater in which we are sitting. This union between text and visual image continues in the following lines: "Nothing. Empty dark. Till first word always the same. Night after night the same. Birth." These words describe not only the man in the room, but also the situation of the audience awaiting the opening of *A Piece of Monologue*. During the play's run, the spectators sit, night after night, in the empty dark, waiting for the Speaker's first word, which is always the same: "Birth." The next lines are also written in the form of a stage direction: "Then slow fade up of a faint form. Out of the dark." Yet the text here does not correspond to the opening scene that we have witnessed, since the lights went up before the Speaker began his monologue. With the next words we move even further from the stage setting in front of us, back to "a window. Looking west."

Through the window that we do not see, the man perceives the fading light of evening: "Light dying. Soon none left to die. No. No such thing as no light. Starless moonless heaven. Dies on to dawn and never dies."[10] Whether speaking of the light in the room, or of that of the world outside, the Speaker always describes it in terms that could apply equally well to the faint light in which the stage is bathed, and he consistently compares its fading to the process of dying. The man turns his eyes from the window "to face the darkened room" (p. 75). His movements and perceptions thus follow the same path as those of the other Beckettian characters in this study; from the darkness of the outer world to an inner space that is equally obscure. He lights the lamp, following the same set of precise directions we have heard before, yet the Speaker insists this time upon the disembodied image of the man's hands:

> There in the end slowly a faint hand. Holding aloft a lighted spill. In light of spill faintly the hand and milkwhite globe. Then second hand. In light of spill. Takes off globe and disappears. Reappears empty. Takes off chimney. Two hands and chimney in light of spill. Spill to wick. Chimney back on. Hand with spill disappears. Second hand disappears. Chimney alone in gloom. Hand reappears with globe.

This emphasis on the hands to the exclusion of the rest of the body evokes a striking mental image of a very dark room where only the objects closest to the light source are visible. It also serves to underscore the detachment the Speaker feels from the self he is perceiving and describing: not only does he speak in the third person and in a cold, terse style, he objectifies himself even further by separating his hand from the rest of his body in order to observe it from a distance as if it were an independent, disembodied agent. Such fragmentation of the body is prevalent in Beckett's work. In *Happy Days*, for instance, we see first the upper portion of Winnie's body embedded in a mound, then only her head, while *Play* presents three heads protruding from urns. *Not I* offers a stark image of a disembodied mouth, and in *That Time* we perceive an old man's head floating above a darkened stage. The following passages from Laing's *The Divided Self* describe a schizophrenic's feeling of disembodiment and the more common feeling of embodiment:

> The [schizophrenic] individual's being is cleft in two, producing a disembodied self and a body that is a thing that the self looks at, regarding it at times as though it were just another thing in the world. . . .
>
> Most people feel they began when their bodies began and that they

> will end when their bodies die. We could say that such a person experiences himself as *embodied.*[11]

The first description clearly applies to the attitude of *A Piece of Monologue*'s Speaker toward the self he is observing. The second defines the experience of embodiment in terms of time: birth and death are felt to be precise points of beginning and ending for the self, a concept that is consistently questioned by Beckett as untenable in a world where an endless, formless, ceaselessly repetitive time allows for neither the true birth nor the true death of the self.

From the hands lighting the lamp in the darkened room, our inner eyes are called to focus upon the brass bedrail before the dim light is said to fade again. The phrases "Window gone. Hands gone" describe the setting that is now visible in the theater, but the following lines again lead our attention away from the stage: "Light gone. Gone. Again and again. Again and again gone. Till dark slowly parts again. Grey light." The evocative power of these words does not reside solely in the mental image they paint, for they are describing the experience that the spectators of this play are living through: at the beginning of *A Piece of Monologue*, the curtain rises to slowly part the dark and present a faint, grey light which will remain until its extinction at the very end of the play. Again and again it will reappear and be gone, as long as audiences continue to attend productions of the drama.

The phrase "rain pelting" serves as a transition between the image of a man in a room and a memory of a rainy funeral of one of his loved ones. Rain was mentioned earlier, both as one of the faint sounds still perceivable within the still, dark, nearly silent room, and as water "dropping gentle on the place beneath" (p. 73). Here it takes us out of the room to a scene around a grave in a cemetery. The "dark [which] slowly parts again," giving way to "grey light," may thus also be the curtains of the stage of the Speaker's mind, which part to present him with a memory associated with the rain he hears. This memory is described in cinematographic terms: "Umbrellas round a grave. Seen from above. Streaming black canopies. Black ditch beneath. Rain bubbling in the black mud. Empty for the moment. That place beneath . . . . Thirty seconds. . . . Then fade" (pp. 75–76).

When the memory fades, the Speaker repeats an earlier formula: "Dark whole again." He immediately retracts his statement, though, with the familiar disclaimer, "No. No such thing as whole." Since neither darkness nor silence can be whole, the man stands in a dim light, like the one present on stage, listening to faint sounds: "Stands staring beyond half hearing what he's saying." This image of a man in a room, listening to, and only half hearing his own words, closely parallels the ending predicted by the woman's voice in *Eh Joe*: "The whisper . . . The odd word . . . Straining to hear . . . . It stops in the end . . . You stop it in the end . . . Imagine if you couldn't . . . . If it went on . . . The whisper in your head" (p. 38). It also calls to mind the impossibility of finishing the stories of both *Cascando* and *Endgame*, as well as Hamm's vision of his ending as a ceaseless babbling and whispering among the various parts of himself. *Film* uses the sense of sight, instead of hearing, to portray a similar situation of endless perception of the self by the self.

The Speaker next begins to question his use of the third-person singular: "He?" This doubt concerning pronouns recalls the difficulties encountered by Mouth in *Not I*, when it interrupts its third-person monologue five times with the question "who?," which it answers consistently with a vehement "she!" The Speaker of *A Piece of Monologue* has used the pronoun "he" on numerous occasions up till this point. The third-person form has thus far presented no problems to him, since he perceives and expresses the self he is pursuing as an object separate in both time and space from the pursuing subject, whose name would be the absent "I." The grammatical difficulty arises here because the perceiver/perceived dichotomy has been transferred to another level: the subject, Speaker, is perceiving the object, "he," who is in turn engaged in the process of perceiving himself, through "the words falling from his mouth." The Speaker balks at using the same pronoun for both parties to the perception, and the bipartite linguistic solution he has worked out for the narration of his tale breaks down when he confronts the endless chain of perceivers and perceived that inhabit his consciousness. The endless circularity of the process of perception is underscored by the fact that, in descending from the perceiving subject, the Speaker, to the perceived object, "he," who is perceiving another part of the self for which there seems to be no pronoun, we, the perceivers of the entire process, rejoin the image of the Speaker on stage: a man in a darkness that is less than whole, "staring beyond half hearing what he's saying." The Speaker may also realize that his words have momentarily coincided with his present situation, and the question "He?" may be prompted by his recognition that, at least for an instant, the word "I" might have been appropriate. Yet the moment of self-coincidence passes before the Speaker's language can catch up with it, and the text moves away from the image on stage as it speaks of the man lighting the lamp, "as described."

Just as the man "backs away to edge of light," the Speaker seems to have backed away from the insoluble perceptual and linguistic dilemma he has just confronted. The textual image again joins the stage image, as the man "turns to face wall. Stares beyond into dark." He is described in the process of waiting "for first word always the same. It gathers in his mouth. Parts lips and thrusts tongue forward. Birth. Parts the dark." The Speaker is describing his experience of the act of self-expression, which always begins, as this monologue does, with the word "birth." The creative act, for him as for Beckett, consists of giving utterance to the streams of words and emotions that well up from the inner depths of the artist's self, a process nowhere so clearly dramatized as in the radio play *Cascando*. Similarly, *Not I* tells the story of an aphasiac woman who one day suddenly realized that "words were coming . . . . this stream" (p. 18). If the word which the Speaker, and the man he describes, struggle night after night to say is "birth," so is the process by which it is formed. Physical and artistic birth are linked in the description of speaking as an expulsion of the word "birth" through the parted lips of the mouth.

After giving birth to the word with which he began his monologue, the Speaker compresses all the images of the play into a series of very short phrases:

> Birth. Parts the dark. Slowly the window. That first night. The room. The spill. The hands. The lamp. The gleam of brass. Fade. Gone. Again and again gone. Mouth agape. A cry. Stifled by nasal. Dark parts. Grey light. Rain pelting. Streaming umbrellas. Ditch. Bubbling black mud. Coffin out of frame. Whose? Fade. Gone.

The form of this passage, as well as the technical directions "fade" and "out of frame," create the ambiance of a television studio where a playwright like Beckett might be viewing a videotape of a script like *A Piece of Monologue*, whose individual takes would be labelled with concise titles such as "The room," "A cry," or "Streaming umbrellas." When his description of the viewing ends with the word "gone," the Speaker announces his intention to "move on to other matters. Try to move on. To other matters." In his attempt to do so he poses and answers a technical question similar to those that receive so much attention from Beckett both when he writes and when he participates in the staging of his plays: "How far from wall? Head almost touching. As at window. Eyes glued to pane staring out" (pp. 76–77). The reference to the eyes glued to the pane, an image already mentioned in the text (p. 74), draws the Speaker, and us, back into the "matters" with which he has dealt from the beginning, as it introduces a passage that repeats phrases from various portions of the play. Thus, the Speaker's summary of the monologue fails to wrap it up neatly so it can be placed into the film archives of his mind, in order to allow him to proceed to imagine, express, summarize, and conclude other episodes of his life. He is destined to continue his back-and-forth movement, "From mammy to nanny and back," "From funeral to funeral" (p. 70), from bed to window to lamp to wall to bed, from image to image, from word to word, from birth to dying, so long as the faint light and sounds of consciousness remain, i.e., forever.

In spite of its repetitiveness and its concentration upon the theme of dying and going, the text of *A Piece of Monologue* now introduces a nearly new element with the mention of a "faint cry in his ear." "Nearly new," because the preceding summary mentions, for the first time in the text, "A cry. Stifled by nasal" (p. 76). Here, then, is another reason why the Speaker's summary has failed to bring the "matters" of the monologue to a neat conclusion: not only will words and images it repeats from the past continue to be dealt with, but it also contains new elements that are to be developed in subsequent passages. The "faint cry in his ear" both precedes and follows another description of the process of giving birth to language: "Mouth agape. Closed with hiss of breath. Lips joined. Feel soft touch of lip on lip. Lip lipping lip. Then parted by cry as before." This image of the man's lips feeling each other presents an anatomical variation upon the theme of self perceiving self that is so central to *A Piece of Monologue*. It is also reminiscent of Mouth's description, in *Not I*, of the woman who "gradually . . . felt . . . her lips moving . . . . the tongue in the mouth" (pp. 18–19). The cry that parts the lips may be a response both to the painful process of birth (or artistic creation) and/or to the "anguish of perceivedness" (*Film*, p. 11) experienced by a man confronted with concrete evidence of the ineluctable duality of self.

The newly introduced image of a mouth giving birth to words is soon repeated: "Stands there staring beyond waiting for first word. It gathers in his mouth. Parts lips and thrusts tongue between them. Tip of tongue. Feel soft touch of tongue on lips. Of lips on tongue." This repetition underscores the notion that birth is not, any more than death, a clear-cut, unequivocal process which can be situated at an identifiable moment of time. The indeterminacy of time is further accentuated in the following lines, which carry the man, the Speaker, and the spectators from present to past to future, through "thirty thousand odd" nights which are tied together by the images of darkness, stillness, eyes, and windows that are common to them all: "Stare beyond through rift in dark to other dark. Further dark. Sun long sunk behind the larches. Nothing stirring. Nothing faintly stirring. Stock still eyes glued to pane. As if looking his last. At that first night. Of thirty thousand odd. Where soon to be. This night to be" (pp. 77–78). We see the Speaker standing still on a dimly lit stage, describing a man standing still in another dark room, whose vision drifts to yet another dark scene—the larches that were outside his room on the night of his birth. The stillness of the larches gives way to the stillness of the man who gazes out his window "at that first night." All the nights in between are brought together in the undifferentiated bundle of "thirty thousand odd," to which "this night," too, and the self that exists in it, will soon be relegated. The unperceivable, undefinable manner in which these various nights and selves flow into one another is highlighted in this passage by the use of the verbal form "stare," instead of the third-person singular "stares," which the audience has come to expect in the text. Since the subject of the verb is absent, we can only speculate as to whether the Speaker has chosen the imperative, first-person singular or plural, second-person singular or plural, or third-person plural form.[12] It is clear, however, that some shift in his perception of his own relationship to the man he is describing has taken place. The Speaker may well have momentarily forgotten the grammatical and conceptual distance he has endeavored to establish between himself and the object of his perception, slipping into the use of the verb form that accompanies the subject "I." Such slips are found elsewhere in the text,[13] but they are rare. All but one of them occur after the Speaker's questioning of his use of the third-person singular pronoun "he" (p. 76), indicating, perhaps, a perceptual confusion which has been building up since that time and which will soon reach its climax with the second and final "He?" of the text (p. 78).

The speed with which the man's different selves give way one to the other is suggested by the brevity and rapidity of the terse summary of the nightly lamplighting now offered by the Speaker: "Spill. Hands. Lamp. Gleam of brass. Pale globe alone in gloom. Brass bedrail catching light. Thirty seconds. To swell the two and a half billion odd. Fade. Gone. Cry. Snuffed with breath of nostrils. Again and again. Again and again gone." The enigmatic words of a previous passage—"A cry. Stifled by nasal" (p. 76)—become clear here, as we understand that with each breath he takes, the man snuffs out the previous self to which he had given birth an instant before. The text introduces a possible conclusion to the seemingly endless cycle of birth and death with the lines, "Till whose grave? Which . . . he all but said which loved one's? He?" The question, "He?," may imply that the end will come when the loved one whose grave is seen is the "he" of the text. The graveyard image envisioned is almost the same as the one evoked earlier, seen from above with its black ditch, rain, canopies, and bubbling black mud. One notable exception is the mention of the "coffin on its way," which was absent in the first scene, yet mentioned in the later summary of the text's images. Could this be the coffin of the man in question, being carried to the empty black ditch that has already been dug for him? Perhaps, but the coffin is merely "on its way" to the grave, as the man has been since that first night of his birth. The Speaker next corrects the phrase, "he all but said loved one on his way," to "her way," changing the sex of the coffin's inhabitant, perhaps in an effort to regain the distance necessary to describe a scene with which he has begun to identify too closely. The words "he all but said loved one" have, with slight variations, formed a constant refrain in the monologue, yet their use here is striking since they follow the words, "loved one," uttered for the first time without the qualifying "he all but said."

After the funeral scene fades away, ghosts from the graveyard come into the darkened room as the Speaker describes the man focusing upon the wall in an attempt to regain the lost images of his past, of those "thirty thousand nights of ghosts beyond. Beyond that black beyond" (pp. 78–79). The major images of the text, many of which have been invisible to the audience's eyes from the beginning, have now become invisible ghosts to the Speaker and to the man who stares through the invisible wall into the black beyond at "ghost light. Ghost nights. Ghost rooms. Ghost graves. Ghost . . . he all but said ghost loved ones." There is nothing for the man to do now but "wait . . . on the rip word," the word "birth" which will well up in his mouth, part his lips, and issue forth at the beginning of a piece of monologue similar to the one we are now hearing.

The Speaker describes the man as the words begin streaming from his mouth, while he "stands there staring beyond at that black veil lips quivering to half-heard words." The grey wall, once white, once covered with pictures of loved ones, has now become a black veil over all the images the man is trying to perceive. His auditory perception is failing, too, as it did once before, when he attempted to hear the words he was uttering (cf. p. 76: "Stands staring beyond half hearing what he's saying"). These "half-heard" words are "treating of other matters. Trying to treat of other matters," such as, perhaps, all the matters of which this monologue has treated—birth, death, loved ones, pictures, funerals, rain, lights, windows, walls, sounds, sights, speaking. Yet he realizes, as the Speaker now seems to realize after the long treatment of other matters which he has just delivered, that all attempts to perceive or express anything, from the very beginning of his life, have, as in the text of *A Piece of Monologue*, returned constantly to their starting point, to a man alone in a dimly lit room awaiting his death. For, from the beginning, there "never were other matters. Never two matters. Never but the one matter. The dead and gone. The dying and the going. From the word go. The word begone." Just as the word "go," which marks the beginning of a process, is contained in the word "begone," which signifies departure or disappearance, so is the process of birth, that great beginning, shaped by and directed to the ending that is death. Beckett chose the word "begone" for more than its meaning and its inclusion of the word "go," however. Its sound is extremely close to that of the word "begin," which would be a less surprising choice at this point in the text, and which is, therefore, probably the word awaited by the audience when it hears the initial /big/ sound. The impact of "begone" is therefore double, since it not only conveys a meaning contrary to what might have been expected, but does so only after it has prepared our ears for a word nearly its opposite. The phrase "the word begone" may be read, on another level, as a command that the word depart. *A Piece of Monologue* has linked words and birth, the ending of words and dying, from its very first lines. Since the Gospel According to Saint John tells us that "in the beginning was the Word" (i:1), ordering the word to be gone is a way of demanding the ending so longed for in all of Beckett's work, an ending whose conditions are a silence, a stillness, and a darkness which, because there is "no such thing," will never come.

Silence, stillness, and darkness, though never whole, may be approached, and the end does indeed seem near as *A Piece of Monologue* draws to a close. Beckett's stage directions indicate that "thirty seconds before end of speech lamplight begins to fail" (p. 69), at about the point where the Speaker mentions "the light going now." After his acknowledgement that no other matters exist but "the dying and the going," the Speaker does not attempt to imagine or express anything but the concrete situation in which the spectators perceive him: "The light going now. Beginning to go. In the room. Where else? Unnoticed by him staring beyond. The globe alone. Not the other. The unaccountable. From nowhere. On all sides nowhere. The globe alone. Alone gone." After this last word, the lamp on stage goes out, leaving the Speaker standing in silence, "barely visible in diffuse light" (p. 69), in the "unaccountable" light coming "from nowhere," before the total blackout that ends the play.[14]

The last word of *A Piece of Monologue* is "gone." Its first word is "birth." These words seem appropriate choices for beginning and ending a monologue that tells of a man's birth and of his dying, and they enclose the text in a traditional time-line that begins at its beginning and ends at its end. However, once again, Beckett is merely manipulating an old-fashioned literary technique to his own ends. Just as the word "birth" begins the surprising phrase "birth was the death of him," so the word "gone" concludes a series of phrases that cast doubt upon the possibility of the ending towards which the play has been directed. While one of the lights on stage is now gone, the other, the unaccountable "faint diffuse light" (p. 69), remains. As so often in Beckett, the ending of *A Piece of Monologue* leaves the impression that we may be witnessing a consciousness' final moment—its approach to the void where movement, words, light, and perception will all "begone." Yet, at the same time, we leave the theater with the lingering doubt that all we have just seen and heard may be merely an arbitrarily chosen segment of an endless process of perception which will be renewed, with slight variations, and much repetition, at another time, in another place, before other witnesses. There is no reason not to believe that the light we have just seen go out is merely another instance of text and stage image momentarily coinciding and that the lamp will be relit again at some point in preparation for the speaking of another piece of monologue.

From all the "other matters" of the monologue, the dramatic situation of its end is reduced to one man in a room on one night, standing in a dim light whose source is unaccountable, listening to, and half hearing, himself. Not only, then, does the text of the play rejoin the stage image at its end, it also places *A Piece of Monologue* squarely in the lineage of the other Beckettian dramas analyzed thus far. Such is the situation Hamm envisions for his final moments, as well as the one in which we see him at the end of *Endgame* (the presence of the silent Clov might be seen to correspond to the mention, in *A Piece of Monologue*, of "him staring beyond"). The text of *Cascando* contains all the elements of *A Piece of Monologue*'s conclusion, even if none of them is offered visually to the audience: pursuit of self in solitary darkness in an attempt at self-expression, which is characterized as a desperate, compulsive, painful process with no finality, but only an endless series of beginnings tending toward endings that never come. At the end of *Film*, O finds himself alone in his room in the same situation as *A Piece of Monologue*'s Speaker, with the exception that his self-perception takes the form of seeing rather than of hearing. *Eh Joe* shows its spectators another man alone in his room one evening, straining at the conclusion of the play to hear a relentless internal monologue, whose diminishing volume towards the end corresponds to the fading light that accompanies the final lines of *A Piece of Monologue*.

Much of the foregoing discussion has concentrated upon Beckett's choice of words, his use of repetition, and the interplay between stage image and text in *A Piece of Monologue*. It would be impossible for a spectator to perceive all of the implications of the text described in these pages unless he or she had carefully studied the play before attending the theater. However, the net effect of the dramatic and linguistic techniques used to create the play does have great power over an attentive audience. The image that remains before our eyes for nearly an hour is accompanied by words whose shape, sound, meaning, and repetition draw our minds towards and away from it in their evocation of a life in pursuit of death, of a beginning in search of its end.

Chapter 7

ROCKABY:

"stop her eyes"

Rockaby, a short stage play written in English, premiered in 1981 at the State University of New York at Buffalo, under the direction of Alan Schneider. Beckett's translation of the play into French appeared the following year under the title *Berceuse*.

The sole image of *Rockaby* is that of a woman, prematurely old and dressed in black, who sits in a rocking chair listening to her own recorded voice. Although this is the first of the plays in this study to have a woman as its central character, Beckett had previously created several major roles for women, starting with the character of Maddy Rooney in the 1957 radio play, *All That Fall*. As Charles Lyons notes, *Rockaby*'s "image of a woman, locked in place, listening to some enigmatic story that may describe her past, refers us to *Not I*, its most immediate model, and to *Happy Days*."[1] The male characters of the previously discussed plays also have a great deal in common with the woman of *Rockaby*. Once more, a character has taken refuge in her room after searching for vision in the external world and has embarked upon the endless pursuit of self-perception. Once more, a consciousness is endeavoring to catch up with itself in an attempt to reach the longed-for ending to perception which, though apparently near, may never be perceived by the consciousness that strives for it and thus may never actually arrive. The now-familiar room and window, common to all the plays in this study, are important images in *Rockaby*, although, as in *A*

Piece of Monologue, the stage set does not present them to the spectators' eyes. The dramatic space of these two recent plays is much less concrete than that of the earlier dramas and exists only as the platform upon which we perceive the characters who draw us backward and project us forward into other times and other places.

The text of *Rockaby* comprises four parts, the first three of which are roughly equal in length (fifty-two, fifty-seven, and fifty-eight lines respectively), while the fourth is half again as long as the preceding sections (eighty-four lines). Each successive part contains a limited number of different lines, some of which echo words, lines, and passages from previous sections, with or without variations, and some of which are new, but may be repeated in the following section(s). Beckett's fascination with the process of permutation is once again evident in his skillful manipulation of *Rockaby*'s restricted number of words, sounds, and images.

Each part begins in precisely the same manner: the immobility of the rocker; the woman's voice asking for "more"; another pause; and the simultaneous commencement of the rock (which is controlled mechanically) and the recorded voice, whose first two lines are similar throughout and identical in parts one and three ("till in the end/the day came" [pp. 9, 14])[2] and in parts two and four ("so in the end/close of a long day" [pp. 12, 17]). Each section ends with the simultaneous echo of the last line, the coming to rest of the rock, and a faint fade of light (which becomes a slow total fade-out at the end). The last two verses of each part are either identical ("rock her off/rock her off"—part four [p. 20]) or nearly so ("another living soul/one other living soul"—part two [p. 14]), and parts one and three again repeat each other in their final lines ("time she stopped/*time she stopped*" [pp. 11, 16], with the underscored line being spoken by both the woman on stage and her recorded voice). Such meticulous construction and repetitiveness are not confined to the beginnings and endings of each part of *Rockaby*, but are evident throughout the play. The text of *Rockaby* represents the most carefully controlled, highly structured, and repetitive use of words and sound of all the dramatic works thus far considered.

Rockaby, even more than *A Piece of Monologue*, might be characterized as a dramatic poem. Enoch Brater calls it "a performance poem in the shape of a play."[3] Its language is neither that of everyday life, nor that of the Speaker's internal monologue in *A Piece of Monologue*, but rather a condensed and repetitive chant whose rhythm imitates the regular back-and-forth movement of the rocking chair. The French title, *Berceuse*, means both "rocking chair" and "lullaby," while the English *Rockaby* refers to a traditional lullaby in which a baby's cradle falls from a tree-top, thus bringing together in one song the images of birth and death that are so often juxtaposed in Beckett. Beckett exploits to the maximum all the allusions, images, and emotions that this old popular musical form can evoke to the eyes, ears, and hearts of his spectators, and the poetry of *Rockaby* closely imitates the soft, repetitive, monotonous, hypnotic lyrics that generations of mothers have sung to lull their infants to sleep. The linguistic and imagistic structure of the play also imitates another form of children's music: the repetitive narrative songs that seem to be coming to an end, only to recommence at the beginning in an endless game of mirrors, e.g., "Found a Peanut," or "The Bear Went Over the Mountain." In one of his rare interviews, Beckett recommended that theater be made to imitate "the kind of form one finds in music, . . . where themes keep recurring."[4] *Rockaby*, which borrows both its title and its form from music, is a vivid and successful illustration of this idea. The word "rockaby" may also call to the minds of some spectators the word "good-by," which could also be a fitting title for this dramatic image of a woman approaching her end.

The meaning of the words of *Rockaby* is less important than their form, their sound, and the visual image that they envelop; it is simply one dramatic element among many. In this respect, Beckett responds perfectly to the esthetic recommendations of Antonin Artaud, who called for a theater where the importance of the textual content would be radically reduced in favor of other more specifically dramatic effects such as gesture, lighting, material images, sound, décor, music, etc. Artaud asked the dramatist to consider language as a form of "incantation,"[5] and this seems to have been Beckett's intention in writing the text of *Rockaby*. The "story" told by the words of this play is quite simple, condensing into several oft-repeated formulas the essentials of an entire human existence:

> the day came
> when she said
> time she stopped

going to and fro
all eyes
for another
another creature like herself
went back in
time she went and sat
at her window
facing other windows
all eyes
for another
all blinds down
hers alone up
when she said
time she stopped
went down
down the steep stair
into the old rocker
where mother sat
all in black
sat and rocked
with closed eyes
saying to the rocker
rock her off

Thus, as we learn from the voice to which we are listening, the woman we see upon the stage has spent her life in pursuit of vision, desperately searching to see—another like herself, or herself—and to be seen. In this respect she is like *Endgame*'s Hamm, who continually asks Clov to look out the window of his shelter and report on what he has seen. She is also like Voice and Music of *Cascando*, who strive to see the self named Woburn, and like the protagonist of *Film*, whose existence, as narrated by the sequence of photographs, has consisted of nothing more than a series of instances of percipere and percipi. Similarly, in *Eh Joe*, Joe spends his lonely evening imagining visions of his past, as the perceiving eye of the self, or the camera, zeroes in upon him. The man described in *A Piece of Monologue* is also engaged in a desperate struggle to see—to see outside his faintly lit room, to see his loved ones in his memory, and to see the past and present selves evoked by the Speaker. Like all these characters, who renounce their attempts at vision in the external world to embark upon a voyage into the dimly lit corridors of memory and consciousness, the woman of *Rockaby* retreats from the outer world to the sanctuary of her rocking chair, where she descends into the depths of self-perception in an attempt to reach the end of her compulsion to perceive. Her story, like that of all the other characters we have met, is an indication that human existence is nothing more nor less than a continual, albeit fruitless, struggle for perception. Vision, its conditions and its impossibility, are therefore the central concern of *Rockaby*, as well as of much of Beckett's dramatic oeuvre.

We must remember that the woman we see is listening to her own voice, which is coming to her from outside. Such is also the situation of *Eh Joe*: although a woman's voice is used in this play, it is clear to the spectators that it emanates from within the male character's consciousness. Beckett exploited the situation of a character listening to his own recorded voice in two previous stage plays, *Krapp's Last Tape* and *That Time*. This now-familiar technique serves both to indicate to the spectators that we are penetrating the consciousness of the mute character on stage and to dramatize the dual nature of human perception—the division of every consciousness into a perceiving subject and a perceived object that can never coincide with each other, in spite of all one's desires to join them in a perfect perception of the self.

The lighting, consisting of a subdued light on the rocker that becomes slightly weaker at the end of each part and a constant spot on the woman's face, suggests the light of human consciousness as it endeavors constantly, yet unsuccessfully, to perceive itself up till the very moment of its extinction. The subdued, concentrated, and fading light, the woman's black costume, her grey hair, her white hands and face, produce the visual impression of a life and a world that are in the process of disappearing. Black and white, the predominant colors of Beckett's latest works, evoke for him the undifferentiation of the void, towards which tend human life and all the perceptual efforts of which it consists from the very moment of birth. At the end of the play, the light, the voice, and the movement of the rocker fade away simultaneously with our visual and auditory perception of this diminishing human existence.

Having given up her travels in the outer world where she had searched, all eyes, all sides, high and low, for another like herself, the woman has come back inside. At first she sits quietly at her window, waiting for the appearance of her other at a neighboring window, but she finally renounces even this hope and descends the steep stair of her consciousness where she meets, not herself, but the image of her mother who had spent her life seeking the same impossible goals. As in all the other plays in this study, the voyage in search of vision which commenced in a spatial dimension as a search for other people, becomes an internal, temporal journey, as the woman closes her eyes and descends into her own consciousness. While Beckett's characters may not be the only inhabitants of the universe, they are the only inhabitants of the particular time and space they occupy at any given moment in their trajectory, and their perspective can never coincide with that of any other being. They are isolated seekers in a world of other unknowable, isolated seekers. Nowhere does Beckett render this notion more clearly than in the haunting text of *The Lost Ones*, which describes a cylindrical "abode where lost bodies roam each searching for its lost one" (p. 7). The woman of *Rockaby* may very well be simply one of the lost ones, searching high and low, in vain, for another face which is itself seeking hers. *Rockaby*'s narration of all these voyages, both exterior and interior, follows the slight, slow, regular rhythm of the rocking chair, a privileged image for Beckett ever since the novel *Murphy*, where the character sought refuge in his rocking chair in order to live and see clearly in his mind. Since the time of *Murphy*, Beckett seems to have lost faith in the possibility of freeing the mind from all influences of the external world, but he has retained his predilection for the controlled, rhythmic movement of the rocker, which also played an important role in *Film*. For Beckett, movement is the fundamental characteristic of all that exists in time and space, and it is the veil which hinders our vision of both the external world and our interior selves (*Proust*, p. 41). All of his characters wander through time and space in pursuit of another living soul or of themselves. From the voyages in geographical space of his early novels to the internal explorations of consciousness undertaken by the characters of his latest plays, the difficulty remains the same: the inexorable flux, change, and movement which preclude the attainment of a fixed, stable point that would finally permit vision. Realizing that it is impossible to become immobile in time and space, the Beckettian character nevertheless prefers to bring the ineluctable movement of life under control by making it as continuous and steady as possible. If all movement is without goal or direction, if every step forward is negated by a step backward, if all hope of meeting the longed-for other is merely an illusion, then wisdom consists of accepting this situation and giving oneself over to the comforting sway of the old rocker which goes continuously back and forth with no other goal than to control and give form to the movement that cannot be escaped so long as one is alive.

Here, then, is what we the spectators of *Rockaby* see with our eyes as we look at the stage: a woman sitting in a rocker listening to herself. But, just as *Eh Joe* and *A Piece of Monologue* present a stage image which is only a starting point for a succession of scenes that we are called upon to create in our imaginations, *Rockaby* causes us to "see" something else in our minds, a vision at one remove, as we listen to this woman's words describe the endless struggle for vision that has characterized her life. The following analysis will examine her words closely in order to discover what she sees, what she has attempted unsuccessfully to see during her life, and the way in which she, and Beckett, communicate these perceptions to the spectators. The fourth part of the text will be used to structure this analysis, since most of the lines and images of the previous parts are repeated in this final section, but reference will be made to the other sections when appropriate.

The voice begins its fourth set of lines with the same words it spoke at the beginning of part two: "so in the end/close of a long day" (p. 17).[6] But here it is referring to *another* long day: at the end of the day in part two, the woman had come back in from her wanderings in the outside world where she had gone to and fro in search of another like herself. This time, however, she abandons her wait at the window, where she had at first been looking for her other, sitting at a window facing hers, and then, simply another blind up, like hers, "one blind up no more" (p. 16). Renouncing her hope ever to be able to see or be seen by *another* living soul in the external world, she has let down her blind and descended the steep stair to sit in the old rocker where her mother had once sat, and where we now, perhaps, see her upon the stage. The word "down" is repeated six times in the first seven lines of this final section, while it is used only once in the preceding sections ("all blinds down"—p. 15). This repetition of "down," coupled with the play's first mention of the "steep stair," gives verbal shape and force to the internal descent that is about to be recounted. The woman is descending into the depths of her self, embarking upon an internal voyage in pursuit of that inaccessible essence where the perceiving "I" and the perceived "me" would coincide, where the desire for perception would be fulfilled, where the ceaseless, obsessive, and futile wandering that characterizes human existence might finally reach its goal.

The language of the text suggests the labyrinthine character of these inner depths. No image or situation evoked brings the description to even a momentary resting place, but each leads imperceptibly into another. The word "down," for instance, ties together a series of actions that are presented nonchronologically: the woman's descent of the stairs, her letting down of the blind, and her sinking into the rocking chair. The fourth line, "in the end went down," combines words from both lines one—"so in the end"—and three—"went down,"—just as the entire fourth section, from its very beginning, repeats many words and lines heard previously in the play. The nonchronological, repetitious, spiraling, cumulative, fluid language of *Rockaby* corresponds to the nature of the consciousness it is intended to portray.

When the voice says "into the old rocker," referring for the first time to the rocking chair we have been looking at since the beginning of the play, we have the momentary impression that the words to which we are listening have finally caught up with the image before our eyes. However, this encounter is fleeting and uncertain, because the text immediately resumes its distance from the stage image as it draws us into a verbal and imagistic game of mirrors, using the word "rocker" to link images of present and past: the "old rocker" where the woman sits becomes first a "mother rocker," then the rocker "where mother sat," "sat and rocked," "all the years/all in black/best black," "till her end came" (pp. 17–18), just as her daughter, at whom we are looking, and who is also dressed "all in black/best black," will rock on till the end of the play. The end of the mother, alluded to in the lines "till her end came/in the end came," echoes the end of the long day mentioned in the first lines of this section, where the voice was describing the end of a day in the daughter's life. The text has thus gone back in time, from the close of one day in the past of the woman on stage, to rejoin the image of her mother, "gone off her head," who had sat and rocked, and has journeyed forward from that time to the moment of the mother's death, which occurred one night: "dead one night/in the rocker/in her best black/head fallen/and the rocker rocking/rocking away." It may also be anticipating here yet another time, a future point in the life of the woman on stage, which we shall witness at the play's conclusion as her "head slowly sinks, comes to rest" (p. 21) before the final fade-out. The boundaries between mother and daughter become less and less defined as the text moves back and forth in time, from one black-clad woman in a rocker to another, using similar or identical words, phrases, and rhythms to tie together a series of nonidentical, yet somehow indistinguishable, images.

Here we are, thus, in the middle of part four, at our starting point: "in the end/close of a long day." But which one? The close of the day when "her" mother died? Or the "close of a long day" of the beginning of the play? Or the one which begins part two? Or part three? Or part four? Or perhaps the one we witness at the conclusion of the play? All we can know for certain is that we are moving in time, accompanied by the rhythmic, repetitive words of the voice and the concrete image of the slowly moving rocker which lull our minds just as they do the woman on stage. In other words, the reconstruction of this woman's life in linear perspective is impossible for the spectator, whom she draws into the depths of her consciousness. The lack of traditional syntax and punctuation in the text, as well as the dull, expressionless voice of the actress,[7] contribute to this destruction of geometric perspective: one never knows exactly at which point one image or memory ends and another begins.

Cohn contrasts the temporality of Beckett's drama with that of classical theater as follows: "Whereas classical peripetias thrill through to a conclusion, Beckett's plays are unfinal. Rather than Aristotelian beginning, middle, and end, Beckett's plays are endless continua."[8] To the endless continuum of *Rockaby*, Beckett joins a boundless theatrical space that Cohn has labelled "theatereality":

> In the pre-*Play* [1962] plays Beckett gains tension between a strange setting and verbal glimpses of other places, in the post-

> *Play* plays fictional and theater situation and place can converge—theatereality. . . .
>
> In Beckett's theater plays of the 1970s [and 1980s], containing theatereality, tension grows between the spare invariant settings and the memories of lived-in places.[9]

So we find ourselves, with the woman at whom we are looking, at the end of one long day or another, in an indeterminate space that is nevertheless presented to our eyes—it little matters which day or which place, since they are all basically so alike. A woman—mother? daughter? or another?—dressed in her best black, just like the character on stage, rocks away in her rocker, and the text repeats exactly the first eight lines of the beginning of part four: "so in the end/close of a long day/went down/in the end went down/down the steep stair/let down the blind and down/right down/into the old rocker." This time, instead of calling the rocker "mother rocker," the voice alludes to the rocker's maternal embrace with the words, "those arms at last." This woman has spent her entire life trying to see and be seen by another. Having finally admitted the impossibility of her quest, she consoles herself as best she can in the embrace of the old "mother rocker" (p. 17). She is far from the first Beckettian character to seek her mother's arms at the end of her life, to attempt to return to her mother's womb where she would be rocked to her final sleep, just as her own mother had met her end in the arms of the very same rocker.

Beckett's notes to *Rockaby* indicate that the woman on stage, whose eyes are "now closed, now open in unblinking gaze," and increasingly closed as the play advances, are "closed for good halfway through [section] 4" (pp. 21–22), presumably at the lines: "with closed eyes/closing eyes" (p. 19). The words of the text thus correspond once again, momentarily, to the image on stage, but they reestablish their distance immediately as they resume telling the story of this woman, or another, who had searched high and low, to see, to be seen. The word "eyes" is used to unify the various temporal levels of the text at this point, as it appears in four successive lines: "with closed eyes/closing eyes/she so long all eyes/famished eyes." The closed eyes, which might be thought to indicate a conclusion to the compulsive pursuit of vision of which this woman's life has consisted, do not afford her consciousness even a momentary respite from the process of perception. While the eyes on stage remain closed, the woman's inner vision is related to us by her recorded voice, as the closed eyes move backwards in time to become "closing eyes," and then the wide-open eyes of a person famished for an impossible vision, the eyes of the woman who cannot escape her need "to see/be seen" even when she closes her eyes in the dark sanctuary of her mother rocker. She will acknowledge this inevitablity of perception in the play's final lines, when, with her eyes closed, her voice begs the rocker to "stop her eyes/ rock her off" (p. 20).

The blind which the woman had let down over her window and which is mentioned both before and after the closing of the eyes, corresponds to the lids she has just closed over her eyes, those "posterns of the mind" (*More Pricks Than Kicks*, p. 161), which had for so long gazed out upon a world where there was nothing to see, just as the window of her house had never offered any nourishment to her famished eyes. However, neither the lowering of the blind nor that of the eyelids has stemmed her desire to perceive.

After hearing the voice's final recollection of the woman's fruitless travels "high and low/to and fro," and then of her vigil "at her window," in hopes of seeing or being seen by another, we are told once more of her decision to stop seeking her other at her window. This decision was first announced in part three by the lines, "till the day came/in the end came/close of a long day" (p. 16), reiterated at the opening of part four, beginning with the words, "so in the end/close of a long day" (p. 17), again in the middle of this part with the same introduction, "so in the end/close of a long day" (p. 18), and here prefaced by similar lines, "till in the end/close of a long day."

As the woman leaves the window, she says "to herself/whom else/time she stopped." It is time she stopped looking for another in the outside world, since there is nobody to see, or even talk to, but herself. She wishes therefore to be henceforth "her own other," the "other living soul" she has always sought, but she will not succeed in seeing herself either. The repetition of the familiar refrain, "so in the end/close of a long day," just before the final lines that deal with the woman's efforts to be "her own other," suggests that this last attempt at perception will repeat the failure of all the previous ones.

Several times during the play the voice (usually joined by the voice of the woman on stage) has told us that the woman said to herself, "time she stopped," but now the line "saying to herself" is corrected by a "no/done with that" (p. 20), and the voice tells the rocker to "rock her off." This phrase calls to mind the expression "off her rocker," which further links the woman in question to her mother, who had "gone off her head" (p. 18). Insanity is a prevalent leitmotiv in Beckett's work, from the schizophrenic Mr. Endon of *Murphy*, to Hamm's mad painter friend in *Endgame*, to the aphasiac woman of *Not I*, to the obsessed, pacing May of *Footfalls*, to the woman of *Rockaby*. Schizophrenia can be seen as the extreme case of suffering caused by the separation of self from self and therefore from the rest of the world with which Beckett's entire work deals. The catatonic state, by which schizophrenics resist this split, fascinates Beckett, and seems to represent to him the nearest a human being can come to achieving a sense of unity within the self, a condition he once called "the rare dispensation of waking madness" (*Proust*, p. 19). Schopenhauer posited a close relation between madness and artistic genius, characterizing both conditions as atemporal, capable of transcending phenomena and causal relations in order to reach the changeless essence of the world. His description of the loss of memory suffered by mad people could have been written in the 1980s by a reviewer of *Rockaby*: "The thread of memory is broken, the continuity of its connection destroyed, and no uniformly connected recollection of the past is possible. . . . there are gaps in their recollections which they fill up with fictions."[10]

By asking the rocking chair to "rock her off," the woman of *Rockaby* expresses her desire to give up talking to herself because the creature she has been seeking, first in the external world, eyes open, then inside herself, eyes closed, can never be reached by her eyes or by her words: "We cannot know and we cannot be known" (*Proust*, p. 49). The internal self is as multiple, fugitive, and nonexistent as are the other living souls she had sought from her window before her descent down the steep stair of consciousness. We become lost in the text to the extent that we no longer know whether "she" refers to the woman on stage, another, her mother, or even the rocking chair (especially in the French version, where "la berceuse" is referred to as "elle"—p. 52), because Beckett has succeeded in making us reproduce the unfocused and fleeting vision of a consciousness that meets the object of its desire only temporarily and in a fragmented form, losing sight of it at the very instant when that consciousness, and we the spectators, believe we have finally achieved our goal of vision.

What Cohn has written of Beckett's earlier play *Not I* applies equally well to the effect produced by *Rockaby* upon its spectators:

> We see and hear through the voice-brain conflict. Our minds "pick it up," seeking sense through the segmented syntax, staccato rhythms, and few swiftly sketched events. Beckett has conceived a whole play as soliloquy, in which he withholds knowledge of its protagonist only to immerse us all the more deeply in an emotional relationship with her.[11]

"She" must now be content to feel the arms of the rocking chair and to speak to it, in the third person, of herself and of her aborted existence which has consisted merely of one long effort to see and be seen, to see another or herself, to be seen by another or by herself. This hope, which proved to be so futile, has nevertheless motivated the entire life which she has just described and which we have seen pass before our eyes and in our imagination in the form of fluctuating and inextricably interwoven characters, moments, images, and words. Beckett once wrote about the painting of the van Velde brothers in words that apply equally well to the esthetics of *Rockaby*: "Un dévoilement sans fin, voile derrière voile, plan sur plan de transparences imparfaites, un dévoilement vers l'indévoilable, le rien, la chose à nouveau."[12]

The line, "stop her eyes," which is repeated twice near the end of the text, was omitted in the French translation. Such an omission is characteristic of Beckett's translations, which are often less explicit and more ambiguous than the original texts. The voice's order to "stop her eyes" indicates that, in order for the woman to be able to "stop," a desire she has often expressed since the beginning of the play, her eyes must first cease to function. For life is nothing more nor less than the act of perception or the state of being perceived, or, in the words of Berkeley, "esse est percipi."

The final ten lines of text are the least repetitive of the entire play. Although they contain many familiar words and sounds, only one of these lines has been heard before ("those arms at last"). The novelty of the last lines is all the more striking because they follow a group of eleven lines that echo previous passages of *Rockaby*. The newest and most shocking of the concluding lines is "fuck life"; its effect is extremely strong not only because of the obscenity it contains, but also because neither word in it has yet been spoken during the play. The corresponding French line, "aux gogues la vie" (p. 52), has a similar shock effect, although its meaning is somewhat different. "Gogues" is a little-used vulgar word for "chamber pot," or "toilet," and Beckett's choice of it is proof that, in translating, he pays at least as much attention to the sound of words as to their meaning.

At the end of the play we perceive the nearly simultaneous cessation of the voice, the rocking, and the image of the woman in the rocker. It almost seems that her prayers have been answered, that her relentless pursuit of self, and the third-person commentary she has been offering upon it, have finally come to an end, with her life and with her consciousness, which are extinguished at the same moment as the stage lights. However, at the last moment of the play, when everything comes to a standstill, the lighting does not go out all at once: we see it fade first upon the chair and, after a "long pause with spot on face alone," when the "head slowly sinks, comes to rest," the final light fades slowly out and the woman's face disappears into the void. The brief interval between the extinction of the two stage lights of *Rockaby* calls to mind a similar use of lighting at the end of *A Piece of Monologue*. In both cases, Beckett is dramatizing a problem which has long intrigued him: the temporal gap that must occur at the moment of death between the perceiving consciousness and its object, the perceived self. For, at the very moment when the object of perception, the woman, finally becomes immobile in time and space, i.e., a fixed and therefore visible object, she ceases to exist, she is no longer herself. Her consciousness thus goes out without ever fulfilling its goal, since it can succeed in being its own "other" neither in life nor in death. However, the image of this woman and of her consciousness, which we have just penetrated, will remain for quite a while before our eyes and in our minds, just as those of her mother had not been completely extinguished at the close of that long day when she died, but continue to be present to the perception of her daughter, and thus to ours. And they may well reappear to this daughter's daughter when she closes her eyes and rocks till her end in the arms of her mother rocker one night, at the close of a long day. And perhaps also to *this* daughter's daughter, who will set the entire process in motion once again when she asks the voice to tell her about her own life, which is so like that of her mother and her mother's mother, and so like that which we all live. It is a life which, just like this play which begins with the command "more," has neither beginning nor end and is simply a search to see and be seen, but where vision occurs only in bits, pieces, and obscure reflections in an infinite game of mirrors.

Rockaby offers a visual image of a dying consciousness that is carrying away with it the world it has created. From the very beginning of the play, everything is designed to produce an impression of slow and ineluctable entropy: the premature aging of the woman; her grey hair and black clothes; the subdued lighting which fades slightly at the end of each part and finally goes out altogether; the eyes which close more and more often until they shut definitively near the end; the softening of the woman's voice with each line she utters, and the gradual diminishing of the recorded voice's volume towards the end; the repetition of the words "end" and "close" from the very beginning; and the line spoken together, several times, by the woman and the voice—"time she stopped." In *Rockaby*, Beckett offers neither plot, psychology, philosophy, nor entertainment. He presents in their stead a dramatic image of an end, of a disappearance, which he has carefully orchestrated using all the dramatic techniques he has mastered during his years in the theater: lighting, décor, costume, movement, gesture, silence, color, sound, and, of course, the text, which he integrates perfectly with all these other aspects of the theater so that, as Artaud desired, it addresses itself to the senses rather than to the mind, becoming a "poésie dans l'espace, capable de créer des sortes d'images matérielles."[13]

From *Waiting for Godot* to *Rockaby*, Beckett's theater has evolved consistently in the direction of reduction, compression, and the economy of artistic means. What he has to "say" today is, in fact, not very different from what he had to "say" in the beginning, for, as Malone says in the Trilogy, "life and death . . . nothing was ever about anything else to the best of my recollection" (p. 225). What has changed is the dramatic form Beckett uses to communicate his vision of life and death, and of the temporal and spatial conditions to which human existence is subject. His drama has become more and more of a minimalist art: for each play, he chooses an extremely limited number of elements whose dramatic possibilities he exploits to the maximum by combining, repeating, and permuting them in carefully controlled structures. Ever since *Godot*, there has been a progressive reduction and concentration of stage space and time, movement, language, the human body, and images. Beckett seems to have been guided by the idea he wrote in a marginal note on *That Time*: "Less is more."[14] In *Rockaby*, Beckett concentrates an entire human life in one image, several minutes, one movement, and a very few simple, short, and repetitive lines of text. By so doing, he insures that each element will produce its maximum effect upon the spectators, for, in the theater as in the scientific laboratory, condensation entails intensity. By reducing dramatic action and language to their bare minimum, he endows each small change with enormous power: the eyes closing, the light that fades slowly, a new line of text introduced in the middle of a group we have already heard several times before. The progressive minimization of Beckett's dramatic repertory corresponds to his characterization, in *Proust*, of art as a reductive process: "The artistic tendency is not expansive, but a contraction. . . . The only fertile research is excavatory, immersive, a contraction of the spirit, a descent. The artist is active, but negatively, shrinking from the nullity of extracircumferential phenomena, drawn in to the core of the eddy" (pp. 47–48).

Although the dramatic elements of *Rockaby* are extremely limited, this play nevertheless contains echoes of all the Beckettian dramas in this study, presented here in an intensely concentrated form. For example, the couple of *Endgame*, which could stand to be neither together nor apart, has become the memory of the other, like herself, that the woman of *Rockaby* has always sought but never found. The mother, whom we see in her ashbin on the stage of *Endgame*, is evoked only by words in *Rockaby*. Just as the voice of *Rockaby* continues to evoke "the end" from the very beginning of the play, Clov announces at the opening of *Endgame*: "Finished, it's finished, nearly finished, it must be nearly finished" (p. 1). Indeed, *Endgame* presents, in a more traditional form, the same situation as *Rockaby* of a life and a world that are in the process of disappearing. *Cascando* uses only voices to recount its quest for perception which, like that of *Rockaby*, begins in the outer world and becomes an internal pursuit of vision and expression of the self. Like the voice of

Rockaby, *Cascando*'s voice alludes to an ending in its very first lines. The images of room and window are also present in this radio play, although not as prominently as in *Rockaby*. The Beckett work which has perhaps the most in common with *Rockaby* is *Film*, where we see presented in concrete fashion all that the voice of *Rockaby* merely alludes to in fragmentary language and images: a man returns from his wanderings in the street to his mother's room, which he reaches by going up, not down, a stair and where he covers the window, sits in a rocking chair, closes his eyes, and tries in vain to escape the perception of others as well as his own. While *Film* emphasizes the inevitability of perception, *Rockaby* concentrates more upon its impossibility, describing its character's past yearnings for visions of others and self. Both dramas, however, reach similar conclusions: esse est percipi, and in order for vision to cease, being itself must come to an end. The woman of *Rockaby* finally comes to know that in order to be "rocked off," her eyes must stop, or vice versa, a discovery also made by O as he sits in his own rocker at the end of *Film*. In *Eh Joe*, a man sits alone, in his room with a window, listening to his inner voice tell him of his past, as the inevitable eye of self-perception zeroes in upon him. The early manuscripts of *Eh Joe* also called for a rocking chair.[15] And in *A Piece of Monologue*, windows, rooms, memories, light, death and birth, and internal monologue are combined to produce a visual poem very close in meaning and effect to those of *Rockaby*. By condensing all these elements of previous plays, and others, into the single image and austere text of *Rockaby*, Beckett has succeeded in creating a tight, unified, extremely powerful play where not one word, gesture, lighting or sound effect seems superfluous and where all the elements are tied together in a rigorous, precise, dense, and harmonious form.

Beckett's thematic content is relatively limited and remarkably coherent. The interest of his work lies not so much in the ideas or situations he expresses, as in the variety of new forms he uses to shape them. In one of his earlier works, a poem written in 1948 (originally in French), we encounter a summary of the entire subject matter of *Rockaby*:

> peering out of my deadlight looking for another
> wandering like me eddying far from all the living
> in a convulsive space

among the voices voiceless
that throng my hiddenness

(*Poems in English*, p. 59)

From 1948 (and even earlier) to the present, Beckett has been dealing with the same basic problems of perception, movement, space, time, and isolation from self and others. *Rockaby* is one of his latest attempts to explore these problems using the dramatic repertoire he has created over his years of work in the theater. Like a musical composer, he strives to discover how many variations of form he can create around the same themes, and the result is an oeuvre in which each work is closely related to all the others, yet capable of standing on its own as a complete, original, dramatic composition.

CONCLUSION

If Beckett has abandoned traditional dramatic perspective because of his loss of faith in the world order that made such a perspective possible, he has had to discover new techniques to tie together the elements of his drama. For, even though he presents a vision of a fragmented, diminishing, unseeable, purposeless universe and of a humanity which can find no place or identity in it, he does so in a highly formalized, controlled, and systematic manner. His drama does indeed portray the "mess" in which we all exist, yet it succeeds, if not in lending meaning to the objects of his representation, at least in endowing them with form. Beckett has achieved a new vision, one might even say a new perspective, to bind the fragments of his dramatic universe into a tightly structured, esthetically pleasing whole. He exploits all of the diverse ways in which drama can appeal to its spectators' senses and imaginations, creating visual and aural echoes that provoke profound resonances within the hearts and minds of his audiences. However, even though Beckett's meticulous craftsmanship and dramatic genius produce highly unified works, he leaves no doubt that what is being portrayed is a world where vision is impossible, due to the continual movement in time and space that infects all its inhabitants, observer and observed alike.

Beckett refuses the time-honored technique of using an external, omniscient point of view to organize the elements of his drama. Instead, he forces his spectators to adopt the mobile, partial vision of his characters. As his work has progressed, he has drawn audiences further away from the concrete, stable space of the stage, and deeper into the abstract, fluctuating space of his characters' minds, where we join them in their compulsive, yet fruitless, attempts to reach, see, and express their constantly changing inner selves. In *Endgame*, four separate characters exchange dialogue in a recognizable, if somewhat bizarre, stage space. Although this "family" in a room may be viewed, on one level, as a representation of the diverse aspects of a single consciousness, it nevertheless remains a rather conventional dramatic representation of human interaction, especially in comparison to Beckett's later plays. At certain points in *Endgame*, our imagination is obliged to leave the space on stage to follow the course of the drama: we "see" the world outside the windows only through Clov's descriptions of it, and the characters occasionally call up memories of their past in order to add color to their grey, darkening world. Even more significantly, Hamm's story and monologues prefigure Beckett's later, more sustained, attempts at translating into dramatic terms the endless search for self which he had already formalized so strikingly in the novel, with *The Unnamable*. In the next play studied, *Cascando*, Beckett uses the purely abstract space of the radio medium to portray the mental and emotional strivings of an artist at work in the formless depths of his own consciousness. With *Film*, Beckett returns to visual drama and concrete, realistic space, only to deny his spectators a full perspective upon that space by the camera's unconventionally limited angle of vision. Furthermore, the audience is required to switch back and forth between two separate points of view—E's and O's—both of which are recorded by the camera eye, which is no longer a neutral, outside observer but a symbol and agent of self-perception, an observer inserted squarely into the middle of the drama it is meant to observe. The television play *Eh Joe* also makes of the camera a character which represents one aspect of Joe's consciousness, and here Beckett adds another effect—the woman's voice—to convey the inner workings of Joe's memory. This play begins with the camera recording Joe's movements in the space of his room, but renders the dramatic space ever more abstract as the camera zooms progressively inward upon Joe's face, following the same path from external, geographical space to the inner mental settings that has characterized Beckett's drama as a whole. The two recent plays in this study, *A Piece of Monologue* and *Rockaby*, both present stark visual images anchored on a stage whose space is undeniably real, yet undefined by any boundaries. The texts draw our attention both towards and away from the image before our eyes, producing within us the same impression of visual fluctuation and spatiotemporal disorientation that the characters themselves are describing. Both plays use a dual light source to suggest the split nature of the consciousness they portray. This dichotomy is extended in *A Piece of Monologue* by the Speaker's use of the third person in his internal monologue, and in *Rockaby* by the technique of having the woman on stage listen to her own recorded voice, which also speaks in the third person.

In all of these plays, we observe characters trapped within an enclosed space—a room, a mind, or, usually, both—from which there is no issue, endeavoring vainly either to see or to put an end to the painful process of imperfect perception that characterizes the life of human beings endowed with eyes and consciousnesses in an unseeable, unknowable, and inescapable universe. In one of his recent nondramatic texts, *Company*, Beckett has summarized the perceptual problems that form the core of his drama as well of his writing in general:

> In another dark or in the same another devising it all for company. This at first sight seems clear. But as the eye dwells it grows obscure. Indeed the longer the eye dwells the obscurer it grows. Till the eye closes and freed from pore the mind inquires, What does this mean? What finally does this mean that at first sight seemed clear? Till it the mind too closes as it were. As the window might close of a dark empty room. The single window giving on outer dark. Then nothing more. No. Unhappily no. Pangs of faint light and stirrings still. Unformulable gropings of the mind. Unstillable. (Pp. 22–23)

Beckett might be describing in this passage the experience of the spectators who accompany his characters on their endless journeys within themselves. In a dark theater, we witness other people keeping themselves company with a stream of words. Although the image on stage is bold and clear, the more we look at it, while listening to the text, the more unsure we become as to what we are perceiving, an esthetic effect described by Beckett in one of his earliest writings: "the object that becomes invisible before your eyes is, so to speak, the brightest and best."[1] We abandon our reliance upon our eyes of flesh, and give ourselves over to the workings of our minds, only to find that no answers are to be found there, either. Only by attempting to still the gropings of our consciousness can we approach the key to understanding the peace and unity so earnestly desired by Beckett's characters, yet we cannot do so any more than they: even when eyelids close, and windows of dark empty rooms are covered or look out only onto a dark beyond, a "faint light and stirrings" remain—the consciousness that cannot meet itself cannot abandon itself, either. We are never able to see the object sought in Beckett's drama, because we reproduce the fleeting, partial, fragmented vision of his perpetually frustrated characters. What we do see, hear, feel, and recognize in the depths of our being is the dramatization of the search for vision which is the substance of our lives.

The constant mobility of space and time render vision impossible in the Beckettian universe, and movement is a major feature of his dramatic esthetic. The extensive, often comical, physical movement of early works like *Waiting for Godot* and *Endgame* borrows heavily from the music-hall and vaudeville traditions. Some of Beckett's later works also depend greatly upon movement on stage for their dramatic effects—the camera moves in *Eh Joe*, the exits and entrances of *Come and Go*, May's pacing in *Footfalls*, the man passing in and out of the circle of light in *. . . but the clouds . . .*, the sway of the rocker in *Rockaby*, the hooded figures shuffling along the sides and diagonals of a square in *Quadrat I + II*. All of this movement is, however, carefully orchestrated and rigidly controlled, tending to create an image that is, if not static, circumscribed and predictable, affording at least one measure of order to the spectators' fluctuating perceptions. Another group of plays offers much more static stage images: Winnie in her mound in *Happy Days*, the heads in urns of *Play*, the mouth of *Not I*, the face of *That Time*, the Speaker of *A Piece of Monologue*. Movement is by no means absent in these plays, however. Even when the image remains fixed, or nearly so, the language of the text carries the spectators along on the characters' mental voyages in time and space. Indeed, one of the most significant aspects of the evolution of Beckett's drama through the years is the fact that, as movement upon the stage has been minimized and/or strictly regulated, the imaginary mobility required of his spectators has progressively increased. The characters compel us to follow their own perceptions, which shift ceaselessly from past to future, brushing by but never resting upon, the stage images that serve as springboards for their explorations of other times, other places, and other selves. The increasingly abstract stage space of Beckett's later plays contributes to the aura of indeterminacy that surrounds his dramatic situations; as scenic boundaries, e.g., the walls of Hamm's, O's, and Joe's rooms, disappear, we find it easier to enter the boundless, formless space of the characters' consciousnesses. It is often impossible to situate the exact time, place, and character alluded to by a given line of text, because images and phrases in Beckett's drama melt imperceptibly into one another, like the disparate, unordered, repetitive, boundless points of his time and space. Thus, although Beckett's drama may be very rightly characterized as imagistic, and fruitfully analyzed in terms of its relationship to the art of painting, his plays are by no means the frozen tableaux called for by Diderot, who also imagined a theater conceived along the lines of the visual arts. They are, rather, abstract paintings that decompose their subjects, splitting them internally into irreconcilable fragments, images of ruptured objects propelled in an endless, disordered space and time by their own internal mobility.

Beckett's characters all move through a universe where time and space are ever-changing, strangely repetitive, yet somehow always diminishing. The goal of their journeys is either perfect perception or an end to perception, both unrealizable aims that are merely two sides of the same nonexistent coin. They are shown nearing these goals, coming closer and closer to an end that always remains just out of their grasp. Beckett often suggests the approaching end by his characters' faded, deteriorating, colorless physical appearance and their somber costumes, as well as by the bareness and black/white/grey color scheme of the stage décor and lighting. His men and women frequently take refuge in enclosed interior spaces whose windows look out onto nothing, and they refer to colored, vibrant, natural landscapes as irrelevant vestiges of an unretrievable past. The language of the texts refers constantly to the end, and the volume and tempo of the sound, as well as the intensity of the lighting, often diminish as the plays draw to a close.

Beckett employs an equal if not greater number of techniques to dramatize the improbability of ending. Just as his plays almost always begin by breaking in upon the characters in the middle of a situation that seems to have been going on forever, and make frequent references to the ending from their very first lines, when they end, they leave us with much doubt as to whether what we have just witnessed has actually come to a close. The visual and textual similarities of the beginnings and endings of Beckett's plays formalize the indefinite boundaries of the time and space that inform them. These dramas all appear to portray merely abitrarily selected segments of their characters' lives, which, since they are sustained by an interminable process of self-perception, do not depend upon the spectators' physical arrival and departure for their existence. Obviously, on one level, they do—given the nature of theater as a public spectacle in an appointed place that begins and ends at conventionally agreed upon times, which even Beckett has not been able to circumvent, every Beckettian performance must start and stop at given moments and his fictional characters must pass in and out of existence before our eyes. Yet Beckett manages to accept these constraints even as he strives to overcome them. While we "know" that a certain play has begun or ended, Beckett makes us doubt the reality of our perception. He blurs the boundaries between the first and last moments of the play, between tonight's performance and tomorrow night's, and between one play and the next to such an extent that we question if the process we are perceiving will ever reach a conclusion.

The intra- and intertextuality of Beckett's work, both in his plays and in his narrative fiction, promote the impression among his audiences that we have stepped into a world from which there may be no exit. Characters, situations, movements, images, language, concepts, and technical procedures recur frequently, in slightly altered forms, within each piece as well as from one work to the next. The resonances produced in the memories of his spectators by this subtle, complex, and pervasive repetition help to explain why the experience of reading, seeing, and listening to Beckett's works becomes richer and more evocative as one is more and more exposed to them. We gain the impression that, in confronting each new Beckettian creation, we are entering an echo chamber and/or a hall of mirrors, where we can expect to encounter series of sounds and sights already somewhat familiar from previous experiences, but presented in a slightly different manner than before. Beckett exploits to the fullest language, situations, and images that are rich with meanings derived not just from his own work, but from everyday life as well as from the vast body of Western literature he knows so well. The effect of all this repetition, with variations, is to make us feel that we *almost* recognize what we are perceiving, yet can never quite grasp it, because it is not exactly the same as what we saw or heard the last time. We are thus led to experience the same perceptual difficulties as Beckett's characters: the inability to fix images and sounds so we can identify them with certainty in a world whose fluctuating time and space keep them in constant motion, changing them just enough to make them other than what we expected to encounter, though never enough to separate them into definable, perceivable, and expressible entities.

Another way in which Beckett induces perceptual disorientation among his audiences is his extensive use of the play-within-a-play, story-within-a-story, or film-within-a-film technique. In this respect, his drama is truly Pirandellian in its exploration of the boundaries between life and art, leading his characters and spectators into a mental labyrinth from which there is no issue. His work is intensely self-reflective: the characters as well as the plays reveal an acute consciousness of themselves as works of art. The characters' search for perception and expression of self replicates the artist's unending quest for vision and form. Nowhere is the connection between pursuit of self and the artistic process more conspicuous than in *Cascando*, a play whose subject is the creation of a work of art, but the equation of self-perception and artistic potency pervades Beckett's entire oeuvre. The self-conscious form of his drama corresponds perfectly to the nature of the process it is intended to convey.

The nonsyntactical structure of Beckett's language is another formal device that conveys the notion of an unending universe where time and space are circular, as opposed to the linearity of classical language, perspective, and spatiotemporal concepts. Over the years, Beckett's writing has evinced a progressive destruction of syntax—the loss of traditional grammatical links such as conjunctions, prepositions, and subordinate clauses; confusion regarding pronouns and their referents; suppression of punctuation; questioning of tenses; interchangeability of subject and object. He first carried out his linguistic experiments in the novel, coming as close as any author ever had to the annihilation of language itself in *The Unnamable*, about which he said in a 1956 interview, "At the end of my work there's nothing but dust—the namable. In the last book—*L'Innom-*

mable—there's complete disintegration. No 'I,' no 'have,' no 'being.' No nominative, no accusative, no verb."[2] Beckett's dramatic language remained more traditional for a longer period of time. In *Godot* and *Endgame*, for example, although the content of the dialogue was often unusual, absurd, surprising, and even shocking to the ears of many spectators, the grammatical structure of the sentences themselves was rather conventional. (One notable exception is Lucky's speech in *Godot*, whose form prefigures that of Beckett's later dramatic monologues.) The text of these early plays was also delivered in the traditional form of dialogue among diverse players. The language of Beckett's recent plays contrasts sharply with that of his first dramatic writing. In *Rockaby*, for example, punctuation is gone, most of the linguistic liaisons characteristic of syntactical construction are either absent or have ceased to perform their customary functions, and the language consists of repetitive phrases that stand in a circular, indefinite relation one to another, creating a text that defies linear analysis. In addition, the language is delivered, no longer in the form of a dialogue, nor even as a conventional monologue, since the voice we hear does not come from the character on stage, but from an invisible recorded source.

Syntax is an anachronism in a universe whose elements are no longer thought to be logically, permanently, and harmoniously joined by the providence of God in relationships that can be discovered by the eye of man. The major characteristic of syntax is its linearity, or the way in which sentences are constructed in an orderly, progressive fashion that clearly delineates their beginning, middle, and ending. In a world where finality is unthinkable, it is no surprise that language should lose its progressive, coordinated structure. Or, in the words of the voice of *Texts for Nothing*, "it's for ever the same murmur, flowing unbroken, like a single endless word and therefore meaningless, for it's the end gives the meaning to words" (Text 8, p. 111). In another of these texts, the same problem is phrased somewhat differently: "The words too, slow, slow, the subject dies before it comes to the verb, words are stopping too" (Text 2, p. 82). The stable rapport between subject and verb, subject and object, self and not-self, I and me, has ruptured into the fragments of language and selves that circulate independently, without end, in a work, and a world, where nothing, and nobody, ever remain unchanged enough from one second to the next to permit clear perception or adequate expression in language.

In an unusually explicit letter to Axel Kaun in 1937,[3] Beckett stated that language is "a veil that must be torn apart in order to get at the things (or the Nothingness) behind it." He called for the "misuse" of language, dismissing grammar and style as irrelevant masks. The materiality of the surface, which had long since been dissolved by music and painting, needed now to be broken in literature as well. Beckett envisioned a language where "through whole pages we can perceive nothing but a path of sounds suspended in giddy heights, linking unfathomable abysses of silence." He concluded the letter with a comment upon the pleasure he took in "sinning willy-nilly against a foreign language," expressing the hope that he might someday be able to do likewise against his own.

The recent plays Beckett has composed in his native English—*A Piece of Monologue*, *Ohio Impromptu*, and *Rockaby*—dissolve the veil of language to reach into the silent abysses that lie below its surface, coming very close to creating the "literature of the unword" Beckett described in the letter to Kaun. He achieves this new art form in drama both through a highly original use of language, which corresponds in form to the messages that it conveys, and through a number of nonverbal techniques that are equally essential components of his dramatic esthetic. For each of his plays, Beckett composes a second text to accompany the spoken words that prescribes in rigorous detail every technical effect he can envision to give them shape. In the television plays *Ghost Trio* and *. . . but the clouds . . .*, Beckett took a major step towards liberating his dramatic images from the spoken text of the script, using words only to "instruct the viewer, to teach him how to look at and contemplate the actual, wordless visual experience."[4] Moreover, in two very recent pieces for television, *Quadrat I + II* and *Nacht und Träume*, Beckett dispenses with the spoken text altogether, creating wordless visual images that belong as much to the realm of the plastic arts as they do to drama.

Beckett's insistence that his plays be performed precisely according to his prescriptions,[5] and the active role he has taken in their production, derive from his understanding of drama in the Wagnerian sense of a "composite art work" (*Gesamtkunstwerk*). If linear perspective no longer serves to unite the elements of his drama, Beckett has found other means of creating esthetic unity, and principal among these are the visual liaisons between characters and text, décor and characters, that he calls for in his stage directions. His longstanding predilection for the radio and television media is due, at least in part, to their ability to record directly, and fix for posterity, the exact intent of the dramatist. By carefully envisaging and controlling all the elements of his plays, he has succeeded in performing the dramatic "miracle" referred to by Pirandello's Dr. Hinkfuss in *Tonight We Improvise*—the direct translation of an author's text onto the stage, undistorted by the various interpretations that directors or actors might choose to give it:

> Does this not impress you as going to prove that, in the theatre, the thing on which one forms an opinion is never the writer's work (which consists solely of his text) but rather, this or that scenic creation which has been made out of it, one creation being quite different from another, and there being a number of them, whereas the writer's work is a unit? In order to form an opinion of his text, we should have to know it; and in the theatre, this is not possible through the medium of an interpretation which, provided by certain actors, is one thing, and something else again when provided by other actors. The only way out would be, if the work could perform itself, no longer making use of actors, but making use of its own characters, miraculously endowed with flesh, blood and speech. In such a case, I grant you, the writer's work might be judged directly in the theatre. But is any such miracle possible? No one has ever witnessed it.[6]

Although Beckett allows his actors very little freedom of interpretation, an international group of fiercely dedicated, highly talented Beckettian actors has emerged over the years. The actors themselves have become part of the Beckettian dramatic oeuvre, further blurring the boundaries between art and life, between the actors we see on stage and the characters they are portraying. They reappear in various forms from one play to the next just like his characters, who do indeed seem thereby to become "miraculously endowed with flesh, blood and speech."

In his early essay, "Dante . . . Bruno . Vico . . Joyce," Beckett praised James Joyce's *Work in Progress* with the judgment, "Here form *is* content, content *is* form."[7] The same might be said of Beckett's drama. The content to which Beckett's innovative dramatic forms correspond is not new; he treats of the same preoccupations with the relations between the human consciousness and reality, between self and other, between subject and object, as have the major scientists, philosophers, writers, and artists of our century. His, and our, universe is an incoherent, fluctuating, and imperceptible domain where stable, unequivocal vision is impossible. Each human being that inhabits it creates its own reality, which is never the same from one moment to the next, because the subject itself is constantly changing in both space and time. Such a universe poses an obvious dilemma for a dramatist whose works address themselves, by definition, to a group of spectators: if even one consciousness cannot attain a fixed perspective upon either the world around it or itself, how can a modern artist ever hope to capture and formalize any vision, even for himself, let alone for an audience composed of other consciousnesses that are just as mobile in space and time as his own? Beckett's answer to this question has been consistently pessimistic over the years: he cannot. Yet knowledge of the impossibility of the task at hand seems to have served more as an impetus than as a hindrance to Beckett's creative efforts. The "obligation to express" of which he spoke in his "Three Dialogues"[8] has compelled him to continue seeking an unattainable solution to the problem of expressing the inexpressible, naming the unnamable, and seeing the unseeable, in much the same way that his characters doggedly pursue the realization of their impossible goals. In spite of the admitted futility of his mission, or perhaps because of it, Beckett has come closer than any modern author to creating a drama of and for his era. His solutions are never final, as the evolution of his work makes clear, and as befits an indeterminate world bereft of finality. After all these years, Beckett is still hard at work trying to find "a form that accommodates the mess."[9]

NOTES

From time to time, Beckett uses three dots to separate phrases. In those cases, instead of the conventional ellipses used within quotations, the author has added a fourth dot to Beckett's three to indicate an omission. —Editor

Introduction

1. Samuel Beckett, "Recent Irish Poetry," in *Disjecta: Miscellaneous Writings and a Dramatic Fragment*, intro. and ed. Ruby Cohn (London: Calder, 1983), p. 70.

2. Beckett, as quoted in Tom Driver, "Beckett by the Madeleine," *Columbia University Forum*, 4 (Summer 1961), 23.

3. For a thorough discussion of the sources of Beckett's ideas in Western philosophy, see David Hesla, *The Shape of Chaos: An Interpretation of the Art of Samuel Beckett* (Minneapolis: Univ. of Minnesota Press, 1971).

4. Beckett, as quoted in Driver, p. 23.

5. Billie Whitelaw, in a telephone conversation with Ruby Cohn, as quoted in Ruby Cohn, *Just Play: Beckett's Theater* (Princeton: Princeton Univ. Press, 1980), p. 31.

6. Ibid.

7. See Pierre Francastel, *La Figure et le lieu* (Paris: Gallimard, 1967), for a discussion of the relation of esthetic techniques to the imaginary structures of artists and their public.

8. Michel Foucault, *Les Mots et les choses* (Paris: Gallimard-NRF, 1966), p. 86.

9. Beckett, as quoted in Driver, p. 23. (Beckett is here referring specifically to Paris' "La Madeleine" church and its surroundings.)

10. Jean-Marie Apostolidès, "Perception du temps et catégories dramatiques au 17è siècle," *Stanford French Review*, 3 (Winter 1979), 384.

11. Albert Flocon and René Taton, *La Perspective* 3d ed.

Presses Universitaires de France-Que sais-je?, 1978), pp. 41–42; Erwin Panofsky, *La Perspective comme forme symbolique et autres essais* (Paris: Minuit, 1975), p. 129.

12. Jean-Marie Apostolidès, "Le Regard en perspective" (unpublished manuscript).

13. George Kernodle, *From Art to Theater: Form and Convention in the Renaissance* (Chicago: Univ. of Chicago Press, 1944). p. 175.

14. See, for example, Diderot's advice to actors: "Imaginez, sur le bord du théâtre, un grand mur qui vous sépare du parterre; jouez comme si la toile ne se levait pas." "De la poésie dramatique," in *Oeuvres complètes de Diderot*, ed. J. Assézat, VII (Paris: Garnier, 1875), p. 345.

15. Marcel Proust, *A l'ombre des jeunes filles en fleurs* (Paris: Gallimard-Pléiade, 1954), pp. 446–47.

16. Apostolidès, "Perception du temps," p. 386.

17. Erich Auerbach, *Mimesis: The Representation of Reality in Western Literature*, trans. Willard R. Trask (Princeton: Princeton Univ. Press, 1953), pp. 551, 549.

18. Marcel Proust, *La Prisonnière* (Paris: Gallimard-Folio, 1954), p. 80.

19. Ibid., p. 227.

20. Beckett, *Proust* (New York: Grove, 1957), p. 32. Hereafter, insofar as possible, all references to Beckett's works will be to the American Grove Press editions and will appear in the text. If another edition is cited, it will be referenced by a note. I have chosen to cite Beckett's works in English, wherever possible, to lend unity to the style of this essay, since Beckett himself has translated nearly all of the works which he did not originally compose in English. When an English text is unavailable or if the French text conveys a different stylistic or conceptual point than the English, I shall cite the French version; and references for French citations that appear in the text will be to the Editions de Minuit.

21. Marcel Proust, *Le Temps retrouvé* (Paris: Gallimard-Folio, 1954), p. 262.

22. Ibid., pp. 257–58.

23. Apostolidès, "Perception du temps," p. 385.

24. Wylie Sypher, *Rococo to Cubism in Art and Literature* (New York: Vintage, 1960), pp. 289, 294.

25. Luigi Pirandello, *Tonight We Improvise*, trans. Samuel Putnam (New York: E. P. Dutton, 1932), p. 115.

26. Dominique Fernandez, "Pirandello: un trou dans le ciel de papier," *L'Express*, 22 Oct. 1982, p. 19.

27. Sören Kierkegaard, *The Concept of Dread*, trans. Walter Lowrie (Princeton: Princeton Univ. Press, 1944), p. 55.

28. Ilya Prigogine, lecture delivered at the International Symposium on Disorder and Order, Stanford University, 14 Sept. 1981.

29. Corneille Castoriadis, "Science moderne et interrogation philosophique," *Encyclopaedia universalis*, 1977 ed., XVII, 45.

30. B. S. de Witt, "The Many-Universes Interpretation of Quantum Theory," in *Foundations of Quantum Mechanics*, ed. B. d'Espagnat (New York: Academic Press, 1971), p. 226, as quoted in Castoriadis, p. 49.

31. Sigmund Freud, *Introductory Lectures on Psychoanalysis*, trans. and ed. James Strachey (New York: Norton-Liveright, 1977), p. 22.
32. Ibid., p. 285.
33. R. D. Laing, *The Divided Self* (New York: Penguin, 1965), pp. 180–81.
34. Ibid., pp. 39–43.
35. Franz Kafka, "Conversation with the Supplicant," in *The Penal Colony*, trans. Willa and Edwin Muir (New York: Schocken, 1961), p. 14.
36. Jean-Paul Sartre, *L'Etre et le néant: Essai d'ontologie phénoménologique* (Paris: Gallimard, 1943), p. 533.
37. Eric Bentley, *The Playwright as Thinker* (New York: Meridian, 1955), p. 229.
38. Beckett, "La Peinture des van Velde ou le monde et le pantalon," in *Disjecta*, p. 127.
39. Ibid., p. 128.
40. Ibid., p. 129.
41. Beckett, "Peintres de l'empêchement," in *Disjecta*, p. 135.
42. Ibid., p. 137.
43. Stéphane Mallarmé, "La Musique et les lettres," in *Oeuvres complètes*, eds. Henri Mondor and G. Jean-Aubry (Paris: Gallimard-NRF, 1945), p. 647.
44. Beckett, "Three Dialogues," in *Disjecta*, p. 139.
45. Beckett, "La Peinture des van Velde," p. 129.
46. Flocon and Taton, pp. 89–90.
47. Susan Sontag, *On Photography* (New York: Delta, 1977), p. 92, note.
48. H. W. Janson, *History of Art: A Survey of the Major Visual Arts from the Dawn of History to the Present Day* (Englewood Cliffs, N. J.: Prentice-Hall; New York: Harry N. Abrams, 1962), p. 492.
49. Guillaume Apollinaire, *Les Peintres cubistes* (1913; rpt. Paris: Hermann, 1965), pp. 51–52.
50. Janson, p. 523.
51. Alberto Giacometti, interview with André Parinaud, "Pourquoi je suis sculpteur?" *Arts*, 13 June 1962, p. 5.

Chapter 1. "In Boundless Space, In Endless Time"

1. Beckett, as quoted in Paul-Louis Mignon, "Le Théâtre de A jusqu'à Z: Samuel Beckett," *L'Avant-Scène*, 313 (15 June 1964), 8.
2. Hugh Kenner, *Samuel Beckett: A Critical Study*, rev. ed. (Berkeley: Univ. of California Press, 1968), p. 133.
3. Lawrence E. Harvey, *Samuel Beckett Poet and Critic* (Princeton: Princeton Univ. Press, 1970), p. 427.
4. Ibid., p. 356.
5. Beckett, as quoted in Cohn, *Just Play* (see Intro., n. 5), p. 252.
6. Henri Bergson, *Essai sur les données immédiates de la conscience* (1888; rpt. Geneva: Editions Albert Skira, 1945), p. 178.
7. Arthur Schopenhauer, *Selections*, intro. and ed. DeWitt H. Parker (New York: Scribner's, 1928), p. 177.

8. René Descartes, *Discours de la méthode*, ed. Jean-Marie Beyssade (Paris: Librairie Générale Française-Livre de Poche, 1973), p. 129.

9. Beckett, "Dante . . . Bruno . Vico . . Joyce," in *Disjecta* (see Intro., n. 1), p. 33.

10. Eugène Ionesco, "A Propos de Beckett," in *L'Herne*: *Samuel Beckett*, eds. Tom Bishop and Raymond Federman (Paris: Editions de l'Herne, 1976), p. 150.

11. *Webster's New Collegiate Dictionary*, 1975 ed.

12. This common Beckettian expression may be an allusion to Dante's characterization of Adam as "the man that was never born": *Paradiso*, Vol. III of *The Divine Comedy*, trans. and ed. John D. Sinclair (New York: Oxford Univ. Press, 1979), canto vii, p. 103.

13. Beckett, "Intercessions by Denis Devlin," in *Disjecta*, p. 91.

14. Sartre, *L'Etre et le néant* (see Intro., n. 36), p. 625.

15. Ibid., pp. 169–70.

16. Ibid., pp. 224, 255.

17. Beckett, "La Peinture des van Velde" (see Intro., n. 38), p. 126.

18. Sartre, p. 598.

19. Martin Esslin, Intro., *Samuel Beckett: A Collection of Critical Essays* (Englewood Cliffs, N. J.: Prentice-Hall, 1965), p. 7.

20. Cohn, *Just Play*, p. 57.

21. Ibid., p. 36.

22. Ibid., p. 57. While Cohn does not name the television plays to which she is referring, we may assume them to be *Eh Joe*, *Ghost Trio*, and *. . . but the clouds . . .* .

23. Ibid.

24. Harvey, p. 194.

25. Beckett, *Eleutheria*, unpublished play, ca. 1947, p. 116.

26. Harvey, p. 187.

27. Beckett, "Excerpts from Dream of Fair to Middling Women," in *Disjecta*, p. 48.

28. Sartre, p. 63.

29. The English of *How It Is* is somewhat different: "and you bad to worse bad to worse steadily" (p. 9).

30. *Webster's New Collegiate Dictionary*, 1975 ed.

31. Beckett, "La Peinture des van Velde," p. 128.

32. Beckett, "Le Concentrisme," in *Disjecta*, p. 38.

33. Schopenhauer, pp. 91–92.

34. James Joyce, *A Portrait of the Artist as a Young Man* (1916; rpt. New York: Viking, 1964), pp. 112–13.

35. Dante, canto xxxiii, p. 483.

36. Ibid., canto xxviii, p. 407.

37. Ibid., canto xxii, p. 321; canto xxvii, p. 393.

38. Ibid., canto xxxiii, p. 483.

39. Ibid., canto xxvi, p. 379.

40. Ibid., canto xxxiii, p. 483.

41. Ibid., pp. 483–85.

42. Ibid., pp. 484–85.

43. Ibid., canto xxiv, p. 351.

44. Ibid., canto i, p. 23.
45. Ibid., canto xxxiii, p. 485.
46. Beckett, "Three Dialogues" (see Intro., n. 44), pp. 139, 142.
47. Joyce, p. 240.
48. Ibid., pp. 127–28.

Chapter 2. *Endgame*

1. See Ruby Cohn, *Samuel Beckett: The Comic Gamut* (New Brunswick, N. J.: Rutgers Univ. Press, 1962), pp. 226–42, for a discussion of this as well as numerous other biblical references in *Endgame.*

2. Ibid., pp. 229, 233, 236, and 241, for this and further interpretations of the names of *Endgame*'s characters.

3. Charles Lyons, "Beckett's *Endgame*: An Anti-Myth of Creation," *Modern Drama*, 7 (Sept. 1964), 204–9.

4. Martin Esslin, *The Theatre of the Absurd* (Garden City, N. Y.: Doubleday, 1961), p. 36.

5. Beckett, in a letter to Alan Schneider, 29 Dec. 1957, in *Disjecta* (see Intro., n. 1), p. 109.

6. See, for example, Esslin, *The Theatre of the Absurd*, pp. 30–31, and Lyons, "Beckett's *Endgame.*"

7. J. Huizinga, *Homo ludens* (Paris: Gallimard, 1951), pp. 29–31, 35, 176–77, 217.

8. B. S. Hammond, "Beckett and Pinter: Towards a Grammar of the Absurd," *Journal of Beckett Studies*, 4 (Spring 1979), 37.

9. See Edith Kern, "Samuel Beckett et les poches de Lemuel Gulliver," trans. Paul Rozenberg, *Revue des Lettres Modernes. Samuel Beckett: Configuration Critique, no. 8*, 100 (1964), 69–81, for a discussion of the different world views implied by the treatment of objects such as eyeglasses in Swift and Beckett.

Chapter 3. *Cascando*

1. Critics are not in agreement as to the year of composition. The editors of *L'Herne: Samuel Beckett* (see chap. 1, n. 10) and Ludovic Janvier, in *Beckett* (Paris: Seuil-Ecrivains de Toujours, 1969), give 1963 as the date of writing. The editors of *A Student's Guide to the plays of Samuel Beckett* (London: Faber and Faber, 1978) say *Cascando* was written in 1962. Federman and Fletcher's bibliography, *Samuel Beckett: His Works and His Critics* (Berkeley: Univ. of California Press, 1970), supplies only the date of publication. I have cited the 1961 date supplied by Clas Zilliacus in *Beckett and Broadcasting: A Study of the Works of Samuel Beckett for and in Radio and Television* (Åbo, Finland: Åbo Akademi, 1976), p. 118, because Mr. Zilliacus's documentation of the play's composition is extensive and convincing.

2. See Martin Esslin, "Samuel Beckett and the Art of Broadcasting," in *Mediations: Essays on Brecht, Beckett, and the Media* (Baton Rouge: Louisiana State Univ. Press, 1980), pp. 135–37 and 141–50, for a comprehensive discussion of the close rapport between these two works, as well as an analysis of Beckett's *Roughs for Radio* as preliminary sketches for them.

3. Irving Wardle, intro., *New English Dramatists 12: Radio Plays* (Harmondsworth, 1968), pp. 14–15, as quoted in Zilliacus, p. 14.

4. Charles Hampton, in a staging report for 1967 stage version of *All That Fall* at Univ. of Calgary (directed by Hampton), as quoted in Zilliacus, p. 179.

5. *Cascando* is available in three Grove press editions listed in the Bibliography: *Cascando and Other Short Dramatic Pieces*; *I Can't Go On, I'll Go On*; and *The Collected Shorter Plays of Samuel Beckett*. Page numbers in this chapter refer to the first edition.

6. Cohn, *Just Play* (see Intro., n. 5), p. 76.

7. Esslin, *Mediations*, pp. 77–78, 146–50.

8. Beckett, in a letter to Herbert Myron, 21 Sept. 1962, written to accompany donation of a batch of *Cascando* manuscripts to the Theatre Collection of Harvard College Library, as quoted in Zilliacus, p. 118.

9. Esslin, *Mediations*, p. 78.

10. Schopenhauer, *Selections* (see chap. 1, n. 7), p. 180.

11. Ibid., p. 183.

12. Esslin, *Mediations*, p. 77.

13. Hannah Copeland, *Art and the Artist in the Works of Samuel Beckett* (The Hague: Mouton, 1975), pp. 134–35.

14. According to Federman and Fletcher (p. 70), the play's original title was *Calando*, a musical term indicating diminishing volume and decreasing tempo. Beckett changed it to *Cascando* when French radio officials pointed out that "calendos" is French slang for "cheese."

15. Since this analysis will proceed page by page through the text of *Cascando*, page numbers will be supplied only when discussion of a new page begins or when material from another part of the play is cited.

16. Beckett, "Proust in Pieces," in *Disjecta* (see Intro., n. 1), p. 64.

17. Beckett, "Dream of Fair to Middling Women" (see chap. 1, n. 27), p. 47.

18. Albert Camus, *La Peste* (Paris: Gallimard-Folio, 1947), p. 99.

19. Ibid., p. 100.

20. Zilliacus sees in this phrase a reference to the thousand and one tales of the *Arabian Nights*, "told by another storyteller, kept alive by telling stories," p. 129.

21. Beckett, as quoted in Driver (see Intro., n. 2), p. 23.

22. Beckett, "Three Dialogues" (see Intro., n. 44), p. 139.

Chapter 4. *Film*

1. *Film* is available in three Grove Press editions listed in the Bibliography: *Cascando and Other Short Dramatic Pieces*, *The Collected Shorter Plays of Samuel Beckett*, and *Film: Complete Scenario/Illustrations/Production Shots*. Page numbers in this chapter refer to the last edition.

2. See Sylvie Debevec Henning, "*Film*: A Dialogue Between Beckett and Berkeley," *Journal of Beckett Studies*, 7 (Spring 1982), 89–99, for a discussion of Beckett's reasons for citing Berkeley's phrase at

the beginning of *Film*, and a comparison of the two writers' notions of perception and self-perception.

3. Alan Schneider, "On Directing *Film*," in *Film: Complete Scenario/Illustrations/Production Shots*, p. 65.

4. As quoted in S. E. Gontarski, "*Film* and Formal Integrity," in *Samuel Beckett: Humanistic Perspectives*, eds. Morris Beja, S. E. Gontarski and Pierre Astier (N.p.: Ohio State Univ. Press, 1983), p. 135.

5. I say "almost" because the eyes of both camera and spectators still perceive O even when he believes himself to be totally alone.

6. Raymond Federman, "Film," in *Samuel Beckett: The Critical Heritage*, eds. Lawrence Graver and Raymond Federman (London: Routledge & Kegan Paul, 1979), pp. 279, 281.

7. See Schneider's essay for a lively and fascinating discussion of this and other technical problems involved in the making of *Film*.

8. Kernodle, *From Art to Theater* (see Intro., n. 13), p. 49.

9. See, for example, Ludovic Janvier, *Pour Samuel Beckett* (Paris: Minuit, 1966), pp. 73–74.

10. Schneider, "On Directing *Film*," p. 72.

11. Ibid., p. 88. (The decision to use the eye at the beginning was made during the shooting of *Film*, when the original opening sequence was scrapped.)

12. William Van Wert, " 'To Be is to be Perceived': Time and Point of View in Samuel Beckett's *Film*," *Literature/Film Quarterly*, 8 (Apr. 1980), 136.

13. Schneider, "On Directing *Film*," p. 65.

14. Ibid., p. 85.

15. Ibid., Picture Editor's note, p. 33, and Schneider, "On Directing *Film*," p. 85.

16. Henri Bergson, "The Cinematographic View of Becoming," in *Zeno's Paradoxes*, ed. Wesley C. Salmon (Indianapolis: Bobbs-Merrill, 1970), p. 61.

17. Ibid., p. 62.

18. Beckett, as quoted in Martha Fehsenfeld, "Beckett's Late Works: An Appraisal," *Modern Drama*, 25 (Sept. 1982), 358.

19. Schneider, "On Directing *Film*," p. 90.

20. Beckett, in a letter to Alan Schneider, 29 Dec. 1957 (see chap. 2, n. 5), p. 109.

Chapter 5. *Eh Joe*

1. *Eh Joe* is available in three Grove Press editions listed in the Bibliography: *Cascando and Other Short Dramatic Pieces*; *I Can't Go On, I'll Go On*; and *The Collected Shorter Plays of Samuel Beckett*. Page numbers in this chapter refer to the first edition.

2. Jack MacGowran, "MacGowran on Beckett," interview by Richard Toscan, *Theatre Quarterly*, 3 (July–Sept. 1973), 20, as quoted in Zilliacus, (see chap. 3, n. 1), p. 198.

3. Beckett's recent television play, *Quadrat I + II*, first shows four figures in white, blue, red, and yellow cloaks moving along

the sides and diagonals of a square, accompanied by percussion instruments. Then it shows the same figures moving along the same lines, but much slower, without the percussion accompaniment, and in black and white. Beckett's comment upon viewing the recording of the second portion was: "Good—this is a hundred thousand years later!" (As quoted in Martin Esslin, "A Poetry of Moving Images," unpublished paper delivered in Austin, Texas, 23 Mar. 1984, pp. 14–15).

4. Esslin, *Mediations* (see chap. 3, n. 2), p. 151.

5. Zilliacus (see chap. 3, n. 1), pp. 185–86.

6. Esslin, *Mediations*, pp. 151–52.

Chapter 6. *A Piece of Monologue*

1. This information, as well as certain other details about the staging of the play included in this chapter, comes from a talk delivered by Warrilow to Martin Esslin's seminar on Beckett at Stanford University in April 1980.

2. *A Piece of Monologue* is available in two Grove Press editions listed in the Bibliography: *Rockaby and Other Short Pieces* and *The Collected Shorter Plays of Samuel Beckett*. Page numbers in this chapter refer to the first edition.

3. It is true that Beckett used a single character and no voices in *Film* to achieve this goal, but the dual-vision technique employed there was less than totally successful. Of the plays not included in this study, *Not I* (1972) was Beckett's first dramatization of a consciousness to use a single character who spoke her own text upon stage.

4. Esslin, *Mediations* (see chap. 3, n. 2), pp. 117–24, and seminar on Beckett at Stanford University in April 1980.

5. Since this analysis will proceed page by page through the text of *A Piece of Monologue*, page numbers will be supplied only when discussion of a new page begins or when material from another part of the play is cited.

6. Kristin Morrison, "The Rip Word in *A Piece of Monologue*," *Modern Drama*, 25 (Sept. 1982), 350.

7. If two and a half billion seconds have passed, the man in question is now seventy-nine years old. If, on the other hand, thirty thousand nights have elapsed, the man is eighty-two. Beckett, with his love for numbers, was certainly aware of this discrepancy when he wrote the text. He may have meant it as a joke on his critics who, he knew, would be the only ones to bother making such calculations. Or he may have intended this mathematical inconsistency to subtly underscore the way in which the text moves back and forth through time, seeming to come to rest upon the figure before our eyes only to pass imperceptibly through him and on to another time, and thus another man.

8. Comparison with the French translation shows the first reading to be the favored one: "Né au plus noir de la nuit" (p. 30).

9. Hersh Zeifman notes that these words are an allusion to Shakespeare's *The Merchant of Venice*: "The quality of mercy is not strained, / It droppeth as the gentle rain from heaven / Upon the place

beneath" (IV:i:189–91). "*Come and Go*: A Criticule," in Beja (see chap. 4, n. 4), p. 143.

10. An almost identical passage occurs in the text of *Company*: "Light dying. Soon none left to die. No. No such thing as no light. Died on to dawn and never died" (p. 54).

11. Laing, *The Divided Self* (see Intro., n. 33), pp. 162, 66.

12. Beckett used the third-person singular form in his French translation.

13. "Turn from it in the end to face the darkened room" (p. 75); "Move on to other matters. Try to move on" (p. 76); "Feel soft touch of lip on lip," "Feel soft touch of tongue on lips" (p. 77).

14. This blackout is specified only in the stage directions to the later French translation.

Chapter 7. *Rockaby*

1. Charles Lyons, "Perceiving *Rockaby*—As a Text, As a Text by Samuel Beckett, As a Text for Performance," *Comparative Drama*, 16 (Winter 1982–83), 301.

2. *Rockaby* is available in two Grove Press editions listed in the Bibliography: *Rockaby and Other Short Pieces* and *The Collected Shorter Plays of Samuel Beckett*. Page numbers in this chapter refer to the first edition.

3. Enoch Brater, "Light, Sound, Movement, and Action in Beckett's *Rockaby*," *Modern Drama*, 25 (Sept. 1982), 345.

4. Charles Marowitz, "Paris Log," *Encore*, 9 (Mar.–Apr. 1962), 44.

5. Antonin Artaud, *Le Théâtre et son double* (1938; rpt. Paris: Gallimard, 1964), p. 193.

6. Since this analysis will proceed page by page through the text of the fourth part of *Rockaby*, page numbers will be supplied only when discussion of a new page begins or when material from another part of the play is cited.

7. Specified only in the later French version.

8. Cohn, *Just Play* (see Intro., n. 5), p. 35.

9. Ibid., pp. 28, 31.

10. Schopenhauer, *Selections* (see chap. 1, n. 7), p. 117.

11. Cohn, *Just Play*, pp. 71–72.

12. Beckett, "Peintres de l'empêchement" (see Intro., n. 41), p. 136.

13. Artaud, p. 57.

14. Beckett, as quoted in Cohn, *Just Play*, p. 172.

15. Fehsenfeld, "Beckett's Late Works" (see chap. 4, n. 18), p. 357.

Conclusion

1. Beckett, "Dream of Fair to Middling Women" (see chap. 1, n. 27), p. 44.

2. Beckett, as quoted by Israel Shenker, "Moody Man of Letters," in Graver (see chap. 4, n. 6), p. 148.

3. Beckett, in a letter to Axel Kaun, trans. Martin Esslin, in *Disjecta* (see Intro., n. 1), pp. 170–73.

4. Esslin, "A Poetry of Moving Images" (see chap. 5, n. 3), p. 12.

5. Witness, for a recent example, the controversy surrounding the 1985 production of *Endgame* by Boston's American Repertory Theatre, when Beckett expressed his disapproval of the liberties taken with his staging directions.

6. Pirandello, *Tonight We Improvise* (see Intro., n. 25), pp. 28–29.

7. Beckett, "Dante . . . Bruno . Vico . . Joyce" (see chap. 1, n. 9), p. 27.

8. Beckett, "Three Dialogues" (see Intro., n. 44), p. 139.

9. Beckett, as quoted in Driver (see Intro., n. 2), p. 23.

BIBLIOGRAPHY

WORKS BY SAMUEL BECKETT

This is a list of the most readily available English and French editions of Beckett's works; for information on other editions, see: *Samuel Beckett: His Works and His Critics*, by Raymond Federman and John Fletcher (Berkeley: Univ. of California Press, 1970).

"Assumption." *transition*, 16–17 (June 1929), 268–71.

Cascando and Other Short Dramatic Pieces. New York: Grove, 1968(?). Contains *Cascando, Words and Music, Eh Joe, Play, Come and Go*, and *Film*.

"A Case in a Thousand." *The Bookman*, 86 (Aug. 1934), 241–42.

Catastrophe et autres dramaticules. Paris: Minuit, 1982. Contains *Cette fois, Solo, Berceuse, Impromptu d'Ohio*, and *Catastrophe*.

Collected poems in English and French. London: Calder, 1977.

The Collected Shorter Plays of Samuel Beckett. New York: Grove, 1984. Contains *All That Fall, Act Without Words I, Act Without Words II, Krapp's Last Tape, Rough for Theatre I, Rough for Theatre II, Embers, Rough for Radio I, Rough for Radio II, Words and Music, Cascando, Play, Film, The Old Tune, Come and Go, Eh Joe, Breath, Not I, That Time, Footfalls, Ghost Trio, . . . but the clouds . . ., A Piece of Monologue, Rockaby, Ohio Impromptu, Quad, Catastrophe, Nacht und Träume*, and *What Where*.

Comédie et actes divers. Paris: Minuit, 1972. Contains *Comédie, Va-et-vient, Cascando, Paroles et musique, Dis Joe, Actes sans paroles I et II, Film*, and *Souffle*.

Comment c'est. Paris: Minuit, 1961.

Compagnie. Paris: Minuit, 1980.
Company. New York: Grove, 1980.
Le Dépeupleur. Paris: Minuit, 1970.
La Dernière Bande suivi de Cendres. Paris: Minuit, 1959.
Disjecta: *Miscellaneous Writings and a Dramatic Fragment*. Intro. and ed. Ruby Cohn. London: Calder, 1983. Contains "Dante . . . Bruno . Vico . . Joyce," "Le Concentrisme," "Excerpts from Dream of Fair to Middling Women," "German Letter of 1937," "Les Deux Besoins," "Schwabenstreich," "Proust in Pieces," "Poems. By Rainer Maria Rilke," "Humanistic Quietism," "Recent Irish Poetry," "Ex Cathezra," "Papini's Dante," "The Essential and the Incidental," "Censorship in the Saorstat," "An Imaginative Work!," "Intercessions by Denis Devlin," "MacGreevy on Yeats," "The Possessed," "On *Murphy* (to McGreevy)," "On *Murphy* (to Reavey)," "On Works to 1951," "On *Endgame* (to Schneider)," "On *Play*," "On *Murphy* (to Sighle Kennedy)," "On *Endgame* (program note)," "Geer van Velde," "La Peinture des van Velde ou le monde et le pantalon," "Peintres de l'empêchement," "Three Dialogues," "Henri Hayden, homme-peintre," "Hommage à Jack B. Yeats," "Homage to Jack B. Yeats," "Henri Hayden," "Bram van Velde," "Pour Avigdor Arikha," "For Avigdor Arikha," and *Human Wishes*.
Eleutheria. Unpublished play in three acts, ca. 1947.
En attendant Godot. Paris: Minuit, 1952.
Endgame followed by Act Without Words. New York: Grove, 1958.
Ends and Odds. New York: Grove, 1976. Contains *Not I*, *That Time*, *Footfalls*, *Ghost Trio*, *Rough for Theatre I*, *Rough for Theatre II*, *Rough for Radio I*, and *Rough for Radio II*.
Film: *Complete Scenario/Illustrations/Production Shots*. New York: Grove, 1970.
Fin de partie. Paris: Minuit, 1957.
First Love and Other Shorts. New York: Grove, 1974. Contains "First Love," "From an Abandoned Work," "Enough," "Imagination Dead Imagine," "Ping," "Not I," and "Breath."
Fizzles. New York: Grove, 1976. Contains "Fizzle 1," "Fizzle 2," "Fizzle 3: Afar a bird," "Fizzle 4," "Fizzle 5," "Fizzle 6," "Fizzle 7: Still," and "Fizzle 8: For to end yet again."
Happy Days. New York: Grove, 1961.
"Heard in the Dark 2." *Journal of Beckett Studies*, 5 (Autumn 1979), 7–8.
How It Is. New York: Grove, 1964.
I Can't Go On, I'll Go On: *A Selection from Samuel Beckett's Work*. Ed. Richard W. Seaver. New York: Grove, 1976. Contains "Dante and the Lobster," "From *Murphy*," "From *Watt*," "Whoroscope," "From *Echo's Bones*," "Cascando" (poem), "Saint-Lô," "Dante . . . Bruno . Vico . . Joyce," "First Love," "From *Mercier and Camier*," "The Expelled," *Molloy* (Part I), "From *The Unnamable*," "Texts for Nothing 11, 13," *Waiting for Godot*, *Krapp's Last Tape*, *How It Is* (Part I), "Imagination

Dead Imagine," "Lessness," *Cascando* (play), *Eh Joe*, *Not I*, and *That Time*.
Ill Seen Ill Said. New York: Grove, 1981.
L'Innommable. Paris: Minuit, 1953.
Krapp's Last Tape and Other Dramatic Pieces. New York: Grove, 1960. Contains *Krapp's Last Tape*, *All That Fall*, *Embers*, *Act Without Words I*, and *Act Without Words II*.
The Lost Ones. New York: Grove, 1972.
Malone meurt. Paris: Minuit, 1951.
Mal vu mal dit. Paris: Minuit, 1981.
Mercier and Camier. New York: Grove, 1975.
Mercier et Camier. Paris: Minuit, 1970.
Molloy. Paris: Minuit, 1951.
More Pricks Than Kicks. New York: Grove, 1972. Contains "Dante and the Lobster," "Fingal," "Ding-Dong," "A Wet Night," "Love and Lethe," "Walking Out," "What a Misfortune," "The Smeraldina's Billet Doux," "Yellow," and "Draff."
Murphy. New York: Grove, 1957.
Murphy. Paris: Minuit, 1965.
"Neither." *Journal of Beckett Studies*, 4 (Spring 1979), vii.
Nouvelles et textes pour rien. Paris: Minuit, 1958. Contains "L'Expulsé," "Le Calmant," "La Fin," and "Textes pour rien."
Ohio Impromptu, Catastrophe, and What Where. New York: Grove, 1984.
Oh les beaux jours suivi de Pas moi. Paris: Minuit, 1974.
"One Evening." *Journal of Beckett Studies*, 6 (Autumn 1980), 7–8.
Pas suivi de quatre esquisses. Paris: Minuit, 1978. Contains *Pas*, *Fragment de théâtre I*, *Fragment de théâtre II*, *Pochade radiophonique*, and *Esquisse radiophonique*.
Poèmes suivi de mirlitonnades. Paris: Minuit, 1978.
Poems in English. New York: Grove, 1961. Contains "Whoroscope," "Echo's Bones," "Two Poems," and "Quatre poèmes."
Pour finir encore et autres foirades. Paris: Minuit, 1976. Contains untitled foirades and "Au loin un oiseau," "Se voir," and "Immobile."
Premier Amour. Paris: Minuit, 1970.
Proust. New York: Grove, 1957.
Rockaby and Other Short Pieces. New York: Grove, 1981. Contains *Rockaby*, *Ohio Impromptu*, *All Strange Away*, and *A Piece of Monologue*.
"Sedendo et Quiesciendo [*sic*]." *transition*, 21 (Mar. 1932), 13–20.
Stories and Texts for Nothing. New York: Grove, 1967. Contains "The Expelled," "The Calmative," "The End," and "Texts for Nothing."
Têtes mortes. Paris: Minuit, 1972. Contains "D'un ouvrage abandonné," "Assez," "Imagination morte imaginez," "Bing," and "Sans."
"Text." *New Review* (Apr. 1932), 57.
Three Novels. New York: Grove, 1965. Contains *Molloy*, *Malone Dies*, and *The Unnamable*.
Tous ceux qui tombent. Paris: Minuit, 1957.
Waiting for Godot. New York: Grove, 1954.
Watt. New York: Grove, 1959.

Watt. Paris: Minuit, 1968.
Worstward Ho. London: Calder, 1983.

WORKS ABOUT SAMUEL BECKETT

This is a selective list of Beckett criticism which has proven most useful to my study. For a more complete list of Beckett criticism, see *Samuel Beckett: His Works and His Critics*, by Raymond Federman and John Fletcher (Berkeley: Univ. of California Press, 1970).

In cases where collections of pieces about Beckett appeared either in book form or in a special issue of a periodical, I have listed both the collection and the individual articles which I found most valuable.

Anders, Günther. "Being Without Time: On Beckett's Play *Waiting for Godot*." Trans. Martin Esslin. In *Samuel Beckett: A Collection of Critical Essays*. Ed. Martin Esslin. Englewood Cliffs, N.J.: Prentice-Hall, 1965, 140–51.

Bair, Deirdre. *Samuel Beckett: A Biography*. New York: Harcourt Brace, 1980.

Beja, Morris, S. E. Gontarski and Pierre Astier, eds. *Samuel Beckett: Humanistic Perspectives*. N.p.: Ohio State Univ. Press, 1983.

Benmussa, Simone. "Samuel Beckett." *Livres de France*, 18 (Jan. 1967), 2.

Bishop, Tom and Raymond Federman, eds. *L'Herne: Samuel Beckett*. Paris: Editions de l'Herne, 1976.

Blanchot, Maurice. "Où maintenant? Qui maintenant?" In *Le Livre à venir*. Paris: Gallimard, 1959, 256–64.

Bonnefoi, Geneviève. "Textes pour rien?" Trans. Jean M. Sommermeyer. In *Samuel Beckett: The Critical Heritage*. Eds. Lawrence Graver and Raymond Federman. London: Routledge & Kegan Paul, 1979, 139–45.

Bosquet, Alain. "Poème pour Sam." In *L'Herne: Samuel Beckett*. Eds. Tom Bishop and Raymond Federman. Paris: Editions de l'Herne, 1976, 152–54.

———. Rev. of *Mercier et Camier*, *Premier Amour*, and *Le Dépeupleur*. Trans. Jean M. Sommermeyer. In *Samuel Beckett: The Critical Heritage*. Eds. Lawrence Graver and Raymond Federman. London: Routledge & Kegan Paul, 1979, 316–21.

Brater, Enoch. "Fragment and Beckett's Form in *That Time* and *Footfalls*." *Journal of Beckett Studies*, 2 (Summer 1977), 70–81.

———. "Light, Sound, Movement, and Action in Beckett's *Rockaby*." *Modern Drama*, 25 (Sept. 1982), 342–48.

Brustein, Robert. "An Evening of *Déjà-vu*." In *Samuel Beckett: The Critical Heritage*. Eds. Lawrence Graver and Raymond Federman. London: Routledge & Kegan Paul, 1979, 258–61.

Calder, John. "La Concentration de Samuel Beckett." Trans. Nicole Bonvalet. In *L'Herne: Samuel Beckett*. Eds. Tom Bishop and Raymond Federman. Paris: Editions de l'Herne, 1976, 162–65.

———. Rev. of *The Lively Arts: Three Plays by Samuel Beckett* on BBC 2, 17 Apr. 1977. *Journal of Beckett Studies*, 2 (Summer 1977), 117–21.

Chambers, Ross. "Beckett's Brinkmanship." In *Samuel Beckett: A Collection of Critical Essays*. Ed. Martin Esslin. Englewood Cliffs, N.J.: Prentice-Hall, 1965, 152–68.

———. "Samuel Beckett and the Padded Cell." *Meanjin*, 21 (Dec. 1962), 451–62.

Cohn, Ruby. *Just Play: Beckett's Theater*. Princeton: Princeton Univ. Press, 1980.

———. "Plays and Players in the Plays of Samuel Beckett." *Yale French Studies*, 29 (Spring-Summer 1962), 43–48.

———. *Samuel Beckett: The Comic Gamut*. New Brunswick, N.J.: Rutgers Univ. Press, 1962.

———. "Waiting is All." *Modern Drama*, 3 (Sept. 1960), 162–67.

———. "*Watt* à la lumière du *Château*." Trans. Madeleine Jambon. In *L'Herne: Samuel Beckett*. Eds. Tom Bishop and Raymond Federman. Paris: Editions de l'Herne, 1976, 306–17.

Copeland, Hannah C. *Art and the Artist in the Works of Samuel Beckett*. The Hague: Mouton, 1975.

Cousineau, Thomas J. "*Watt*: Language as Interdiction and Consolation." *Journal of Beckett Studies*, 4 (Spring 1979), 1–13.

Davie, Donald. "Kinds of Comedy." In *Samuel Beckett: The Critical Heritage*. Eds. Lawrence Graver and Raymond Federman. London: Routledge & Kegan Paul, 1979, 153–60.

Dearlove, Judith. "The Voice and its Words: How It Is in Beckett's Fiction." *Journal of Beckett Studies*, 3 (Summer 1978), 56–75.

De Magny, Olivier. "Samuel Beckett ou Job Abandonné." *Monde Nouveau: Paru*, 97 (Feb. 1956), 92–99.

De Martinoir, Francine. "Quelques éclats de voix." Rev. of *Catastrophe et autres dramaticules*, by Samuel Beckett. *Quinzaine Littéraire* (1–15 Oct. 1982), 13.

Driver, Tom. "Beckett by the Madeleine." *Columbia University Forum*, 4 (Summer 1961), 21–25.

Duckworth, Colin. Rev. of *Beckett's "Happy Days": A Manuscript Study*, by S. E. Gontarski. *Journal of Beckett Studies*, 3 (Summer 1978), 100–103.

Eastman, Richard M. "Samuel Beckett and *Happy Days*." *Modern Drama*, 6 (Feb. 1964), 417–24.

Esslin, Martin. *Mediations: Essays on Brecht, Beckett and the Media*. Baton Rouge: Louisiana State Univ. Press, 1980.

———. "A Poetry of Moving Images." Unpublished paper delivered in Austin, Texas, 23 Mar. 1984.

———. intro. and ed. *Samuel Beckett: A Collection of Critical Essays*. Englewood Cliffs, N.J.: Prentice-Hall, 1965.

———. *The Theatre of the Absurd*. Garden City, N.Y.: Doubleday, 1961.

Fabre-Luce, Anne. Rev. of *Le Dépeupleur*. Trans. Larysa Mykyta and Mark Schumacher. In *Samuel Beckett: The Critical Heritage*.

Eds. Lawrence Graver and Raymond Federman. London: Routledge & Kegan Paul, 1979, 313–15.
Federman, Raymond. "Film." In *Samuel Beckett: The Critical Heritage*. Eds. Lawrence Graver and Raymond Federman. London: Routledge & Kegan Paul, 1979, 275–83.
———. "Le Paradoxe du menteur." In *L'Herne: Samuel Beckett*. Eds. Tom Bishop and Raymond Federman. Paris: Editions de l'Herne, 1976, 183–92.
Fehsenfeld, Martha. "Beckett's Late Works: An Appraisal." *Modern Drama*, 25 (Sept. 1982), 355–62.
Fletcher, Beryl S., John Fletcher, Barry Smith and Walter Bachem. *A Student's Guide to the Plays of Samuel Beckett*. London: Faber and Faber, 1978.
Frankel, Margherita S. "Beckett et Proust: Le Triomphe de la parole." In *L'Herne: Samuel Beckett*. Eds. Tom Bishop and Raymond Federman. Paris: Editions de l'Herne, 1976, 281–94.
Friedman, Melvin J., ed. *Samuel Beckett Now*. Chicago: Univ. of Chicago Press, 1970.
Frye, Northrop. "The Nightmare Life in Death." In *Samuel Beckett: The Critical Heritage*. Eds. Lawrence Graver and Raymond Federman. London: Routledge & Kegan Paul, 1979, 206–14.
Gadenne, Paul. "Genêt [*sic*] Dépassé." In *"Molloy" et "L'Expulsé" suivis de "Beckett le précurseur" par Bernard Pingaud et du Dossier de presse de "Molloy."* Paris: Union Générale, 1963, 271–74.
Gontarski, S. E. "*Film* and Formal Integrity." In *Samuel Beckett: Humanistic Perspectives*. Eds. Morris Beja, S. E. Gontarski and Pierre Astier. N.p.: Ohio State Univ. Press, 1983, 129–36.
Graver, Lawrence and Raymond Federman, eds. *Samuel Beckett: The Critical Heritage*. London: Routledge & Kegan Paul, 1979.
Hammond, B. S. "Beckett and Pinter: Towards a Grammar of the Absurd." *Journal of Beckett Studies*, 4 (Spring 1979), 35–42.
Harvey, Lawrence E. *Samuel Beckett Poet and Critic*. Princeton: Princeton Univ. Press, 1970.
Henning, Sylvie Debevec. "*Film*: A Dialogue Between Beckett and Berkeley." *Journal of Beckett Studies*, 7 (Spring 1982), 89–99.
Hesla, David H. *The Shape of Chaos: An Interpretation of the Art of Samuel Beckett*. Minneapolis: Univ. of Minnesota Press, 1971.
Hubert, Marie Claude. Rev. of *L'Anatomie de Samuel Beckett*, by Peter Ehrhard. *Journal of Beckett Studies*, 4 (Spring 1979), 91–93.
Hubert, Renée Riese. "A la trace de 'Bing.' " In *L'Herne: Samuel Beckett*. Eds. Tom Bishop and Raymond Federman. Paris: Editions de l'Herne, 1976, 253–58.
———. "Beckett's *Play* Between Poetry and Performance." *Modern Drama*, 9 (Dec. 1966), 339–46.
Ionesco, Eugène. "A Propos de Beckett." In *L'Herne: Samuel Beckett*. Eds. Tom Bishop and Raymond Federman. Paris: Editions de l'Herne, 1976, 149–51.
Iser, Wolfgang. "Samuel Beckett's Dramatic Language." Trans. Ruby Cohn. *Modern Drama*, 9 (Dec. 1966), 251–59.

Janvier, Ludovic. *Beckett*. Paris: Seuil-Ecrivains de Toujours, 1969.
———. "Beckett et ses fables." *Livres de France*, 18 (Jan. 1967), 4–13.
———. "Lieu dire." In *L'Herne*: *Samuel Beckett*. Eds. Tom Bishop and Raymond Federman. Paris: Editions de l'Herne, 1976, 193–205.
———. *Pour Samuel Beckett*. Paris: Minuit, 1966.
Journal of Beckett Studies.
Karl, Frederick R. "Waiting for Beckett: Quest and ReQuest." *Sewanee Review*, 69 (Oct.-Dec. 1961), 661–76.
Kenner, Hugh. *Samuel Beckett*: *A Critical Study*. Rev. ed. Berkeley: Univ. of California Press, 1968.
———. "Samuel Beckett: Comedian of the Impasse." In *Flaubert, Joyce and Beckett*: *The Stoic Comedians*. Boston: Beacon Press, 1962, 67–107.
Kern, Edith. "Samuel Beckett et les poches de Lemuel Gulliver." Trans. Paul Rozenberg. *Revue des Lettres Modernes. Samuel Beckett*: *Configuration Critique, no. 8*, 100 (1964), 69–81.
Knowlson, James and John Pilling. *Frescoes of the Skull*: *The Later Prose and Drama of Samuel Beckett*. London: John Calder, 1979.
Knowlson, James. *Light and Darkness in the Theatre of Samuel Beckett*. London: Turret Books, 1972.
Kristeva, Julia. "Le Peȓe, l'amour, l'exil." In *L'Herne*: *Samuel Beckett*. Eds. Tom Bishop and Raymond Federman. Paris: Editions de l'Herne, 1976, 246–52.
Lamont, Rosette. "Beckett's Metaphysics of Choiceless Awareness." In *Samuel Beckett Now*. Ed. Melvin J. Friedman. Chicago: Univ. of Chicago Press, 1970, 199–217.
Lawley, Paul. "*Embers*: An Interpretation." *Journal of Beckett Studies*, 6 (Autumn 1980), 9–36.
Leventhal, A. J. "The Beckett Hero." In *Samuel Beckett*: *A Collection of Critical Essays*. Ed. Martin Esslin. Englewood Cliffs, N.J.: Prentice-Hall, 1965, 37–51.
Lodge, David. Rev. of *Ping*. In *Samuel Beckett*: *The Critical Heritage*. Eds. Lawrence Graver and Raymond Federman. London: Routledge & Kegan Paul, 1979, 291–301.
Lyons, Charles R. "Beckett's *Endgame*: An Anti-Myth of Creation." *Modern Drama*, 7 (Sept. 1964), 204–9.
———. "Perceiving *Rockaby*—As A Text, As a Text by Samuel Beckett, As a Text for Performance." *Comparative Drama*, 16 (Winter 1982–83), 297–311.
———. *Samuel Beckett*. New York: Grove, 1983.
Magnan, Jean-Marie. "Les Chaînes et relais du néant." In *L'Herne*: *Samuel Beckett*. Eds. Tom Bishop and Raymond Federman. Paris: Editions de l'Herne, 1976, 259–65.
Marowitz, Charles. "Paris Log." *Encore*, 9 (Mar.-Apr. 1962), 37–46.
Mayoux, Jean-Jacques. "Samuel Beckett homme de théâtre." *Livres de France*, 18 (Jan. 1967), 14–21.
McMillan, Dougald and Martha Fehsenfeld. *Beckett in the Theatre*. London: Calder, 1985.
———. "De *La Dernière Bande* à *Pas*: Structure Dramatique et Con-

trôle Technique." Trans. Marie-Claire Pasquier. Program notes to *Oh les beaux jours.* Paris: Théâtre du Rond-Point, 1982.
Mignon, Paul-Louis. "Le Théâtre de A jusqu'à Z: Samuel Beckett." *L'Avant-Scène*, 313 (15 June 1964), 8.
Mihályi, Gábor. "Beckett's *Godot* and the Myth of Alienation." *Modern Drama*, 9 (Dec. 1966), 277–82.
Miller, J. Hillis. "The Anonymous Walkers." *The Nation*, 190 (23 Apr. 1960), 351–54.
Modern Drama, 9 (Dec. 1966). Ed. Ruby Cohn.
Mooney, Michael E. "*Molloy*, Part 1: Beckett's *Discourse on Method.*" *Journal of Beckett Studies*, 3 (Summer 1978), 40–55.
Morrison, Kristin. "The Rip Word in *A Piece of Monologue.*" *Modern Drama*, 25 (Sept. 1982), 349–54.
Murphy, Peter. Rev. of *All Strange Away*, by Samuel Beckett. *Journal of Beckett Studies*, 5 (Autumn 1979), 99–113.
Nadeau, Maurice. "Samuel Beckett: Humour and the Void." In *Samuel Beckett: A Collection of Critical Essays.* Ed. Martin Esslin. Englewood Cliffs, N.J.: Prentice-Hall, 1965, 33–36.
Oberg, Arthur K. "*Krapp's Last Tape* and the Proustian Vision." *Modern Drama*, 9 (Dec. 1966), 333–38.
O'Hara, J. D. "Beckett Piece by Piece." Rev. of *Ends and Odds*, *Fizzles*, *I Can't Go On, I'll Go On*, by Samuel Beckett, and of *Samuel Beckett and the Pessimistic Tradition*, by Steven J. Rosen. *The Nation*, 224 (19 Feb. 1977), 216–19.
Perloff, Marjorie. *The Poetics of Indeterminacy: Rimbaud to Cage.* Princeton: Princeton Univ. Press, 1981.
Perspective, 11 (Autumn 1959). Ed. Ruby Cohn.
Piater, Jacqueline. Rev. of *Mercier et Camier*, by Samuel Beckett. Trans. Jean M. Sommermeyer. In *Samuel Beckett: The Critical Heritage.* Eds. Lawrence Graver and Raymond Federman. London: Routledge & Kegan Paul, 1979, 307–8.
Pilling, John. Rev. of *For to end yet again and Other Fizzles*, by Samuel Beckett. *Journal of Beckett Studies*, 2 (Summer 1977), 96–100.
"Practical Aspects of Theatre, Radio and Television: Extracts from an Unscripted Interview with Billie Whitelaw by James Knowlson; A Television Recording Made on 1 February 1977 for the University of London Audio-Visual Centre." *Journal of Beckett Studies*, 3 (Summer 1978), 85–90.
Pingaud, Bernard. "Beckett le précurseur." In *"Molloy" et "L'Expulsé" suivis de "Beckett le précurseur" par Bernard Pingaud et du Dossier de presse de "Molloy."* Paris: Union Générale, 1963, 289–311.
———. "Molloy." Trans. Françoise Longhurst. In *Samuel Beckett: The Critical Heritage.* Eds. Lawrence Graver and Raymond Federman. London: Routledge & Kegan Paul, 1979, 67–70.
———. "The School of Refusal." Trans. Kenneth Douglas. *Yale French Studies*, 24 (Fall 1959), 18–21 [erroneously dated 23 (Summer 1959)].

Pouillon, Jean. "Une Morale de la conscience absolue." In *"Molloy" et "L'Expulsé" suivis de "Beckett le précurseur" par Bernard Pingaud et du Dossier de presse de "Molloy."* Paris: Union Générale, 1963, 283–86.
Rabinovitz, Rubin. "Time, Space, and Verisimilitude in Samuel Beckett's Fiction." *Journal of Beckett Studies*, 2 (Summer 1977), 40–46.
Revue des Lettres Modernes. Samuel Beckett: Configuration Critique, no. 8, 100 (1964). Ed. Melvin J. Friedman.
Robbe-Grillet, Alain. "Samuel Beckett, auteur dramatique." *Critique*, 9 (Feb. 1953), 108–14.
———. "Samuel Beckett, or 'Presence' in the Theatre." Trans. Barbara Bray. In *Samuel Beckett: A Collection of Critical Essays.* Ed. Martin Esslin. Englewood Cliffs, N.J.: Prentice-Hall, 1965, 108–16.
Schneider, Alan. " 'Comme il vous plaira': Travailler avec Samuel Beckett." In *L'Herne: Samuel Beckett.* Eds. Tom Bishop and Raymond Federman. Paris: Editions de l'Herne, 1976, 123–36.
———. "On Directing *Film.*" In *Film by Samuel Beckett: Complete Scenario/Illustrations/Production Shots.* New York: Grove, 1970.
Scott, Nathan A. "The Recent Journey Into the Zone Zero: The Example of Beckett and His Despair of Literature." *Centennial Review of Arts and Sciences*, 7 (Spring 1962), 144–81.
Selz, Jean. "L'Homme finissant de Samuel Beckett." *Lettres Nouvelles*, 5 (July–Aug. 1957), 120–23.
Sénart, Philippe. "La Fin de l'homme." *Table Ronde*, 182 (Mar. 1963), 113–19.
Shenker, Israel. "Moody Man of Letters." In *Samuel Beckett: The Critical Heritage.* Eds. Lawrence Graver and Raymond Federman. London: Routledge & Kegan Paul, 1979, 146–49.
Simon, Alfred. "Le Degré zéro du tragique." Trans. Jean M. Sommermeyer. In *Samuel Beckett: The Critical Heritage.* Eds. Lawrence Graver and Raymond Federman. London: Routledge & Kegan Paul, 1979, 266–71.
Solomon, Philip. "Purgatory Unpurged: Time, Space and Language in 'Lessness.' " *Journal of Beckett Studies*, 6 (Autumn 1980), 63–72.
Spender, Stephen. "Lifelong Suffocation." *New York Times Book Review*, 12 Oct. 1958, p. 5.
Tallmer, Jerry. "Beckett's *Endgame.*" Rev. of *Endgame*, Alan Schneider director, at Cherry Lane Theatre, New York. In *The Village Voice Reader.* Eds. Daniel Wolf and Edwin Fancher. Garden City, N. Y.: Doubleday, 1962, 180–82.
Thiel, André. "La Condition tragique chez Samuel Beckett." *La Revue Nouvelle*, 45 (15 May 1967), 449–63.
Torrance, Robert M. "Modes of Being and Time in the World of *Godot.*" *Modern Language Quarterly*, 28 (Mar. 1967), 77–95.
Updike, John. "How How It Is Was." In *Samuel Beckett: The Critical*

Heritage. Eds. Lawrence Graver and Raymond Federman. London: Routledge & Kegan Paul, 1979, 254–57.
Van Wert, William F. "'To Be is to Be Perceived': Time and Point of View in Samuel Beckett's *Film*." *Literature/Film Quarterly*, 8 (Apr. 1980), 133–40.
Wellershoff, Dieter. "Failure of an Attempt at De-Mythologization: Samuel Beckett's Novels." Trans. Martin Esslin. In *Samuel Beckett: A Collection of Critical Essays*. Ed. Martin Esslin. Englewood Cliffs, N.J.: Prentice-Hall, 1965, 92–107.
White, Kenneth Steele. *Einstein and Modern French Drama: An Analogy*. Washington, D.C.: University Press of America, 1983.
Zeifman, Hersh. "*Come and Go*: A Criticule." In *Samuel Beckett: Humanistic Perspectives*. Eds. Morris Beja, S. E. Gontarski and Pierre Astier. N.p.: Ohio State Univ. Press, 1983, 137–44.
Zilliacus, Claus. *Beckett and Broadcasting: A Study of the Works of Samuel Beckett for and in Radio and Television*. Åbo, Finland: Åbo Akademi, 1976.

BACKGROUND MATERIALS

Abraham, Pierre. *Créatures chez Balzac*. Paris: Gallimard-NRF, 1931.
Apollinaire, Guillaume. *Les Peintres cubistes*. 1913; rpt. Paris: Hermann, 1965.
Apostolidès, Jean-Marie. "Perception du temps et catégories dramatiques au 17è siècle." *Stanford French Review*, 3 (Winter 1979), 383–95.
———. "Le Regard en perspective." Unpublished manuscript.
———. *Le Roi-machine: Spectacle et politique au temps de Louis XIV*. Paris: Minuit, 1981.
Artaud, Antonin. *Le Théâtre et son double*. 1938; rpt. Paris: Gallimard, 1964.
Ashbery, John. "No Way of Knowing." In *Self-Portrait in a Convex Mirror*. New York: Viking, 1975, 55–57.
Auerbach, Erich. *Mimesis: The Representation of Reality in Western Literature*. Trans. Willard R. Trask. Princeton: Princeton Univ. Press, 1953.
Baltrusaitis, Jurgis. *Anamorphoses ou Perspectives curieuses*. Paris: Olivier Perrin, 1955.
Barthes, Roland. *Le Degré zéro de l'écriture*. 1953; rpt. Paris: Gonthier, 1965.
Bentley, Eric. *The Playwright as Thinker*. New York: Meridian, 1946.
Bergson, Henri. "The Cinematographic View of Becoming." In *Zeno's Paradoxes*. Ed. Wesley C. Salmon. Indianapolis: Bobbs-Merrill, 1970, 59–66.
———. *Essai sur les données immédiates de la conscience*. 1888; rpt. Geneva: Editions Albert Skira, 1945.
Camus, Albert. *La Peste*. Paris: Gallimard-Folio, 1947.
Castoriadis, Corneille. "Science moderne et interrogation philosophique." *Encyclopaedia universalis*. 1977 ed. Vol. XVII.

Chevalley de Buzon, Catherine. "Rationalité de l'anamorphose." *XVIIè Siècle*, 124 (July-Sept. 1979), 289–96.
Dante. *Paradiso*. Vol. III of *The Divine Comedy*. Trans. and ed. John D. Sinclair. New York: Oxford Univ. Press, 1979.
Deleuze, Gilles. "Peindre le cri." *Critique*, 408 (May 1981), 506–11.
Descartes, René. *Discours de la méthode*. Ed. Jean-Marie Beyssade. Paris: Librairie Générale Française-Livre de Poche, 1973.
Diderot, Denis. "De la poésie dramatique." In *Oeuvres complètes de Diderot*. Ed. J. Assézat. Vol. VII. Paris: Garnier, 1875, 299–394.
Durand, Gilbert. *Les Structures anthropologiques de l'imaginaire*. Paris: Presses Universitaires de France, 1960.
Fernandez, Dominique. "Pirandello: un trou dans le ciel de papier." *L'Express*, 22 Oct. 1982, 18–21.
Feyerabend, Paul. *Against Method: Outline of an Anarchistic Theory of Knowledge*. London: Verso, 1978.
Flocon, Albert and René Taton. *La Perspective*. 3d ed. Paris: Presses Universitaires de France-Que sais-je?, 1978.
Foucault, Michel. *Les Mots et les choses*. Paris: Gallimard, 1966.
Francastel, Pierre. *La Figure et le lieu*. Paris: Gallimard, 1967.
Freud, Sigmund. *Introductory Lectures on Psychoanalysis*. Trans. and ed. James Strachey. New York: Norton-Liveright, 1977.
Giacometti, Alberto. Interview with André Parinaud. "Pourquoi je suis sculpteur?" *Arts*, 13 June 1962, 1,5.
Hazard, Paul. *La Crise de la conscience européenne (1680–1715)*. 3 vols. Paris: Boivin, 1935.
Huizinga, J. *Homo ludens: Essai sur la fonction sociale du jeu*. Trans. Cécile Seresia. Paris: Gallimard, 1951.
Janson, H. W. *History of Art: A Survey of the Major Visual Arts from the Dawn of History to the Present Day*. Englewood Cliffs, N.J.: Prentice-Hall; New York: Harry N. Abrams, 1962.
Joyce, James. *A Portrait of the Artist as a Young Man*. 1916; rpt. New York: Viking, 1964.
Kafka, Franz. *The Penal Colony*. Trans. Willa and Edwin Muir. New York: Schocken, 1961.
Kernodle, George. *From Art to Theater: Form and Convention in the Renaissance*. Chicago: Univ. of Chicago Press, 1944.
Kierkegaard, Sören. *The Concept of Dread*. Trans. Walter Lowrie. Princeton: Princeton Univ. Press. 1944.
Kuhn, Thomas S. *The Structure of Scientific Revolutions*. 2d ed. Chicago: Univ. of Chicago Press, 1970.
Lacan, Jacques. *Le Séminaire. Livre XI: Les Quatre concepts fondamentaux de la psychanalyse*. Paris: Seuil, 1973.
Laing, R. D. *The Divided Self*. New York: Penguin, 1965.
Mallarmé, Stéphane. "La Musique et les lettres." In *Oeuvres complètes*. Eds. Henri Mondor and G. Jean-Aubry. Paris: Gallimard-NRF, 1945, 635–57.
Panofsky, Erwin. *La Perspective comme forme symbolique et autres essais*. Pref. Marisa Dalai Emiliani. Trans. Guy Ballangé. Paris: Minuit, 1975.

Pirandello, Luigi. *Tonight We Improvise*. Trans. Samuel Putnam. New York: E. P. Dutton, 1932.

Planck, Max. "Positivisme et monde extérieur réel." Trans. Cornelius Heim. *Médiations*, 6 (Summer 1963), 49–68.

Poulet, Georges. *Etudes sur le temps humain*. Edinburgh: Edinburgh Univ. Press, 1949.

Prigogine, Ilya. Lecture delivered at the International Symposium on Disorder and Order. Stanford University, 14 Sept. 1981.

Proust, Marcel. *A l'ombre des jeunes filles en fleurs*. Paris: Gallimard-Pléiade, 1954.

———. *La Prisonnière*. Paris: Gallimard-Folio, 1954.

———. *Le Temps retrouvé*. Paris: Gallimard-Folio, 1954.

Sartre, Jean-Paul. *L'Etre et le néant: Essai d'ontologie phénoménologique*. Paris: Gallimard, 1943.

Schopenhauer, Arthur. *Selections*. Intro. and Ed. De Witt H. Parker. New York: Scribner's, 1928.

Sontag, Susan. *On Photography*. New York: Delta, 1977.

Sypher, Wylie. *Rococo to Cubism in Art and Literature*. New York: Vintage, 1960.

Vernon, John. *The Garden and the Map: Schizophrenia in Twentieth-Century Literature and Culture*. Urbana, Ill.: Univ. of Illinois Press, 1973.

INDEX OF NAMES AND BECKETT TITLES